FAMILY AMNESIA

Chinese American Resilience

Images and Text by Betty Yu

Daylight

Cofounder: Michael Itkoff
Creative Director: Ursula Damm
Copy Editor: Gabrielle Fastman

The author has made every attempt to provide information that is accurate and complete.

ISBN: 978-1-954119-44-4

Printed by Ofset Yapimevi, Turkey

Daylight Books
E-mail: info@daylightbooks.org
Web: www.daylightbooks.org

TABLE OF CONTENTS

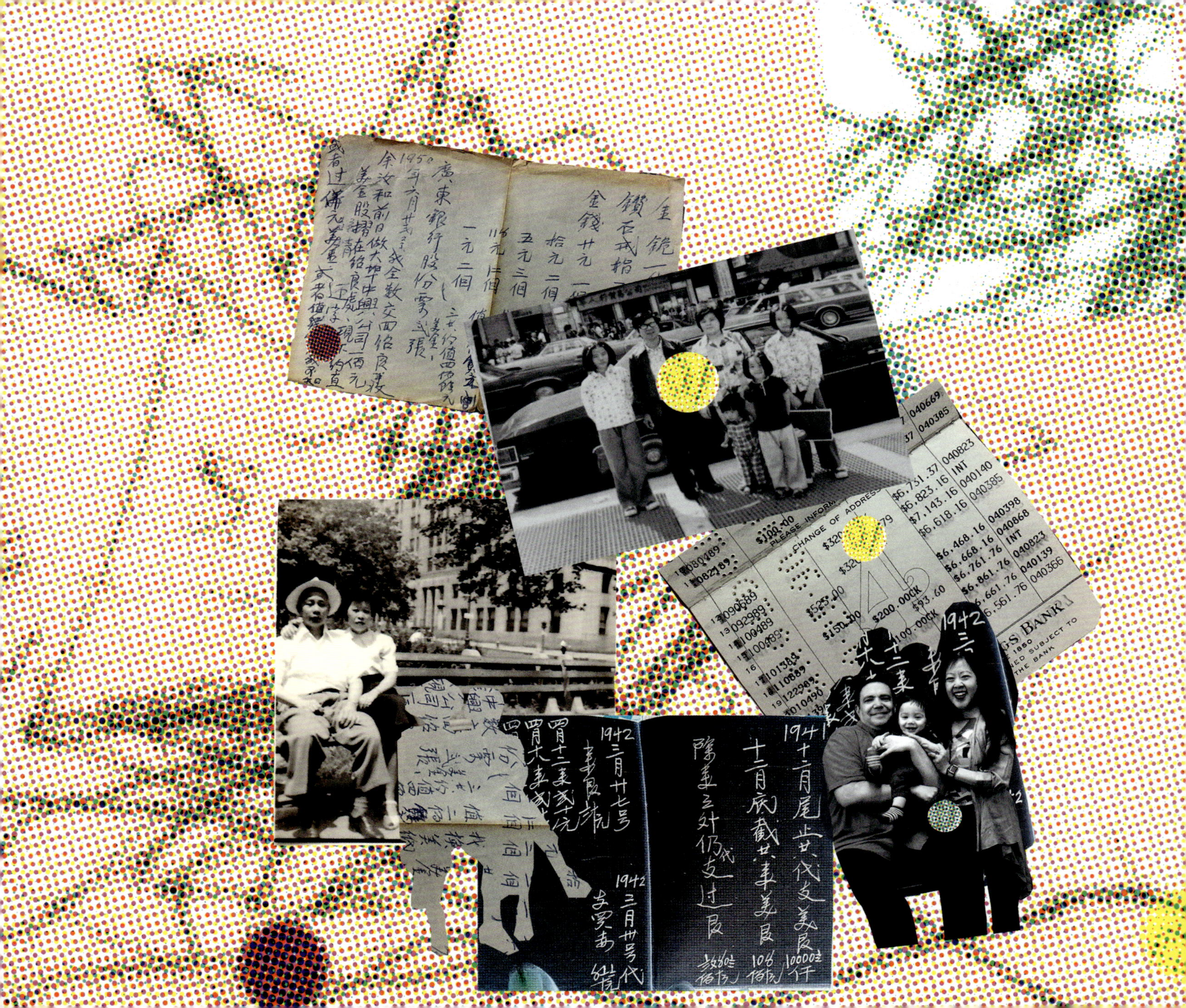

This book is dedicated to my late sister, Virginia Yu, my late father, and late grandparents. Thank you to my partner, John Antush, and my mother, Sau Kwan, for your unwavering support and encouragement. Thanks to my dad and sisters for your patience.

Finally, to my sweet son, Junius Antush-Yu, who is the inspiration and motivation for finishing this book. He is part of our family's continuum and our shared story of resilience that continues on.

Three generations of family and survival
(with background art by the artist's two-year-old son, Junius Antush-Yu), 2024. Mixed-media collage.

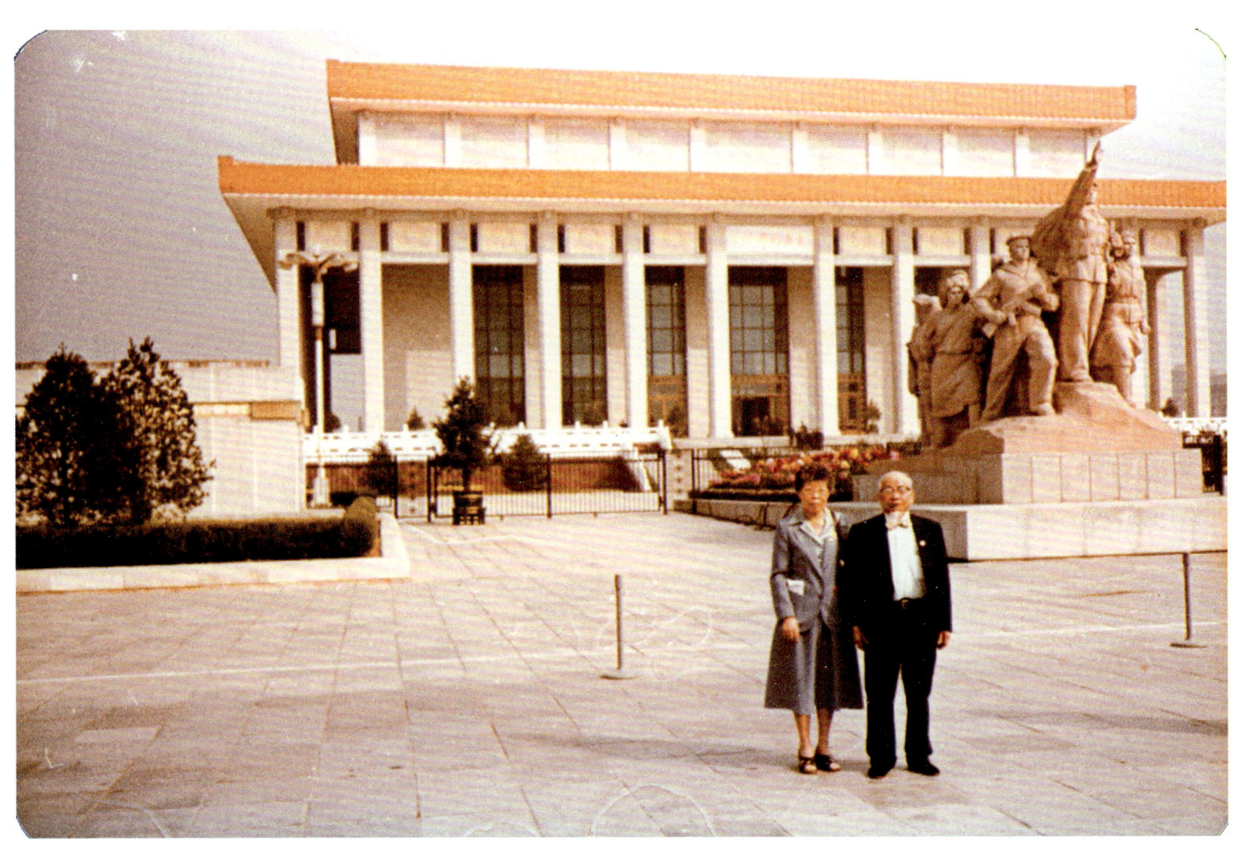

No. 26080
5-18

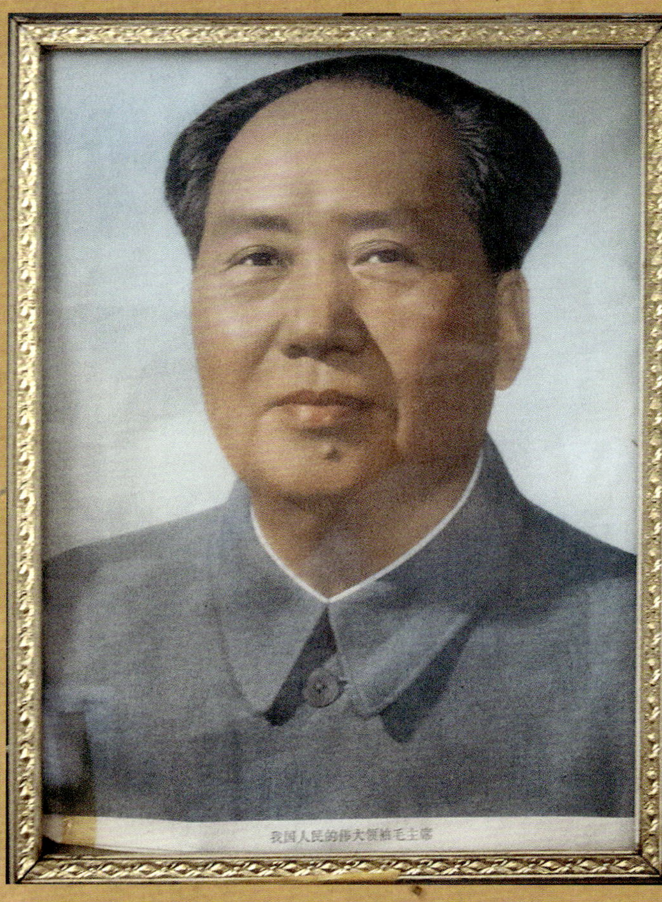

Form 391

IMMIGRATION FILE

U. S. DEPARTMENT OF LABOR
IMMIGRATION SERVICE

SUBJECT: Woo Sui Lean
Ah Woo Fon You

No. 26080/5-18

14—204

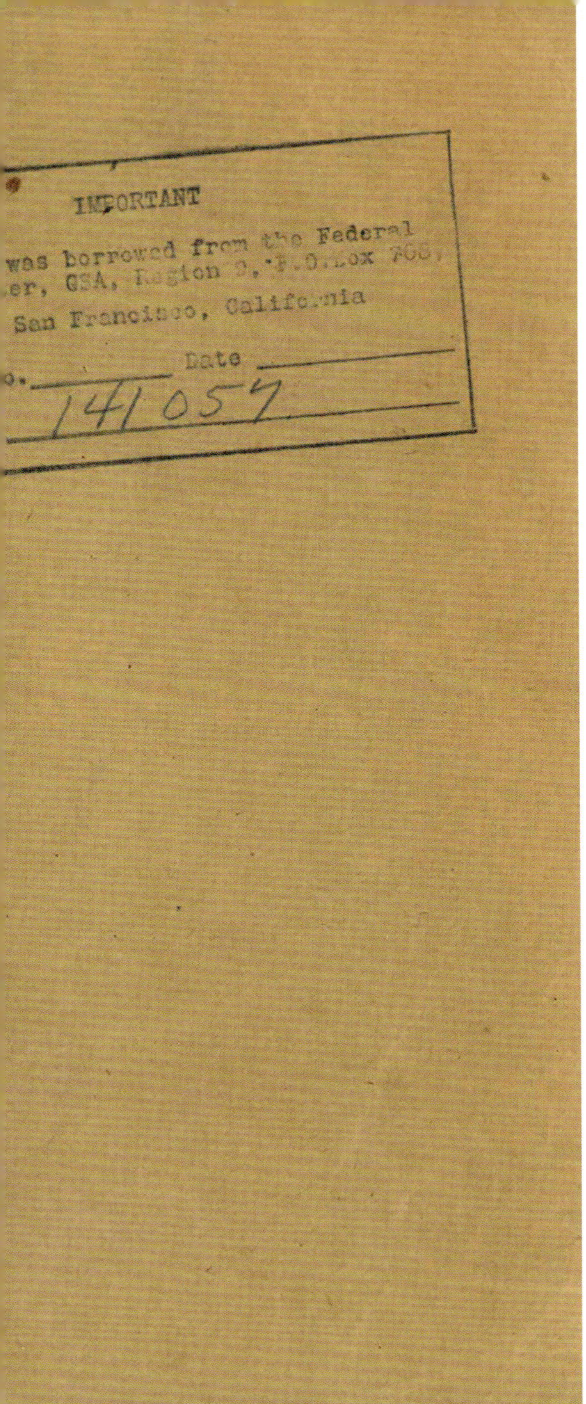

FAMILY AMNESIA: CHINESE AMERICAN RESILIENCE

This is a revised version of an essay originally published as "Acts of Remembering" in Survivance*, the May 2021 issue of* e-flux Architecture*, published by e-flux in collaboration with the Solomon R. Guggenheim Museum.*

Generational resilience and resistance in the United States has been in my blood for four generations. However, like most immigrant families, my family never spoke about the past. It would conjure up too much tragedy, loss, and trauma that has been buried for years. This act of forgetting is common. We want to forget our past, our memories, our struggles, and hardships. I long for those memories I don't have access to. As my grandparents and ancestors have passed, the tools I have available to me are fragmented stories that have been passed on orally, activated in my imagination. These forgotten stories not only honor my ancestors' past but also allow me to live in the present.

NOTES ON EXCLUSION

Like many immigrants and communities of color, the history of systematic discrimination in the United States against

My grandfather's framed photo of Mao Zedong (from the late 1960s); backdrop image is from my grandfather's San Bruno, California, immigration papers from the 1920s.

people of Chinese descent was brutal, driven by white nationalism. The racist and xenophobic 1882 Chinese Exclusion Act prohibited anyone other than a few hundred male merchants from coming to the United States. It remains the only law implemented by the US government preventing members of a specific ethnic or national group from immigrating. My family's story is not unique. It is just one testimony about US history—a history of dispossession of land, of denial of citizenship to non-European immigrants and enslaved people, and of white supremacist/nativist ideology.

It was only five years ago, when I sat down with my father to document our family's story, that I started to understand the depth of our family's roots in the United States, where European nativists (settlers) did all they could to chase away my Chinese ancestors. "Your great-grandfather immigrated to Reno, Nevada, to work," my dad told me. "Wait. What? I had no idea. When was he here? What kind of work did he do?" I asked. "It's all fuzzy. But we think maybe hand laundry. In the late 1800s," Dad replied. Or perhaps he worked on the Central Pacific Railroad or in silver mines. We don't know the full story. My great-grandfather's story is similar to other Chinese immigrants, who came to the US hoping to build roots and find the "golden mountain." During this time, angry white (supremacist) laborers destroyed small Chinatowns that people like my great-grandfather helped build, chasing them away as "a physical and moral threat." Unable to build roots, my great-grandfather went back to China.

GENERATIONS OF MIGRATION: THE UNSPOKEN PAST

The man I knew as my grandfather, Sui Woo, came over in the late 1920s. Like many Chinese immigrants he was a "paper son," someone who bought false papers indicating his dad lived in the United States. He went on to own and operate small hand laundries, one of the few kinds of businesses Chinese could work in because of rampant discrimination. In 1933 he joined other hand-laundry workers to form the Chinese Hand Laundry Alliance (CHLA) of New York, an organization that challenged racist and anti-Chinese policies. In 1942, at age 39, he enlisted in the US Army to fight fascism during World War II. As a veteran he was able to bring his wife over, my grandmother, Yook Ming Woo, through the 1945 War Brides Act. My grandmother worked in the family hand-laundry business, as well as in food and garment factories.

My grandfather became an overseas Chinese nationalist, supporting Mao Zedong and the newly formed People's Republic of China government. From what my relatives and family tell me he was an avid supporter of workers' rights and socialist ideals. Even though I was five when he passed away, I remember visiting my grandfather's apartment and seeing the portrait of Mao Zedong up on the wall along with his published works on the bookshelf in my grandparents' bedroom. It wasn't until I was an adult and became politically conscious that I started to process how divergent my families' experiences and political ideologies were. I started to understand why none of them wanted to talk about their pasts. The trauma, wounds, and grief are profound. My sisters and I were told to never ask too many questions about our family history, our past, and what life was like back in China and Hong Kong. It wasn't until I was in my late teens that I learned that my grandparents were not my biological grandparents. Though they were my real grandparents, they'd adopted my father. This was all unknown to me, and I'm not sure how to begin to understand it.

My father was born in the 1930s in a small countryside village in Taishan, a region of the Guangdong Province in Southern China. These were turbulent times. He rarely talks about his childhood. He refers to those years as "horrific, incredibly violent, and dark." It was a period of constant war. Civil war between the Kuomintang government and the Chinese Communist Party (CCP) began in 1927. The Second Sino-Japanese War began in 1937. Japan invaded in the early 1940s. China became a battle zone of World War II. My dad escaped Japanese troops by running into the fields and hiding out for a time. In 1949 the CCP declared the People's Republic of China, a socialist government based on egalitarian land reform. My dad's family were landholding working peasants. Though they possessed very little land, they were afraid of being targeted by the government as rich landlords. Eventually, my dad and grandmother fled to the city of Guangzhou for several years. Later, at the age of fifteen, he migrated to Hong Kong alone. My dad talks about how his family left his great-grandmother in his house back in the village. She didn't want to leave their home. They found out later she committed suicide, fearing she would be found by CCP Red Guards. That deep trauma left my dad and grandmother silent, creating a void in my family's history.

My mother's family fled the Heshan village of Jiangmen in the southern China province of Guangdong in the 1940s during China's civil war. They went to Hong Kong. My mom shared her father's deep regret that he never returned to China to retrieve his eldest daughter (my mom's sister). Years later, during a 2016 trip to China, my mom reunited with her sister. Her sister harbored no resentment. She talked about how much better life got after the Communist government took over. She explained how the agrarian land reforms benefited her and her family.

My parents married in Hong Kong when it was still a British colony. They tried to escape poverty there by immigrating to Brooklyn, New York's Sunset Park neighborhood in 1972. They arrived with my two oldest sisters, Sheila and Karen, who were five and four, respectively. My mom was pregnant with my sister Virginia. I didn't come into the picture until much later.

INTERGENERATIONAL ROOTS IN ACTIVISM

I still can't believe it was only twelve years ago that I learned about my grandfather's past as not only a labor-rights organizer but also an avid amateur photographer. My parents worked in garment factories for nearly four decades. My mom was a seamstress sewing zippers on to clothing and my dad worked as a button operator. They toiled twelve to fourteen hours a day, six to seven days a week for less than minimum wage, even in unionized factories. My mother suffered deteriorating health conditions, like repetitive stress syndrome, by the time she was in her late forties. My dad is partially deaf as a result of operating a loud button machine for four decades. My grandmother was my main caretaker, since my parents were working long hours to make ends meet.

My own labor activism and love for the arts and photography started when I was a teenager. In 1995, I was taking photography classes and decided to photograph my sister Virginia, who was taking part in a historic student-led hunger strike in front of a Chinatown restaurant, Jing Fong, that was paying their workers seventy-five cents an hour. I became deeply involved in labor-rights organizing, using photography and video to highlight the workers' fight for justice. My mother, Sau Kwan, became curious about this movement that inspired her daughter to go on a hunger strike. She got deeply involved, becoming a leader in the fight against inhumane working conditions. The next ten or so years were special. Organizing alongside my family members felt organic, and at times very challenging. We developed a unique bond. In 2010, my sister Virginia passed away suddenly at the age of 38, leaving behind her husband and two small children. This profound loss still feels devastating. Her commitment to her family and passion for justice was so unwavering. Her death shook me to my core.

Here is an excerpt from a *New York Times* article that featured my sister and me:

Virginia Yu, 27, and Betty Yu, 22, are sisters who grew up in Sunset Park. They said they saw firsthand what working in sweatshops did to their parents, who went for days without seeing their children because of long work hours, and suffered nerve damage from overuse of their hands in sewing and making buttonholes. The young people said they [had] been especially inspired by female sweatshop workers. Women are most often the primary caretakers of children, and are often stuck in the lowest-paying jobs. Many women, they said, work 12-hour days in factories for just above minimum wage, without receiving the overtime pay to which they are legally entitled. They often don't have enough time to go to the bathroom or make telephone calls.

"My mother was working 15 hours days," Betty Yu said. "I didn't know my mother. I didn't know my father. They were at work when I woke up and when I went to bed at night. My mother sewed and my father was a button operator." (Felicia R. Lee, "COPING: Working Overtime to Vanquish Sweatshops," *The New York Times*, Dec. 12, 1999)

Here is an excerpt from *The New Rank and File*, a book by Staughton Lynd and Alice Lynd (Ithaca: Cornell University Press, 2000):

Section: The Hunger Strike

Virginia Yu: Five students did it. It was pretty tough out there. We were right in the street, in front of the Jing Fong restaurant. I remember the first night.

The police gave us a really hard time, especially the captain. At first they said, "Oh, you can put up something for when it rains or gets too sunny." Then they turned around and said, "No." When we tried to put something up to cover ourselves, the police drew a picture of a structure that they thought could not be built. To the police captain's surprise, construction workers actually built what the police had drawn. After all that, the police demolished it.

That was a pivotal moment for me. I saw firsthand what was going on. It was everything the Chinese Staff was talking about: the collusion between the police, the tong, and the Restaurant Association was very clear. I remember seeing gang members across the street. I knew about all this, but being there and seeing it really strengthened me. The police station was across the street from our picket, but they wouldn't let us use the bathroom. The smell of garbage from the restaurant reeked that summer. In the late evening, garbage trucks would drag the garbage right across the area where we had set up tables to sleep. They were trying to intimidate us, but we were even more determined to continue the struggle.

Since we were outdoors, right in the heart of Chinatown, every day, we were able to make an impact on the community. We were able to publicize to the community and to the city that things needed to be changed. Most people stopped to see what was going on. Some students even went into the factories to get people to sign our petitions.

Nelson, my boyfriend, wrote a letter about our campaign to an anchor for Channel 9 News. She was touched by the letter and came out to do an exposé on conditions in Chinatown. Nelson was able to discuss our campaign on TV. We didn't get much rest. I felt I was on display in a museum. I remember waking up with cameras in my face. Every day was a new adventure, since the enemy was on either side of us: to the left was the police and to the right, the restaurant. The sun finally took its toll. In the middle of the week, three of the five students had to go to the hospital because of dehydration.

My whole family didn't want me to do the hunger strike. I didn't tell my mom until the night before, because I knew that if I told her earlier, she wouldn't let me do it. In time, I was able to get my mother and my younger sister involved. My mother wanted to see why I was willing to go without eating for seven days, and if I was part of a cult.

After my mother came around, and saw what the issues were, she began to see what this organization is about. She even began to talk about workers' power and workers' rights. She is now a board member of Chinese Staff [& Workers Association].

My mother has been involved with CSWA for three years. I am constantly amazed by the resilience with which she continues to fight for workers' rights, even though she could be blacklisted. My mother believes in justice and dignity for working people. I have gained so much strength from her determination.

Excerpt from *Sweatshop Warriors* by Miriam Ching Yoon Louie (Boston: South End Press, 2001):

Chapter Four: Extended Families

Small and spry, Mrs. Yu Sau Kwan is the mother of four strong women in their twenties. After immigrating from Hong Kong in 1972, she toiled in unionized Chinatown factories for over two decades, developing deep pains in her back, hip, and fingers from sewing 900 zippers a day. Neither the union nor her employers let her know she was entitled to Workers Compensation for her on-the-job injuries. After seeing the hard work and suffering their mother had to endure, Mrs. Yu's daughters Betty and Virginia joined their peers gravitating to the Chinese Staff and Workers Association (CSWA).

Virginia eventually participated in a 7-day hunger strike protesting the Jing Fong restaurant owners' treatment of the workers in 1995. The passionate identification of her daughters with the restaurant workers in turn drew Mrs. Yu to CSWA. Yu says, "I wondered, What kind of organization is CSWA that it would make my daughter want to fast? So, I decided to go take a look. I ended up joining myself!"

She now organizes her immigrant women worker peers as a member of CSWA's Board and Coordinating Committee of its Brooklyn Center. As a co-founder of the Garment Workers' Health and Safety Project, she works not only with injured Chinese workers, but also Latina/o, Caribbean, and Polish workers.

NOTES ON MY OWN DECOLONIZATION

The land beneath us is not truly ours. It belongs to the Lenape tribe. The Brooklyn neighborhood now known as Sunset Park was home to the Lenape-Algonquian people, specifically the Canarsee. We cannot have a conversation about gentrification and displacement in Sunset Park today without first acknowledging the violence and genocide that was committed against its first inhabitants.

I grew up on 60th Street in Sunset Park. My parents' house sits on stolen land. We are settlers. I do not know the first occupiers of this land. I know that they were forcibly removed. I did not grow up knowing about the enslaved labor that built the city, that paved its streets. I did not grow up knowing about the Black Americans who were displaced from their homes during mid-century urban renewal, dispossessed from their land during the South's Reconstruction era, or were redlined and disenfranchised from buying homes throughout the twentieth century.

In 1771, Brooklyn was made up of farmland and small villages. A third of its population consisted of enslaved people—the same proportion as in Virginia. Emancipation was gradual, taking place between 1799 and 1827. But in the late eighteenth and early nineteenth centuries, Brooklyn was the slaveholding capital of New York State. On average, sixty percent of white families living in Brooklyn were slaveholders. In the town of Flatbush, it was as high as seventy-four percent. Brooklyn's slaveholding percentages surpassed those of South Carolina.

In the 1930s, during a Works Progress Administration's project in Sunset Park, according to a 1911 *Brooklyn Eagle* article, "relics were unearthed at the old water pond by the WPA park crews during the construction of the new pool." What they found was the former village site of the Nyack tribe. Furthermore, according to the article, relics, bones, and graves were also found at Owl's Head Park, a hillock that forms the highest point of the estate also known as Indian Mound. Congressional funds were set aside at the time to build a monument to commemorate the site. Of course, it never materialized.

FRAGMENTS OF HOME/POLITICS OF OUR DISPLACEMENT

There is no direct Chinese translation for "Stop Gentrification." The closest translation is 反对贵族化, or fǎnduì guìzú huà, which literally means "oppose aristocracy." The term that is more widely understood and resonates with the Chinese-speaking community in the United States is 驱赶, or qūgǎn, which means "displacement" or "eviction." The politics of displacement and dispossession are deeply rooted in the fabric of US capitalism, imperialism, colonization, and modern-day state-sanctioned gentrification. One community member made the analogy between the white and wealthy folks who have been gentrifying Manhattan's Chinatown over the past number of decades and the "gentry" of Hong Kong's British colonial rule in the 1840s, when the city's sense of culture and language was stripped away.

Since I was a teenager growing up in New York City in the 1990s, I've been obsessed with documenting my neighborhood of Sunset Park, Brooklyn, which is now New York City's largest Chinatown. I'm not exactly sure why I had this obsession, but I did, and still do. As early as I can remember, I was snapping photos of the neighborhood with a 35 mm film camera. I photographed my family, friends, the kids on the block, and everyday moments. Later, when I went to NYU to study film, I shot hours of footage of my family members. I eventually made a short film about how my mother, a garment worker, and my sister became fierce leaders in the fight against the sweatshop system in the 1990s. Looking back, I was probably trying to capture, preserve, and freeze those moments in time when my sense of home and sanctuary was never in question.

In the late 1970s, working immigrant families like mine were able to afford a house and achieve that slice of the "American Pie." My family was part of the first wave of Cantonese-speaking Chinese families to move into Sunset Park back in the late 1970s. My grandparents started saving money for a house as far back as the 1940s. My parents worked long hours to assist in purchasing a house. I felt privileged to have grown up in the 1980s and 1990s in a neighborhood where I had friends from all backgrounds, but mainly Puerto Rican, Dominican, Chinese, and Northern European.

Since the 1950s, Latinx, and specifically Puerto Ricans, have been moving to Sunset Park. Today, the majority of immigrants (as opposed to Puerto Rican migrants) come from the Dominican Republic, Mexico, and other parts of Central America like Ecuador, Colombia, Peru, El Salvador, and Nicaragua. According to the 2010 census, almost half of the neighborhood is Latinx, and about forty percent is Chinese.

Back in the late 1990s and early 2000s there were dozens of illegal garment factories operating out of warehouses and garages in the industrial parts of the neighborhood. Folks like my mother worked long hours for very low wages in these factories. However, rents and the cost of living were still reasonable. Today, however, real-estate developers aided by millions of dollars in government tax breaks threaten to displace thousands of working-class residents. Many parts of Sunset Park are still zoned for manufacturing, but developers have been trying to change zoning and land-use laws so that they can demolish existing low structures to build tall luxury housing, a real-estate strategy known as "upzoning."

In 2015, the $1 billion Industry City development project was unveiled for the Latinx area of Sunset Park. Industry City was planned to replace Bush Terminal, a manufacturing, shipping, and warehousing complex that was a site of employment for thousands of blue-collar US-born and immigrant laborers from the early 1900s up until the 1970s. The development project rebranded Industry City as an industrial waterfront for a "maker" innovation economy centered on manufactured hipster culture: "high" art, fashion, design, film and TV, tech start-ups, and specialized food sectors.

On the other side of Sunset Park, where I grew up, around 8th Avenue, overseas Chinese and domestic investors (from Flushing, Queens) have been buying up two-story residential homes and other properties and converting them into luxury condos, shopping centers, and other large capital ventures since 2012, with the help of banks in China. These new developments are not meant to serve the tens of thousands of working-class immigrants like my parents who live there, but instead are part of a systematic plan to replace current residents with higher-income new inhabitants. At the same time, the Sunset Park Chinese population is expanding, as it absorbs working-class Chinese people who have been displaced from Manhattan's Chinatown. Meanwhile, longtime Chinese residents of Sunset Park are being subjected to rising rents and forced into smaller, more overcrowded living quarters in houses owned by unscrupulous landlords.

UNMASKING YELLOW PERIL: THE PANDEMIC

The wave of racial justice uprisings in the wake of the murder of George Floyd by police and in the face of anti-Asian violence sparked by the COVID-19 pandemic were a pivotal turning point for many. The pandemic revealed how racist attitudes towards Asians haven't changed much. Today's pandemic-related anti-Asian racism is deeply rooted in the "yellow peril" trope from 150 years ago—language that cast Asians as "perpetual foreigners." Today, we are tokenized as the "model minority." This structural racism is rooted in anti-Blackness. As a longtime activist and avid student of history, I know that we have to actively resist the white-washing of our narratives and challenge divisive "ascension to whiteness" and "model minority" frameworks.

How do these shared histories of living under white supremacy and oppression shape our present and future? As we imagine our liberated futures, how do we create a shared narrative that reveals parallel experiences, common threads of xenophobia, and stories of resilience that are inextricably tied to this country's history of institutionalized racism, nativism, and colonialism?

My cultural collective, the Chinatown Art Brigade, has been joining forces with others in the community to fight the construction of the tallest jail in the world, in the heart of Chinatown. As cultural organizers who identify as abolitionists, we know we have to start with political education. How do we both acknowledge people's lived experiences while challenging the roots of anti-Blackness and structural racism? We begin by asking questions. How do we explain abolition and transformative justice to our elders, our parents, our children, and the working-class immigrants who live and work in our neighborhoods? How do we understand the economic forces that are threatening to displace our neighbors? How can we imagine a safer and more just world? How can we do this while joining abolitionist struggles that oppose increased policing and the construction of new jails?

In Asian communities, the term "abolition" can feel distant and even scary to some. Some are misguided by the Chinatown elite's calls for more police to tackle anti-Asian violence and not-in-my-backyard (NIMBY) ideology. Layers of internalized racism and anti-Blackness must be unpacked. Our popular education and cultural-organizing approaches must meet people where they are, with care and concern, while putting forward a vision of collective liberation that rejects the carceral state.

Excerpt from a conversation that took place as a teach-in entitled "Envisioning Abolition in Our Local Asian American Communities," organized by the Chinatown Art Brigade in partnership with Creative Time as part of Rashid Johnson's Red Stage on June 9, 2021:

Betty Yu: We are an intergenerational collective driven by the fundamental belief that our cultural, material, and aesthetic modes of production have the power to advance social change, racial justice, and economic justice. We are Asian American and Asian-diasporic-identifying artists, video makers, writers, educators, scholars, and activists who have deep roots in Manhattan's Chinatown and the Chinatowns throughout New York City. Together we make work that centers art and culture as a way to support community-led organizing against gentrification, displacement, and racialized capitalism. Gentrification and mass displacement are inextricably tied and part of the same system of the prison-industrial complex that incarcerates and criminalizes and perpetuates state-sanctioned violence against our communities of color.

Linda Luu: This event was inspired by the protests of this past summer in response to the most recent spate of police murders of Black people and the more public dialogue around abolition and defunding the police that followed; the rise in violent public attacks on Asian Americans; the shooting and targeting of massage parlors and vulnerable Asian migrant women workers in Georgia; and, here in the city, the carceral response to these events in the form of the NYPD Asian Hate Crimes Task Force. That the first national conversations on race and racist violence that took place after the events and uprisings of the summer were centered on "Stop Asian Hate Crimes," which is a criminal-justice framework that's centered on the individual perpetrator, and which sets up the expansion of the prison-industrial complex, is consistent with how Asian Americans have historically been used as a wedge between white hegemonic power and racialized groups, particularly Black and brown folks. And it's also not an accurate depiction or understanding of how racist violence actually shows up in our own communities, stratified by class, gender, immigration status, language, and the histories of the places and how people come here. We're holding this event in order to center histories of Asian American organizing and racial-justice work that have been made possible by and which contribute to the rich histories of abolitionist organizing against the racist capitalist settler state that is the US.

Our understanding of abolition is informed by the Black radical tradition and generations of Black freedom fighters who have articulated abolition as a political vision and a practice that demands the abolition of all forms of policing and police because it understands that policing itself is the problem. So, abolition means the fundamental redefinition of ideas of safety and of justice away from the police, the law, and the courts as a way of dealing with our social, economic, political, and interpersonal problems. Meaning that the entire foundation of our political order, which is built on anti-Blackness, settler colonialism, and racial capitalism, must be fundamentally rethought and dismantled.

Betty Yu: I wanted to say a little bit more about why abolition and why are we talking about this within the context of Asian American communities. A lot of Asian groups have been calling for more police presence, which we're absolutely opposed to because it criminalizes folks of color and it pits us against each other. But also, as a working-class kid who grew up in Sunset Park, Brooklyn, with garment-worker parents, I often think about how I talk to folks like my parents, folks of their generation who are in their seventies and eighties. How do we actually see folks where they're at and not use these sorts of words like, you know, abolition or white supremacy? Like, what does that actually mean? How do we talk to people about that? Folks in our communities, monolingual immigrants, Chinese-speaking or Korean-speaking, South Asian–speaking, monolingual immigrants? How do we actually have these conversations with them? And I think that's also where the impetus for this teach-in comes from, and that the carceral state is part of the same system of labor exploitation, gentrification, you know, the system of incarceration, all these things are really tied together.

ACTS OF RADICAL IMAGINATION

How are the struggles for prison abolition, against displacement, for reparations, and for an end to settler colonialism our struggles? What does it mean to decolonize, within our own practices, within our own social movements? How do we build genuine solidarity, one that acknowledges that our liberation is inextricably tied to one another?

Many folks of color, low-income workers, and those organizing on the frontlines are fighting like hell. Frameworks oriented around "futurisms," "reimagining," and "re-envisioning" can feel removed from people's everyday lived material conditions. Many of us are ready for a different system, ready to reimagine a different kind of society that is more just—that upholds racial, economic justice, immigration, health care, housing, and environmental justice. Radical imagination is critical at this historic juncture, because when we give ourselves permission to dream, to reimagine and unleash our visions of emancipatory futures, we make strides toward realizing it.

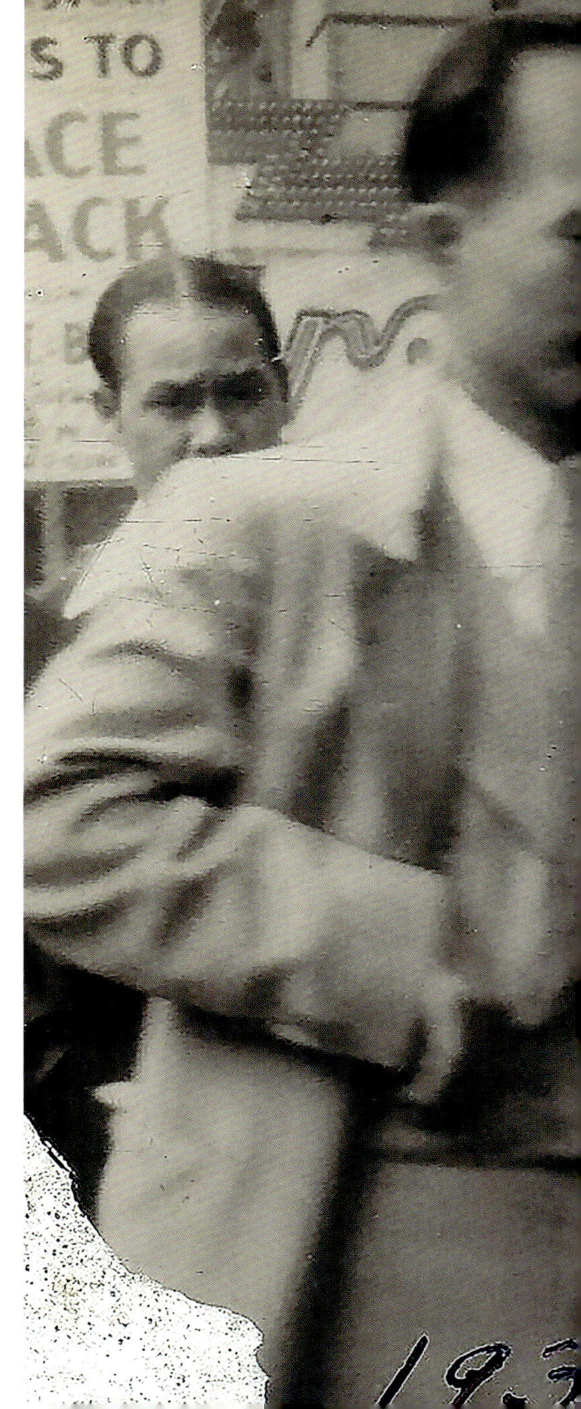
S TO
ACE
ACK

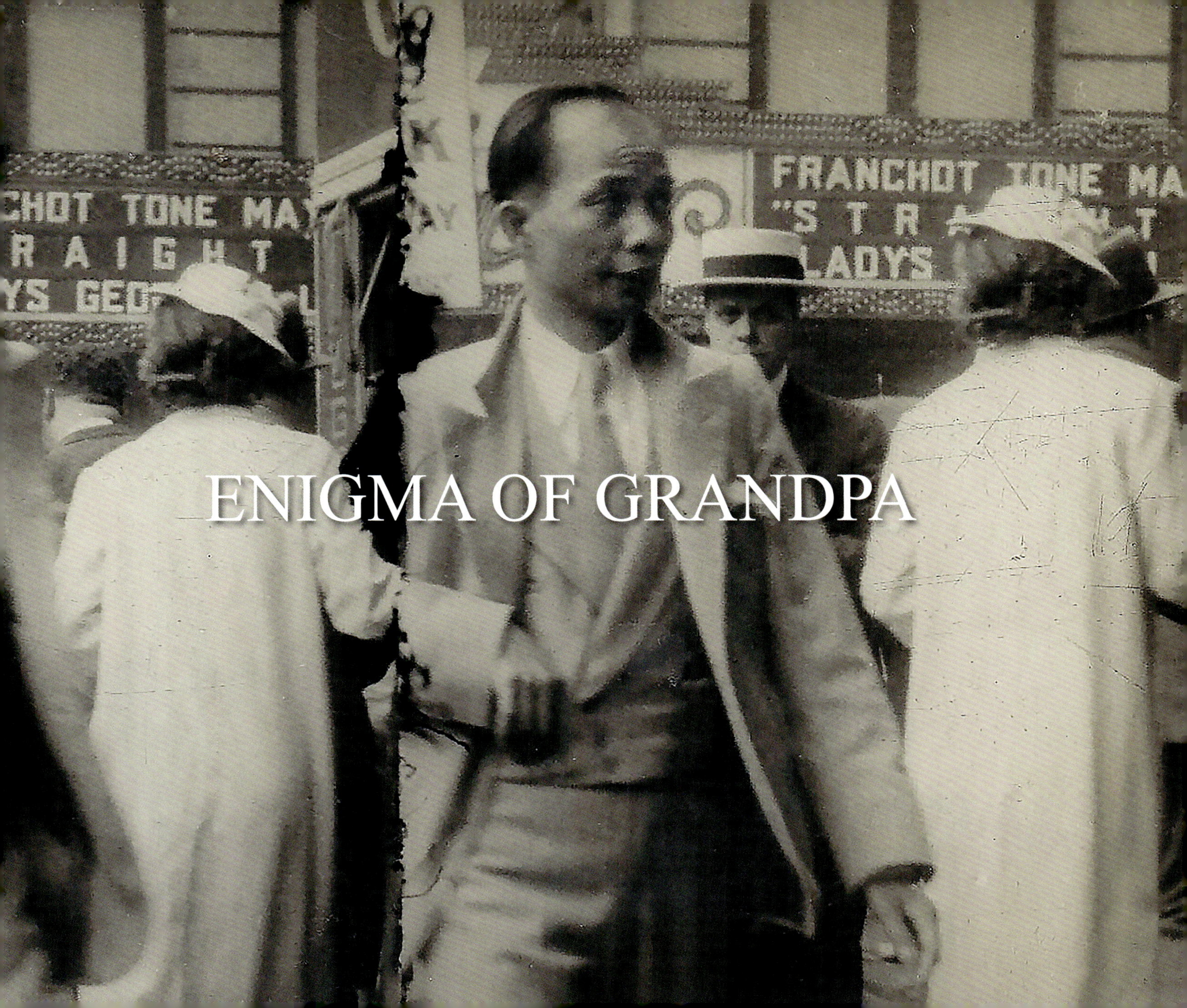

ENIGMA OF GRANDPA

U. S. DEPARTMENT OF LABOR

List 5

LIST OR MANIFEST OF ALIEN PASSENGERS FOR THE UNITED

ALL ALIENS arriving at a port of continental United States from a foreign port or a port of the insular possessions of the United States, and all aliens arriving at a port of said insular possessions from a foreign port, a port of continental United

This (white) sheet is for the listing of

S. S. "President Jefferson" . Passengers sailing from Hongkong, China. , July 4th , 19

ACTION SHEET, FIRST DAY LANDINGS

NAME Woo Sui Lem

APPLICATION AND RECEIPT FOR CERTIFICATE OF IDENTITY

Name Woo Sui Lem Age 20

Place Reno, Nev.

The Chinese Exclusion Act provisions required two white witnesses to testify to a Chinese person's immigration status

24. The Chinese Exclusion Law defines a merchant as follows:

"A merchant is a person engaged in buying and selling merchandise at a fixed place of business, which business is conducted in his name, and who during the time he claims to be engaged as a merchant does not engage in the performance of any manual labor, except such as is necessary in the conduct of his business as such merchant."

From your observation of the applicant, covering the period of the past 12 months, are you fully convinced that he is entitled to be classed as a merchant as the law defines the term "Merchant"?

余永昌余輝

U. S. DEPARTMENT OF LABOR
IMMIGRATION SERVICE

Commissioner of Immigration,
San Francisco, Calif.

Statement of White Witness

Total passengers

U. S. citizens

Aliens

Form 432 [ORIGINAL]

APPLICATION OF LAWFULLY DOMICILED CHINESE LABORER FOR RETURN CERTIFICATE

U. S. DEPARTMENT OF LABOR
IMMIGRATION SERVICE

Office of COMMISSIONER
Port of SAN FRANCISCO
AUGUST 24, 1926 191

To COMMISSIONER OF IMMIGRATION
Chinese and Immigrant Inspector
ANGEL ISLAND STATION, PORT OF SAN FRANCISCO

Sir: It being my intention to leave the United States on a temporary visit abroad, and to depart and return through the Chinese port of entry of San Francisco, I hereby apply, under the provisions of the laws of the United States relating to the exclusion of Chinese (specifically Section 7 of the Act approved September 13, 1888), and of Rules 12 to 14 of the Regulations of the Department of Labor drawn in conformity therewith for pre-investigation of my claimed status as a lawfully domiciled laborer. I submit herewith my Certificate of Residence, No. 38849 (or a certified transcript of a court record of my discharge as a person lawfully entitled to be in the United States). I am prepared to appear before you personally at such time and place as you may designate, and to produce at such time and place witnesses to prove my statutory qualifications for a return certificate, as follows:

Woo Sui Lem 9/2/26

DEPARTED FROM ... PER STEAMER PRES. LINCOLN SEP 18 1926

FAMILY:
Wife, named
Residing
Child or children, named
Residing
Parent, named
Residing
OR

PROPERTY or DEBTS, or both (aggregating at least $1,000 in value) described as follows:
$1,000.00 deposited in the Oriental Branch—The French American Bank, 1000 Grant Avenue, San Francisco, Cal.

I HEREBY AGREE that the above-described claims shall remain as they now exist until my return.

Subscribed and sworn to before me, this 2 day of Sept 1926

Chinese and Immigrant Inspector.

Signature in Chinese 胡瑞廉
Signature in English Woo-Sui Lem
Address 816 Washington St.
Height 5 feet 2½ inches
Physical marks or peculiarities mole under chin; scar above left temple.

SPL 12

U. S. DEPARTMENT OF LABOR
IMMIGRATION SERVICE

ACTION SHEET, ARRIVAL

(Space for filing.)

ARRIVAL. No. 20733 / 6-21
Name Woo Sui Lem
Accompanied by
Class Merchant
Destination
Vessel
Date 1-2-22
Remarks:

(Date) Feb. 21, 1922 Reported Favorably — Inspector.
(Date) Forwarded to Law Section. — Inspector in Charge.
(Date) Action — For Law Section.
(Date) Feb. 24/1922 Action Admit — Commissioner.
(Date) Appealed by
(Date) Department decision
(Date) 2/24/22 Action Landed, 2.30 — J. M. McNamara, For Deportation and Detention Division.
(Date) FEB 28 1922 Issued Certificate of Identity No. 38849

Left: *Grandpa's immigration papers from the 1920s*, 2024. Digital collage.

Immigration of Chinese men required two white witnesses during the Chinese Exclusion Act.

Form 2508

San Francisco, Calif., January 4th 1922.

Commissioner of Immigration,

San Francisco, California,

Sir:

I hereby file notice of appearance in the case of Woo Sui Lern No. 20733/6-21 ex S.S. Golden State, Jan 2nd, 1922, who has applied for admission at this port as a son of merchant Reno, Nevada.

I certify that I am not associated in any way whatever, either directly or indirectly, with any attorney or other person who has been refused permission to practice before your office.

Respectfully,

O. P. Stidger

Attorney for Applicant.

Address: 628 Montgomery St

San Francisco, Cal.

Telephone No. Sutter 5379

(NOTE: This form should not be filed in duplicate; one original is sufficient.)

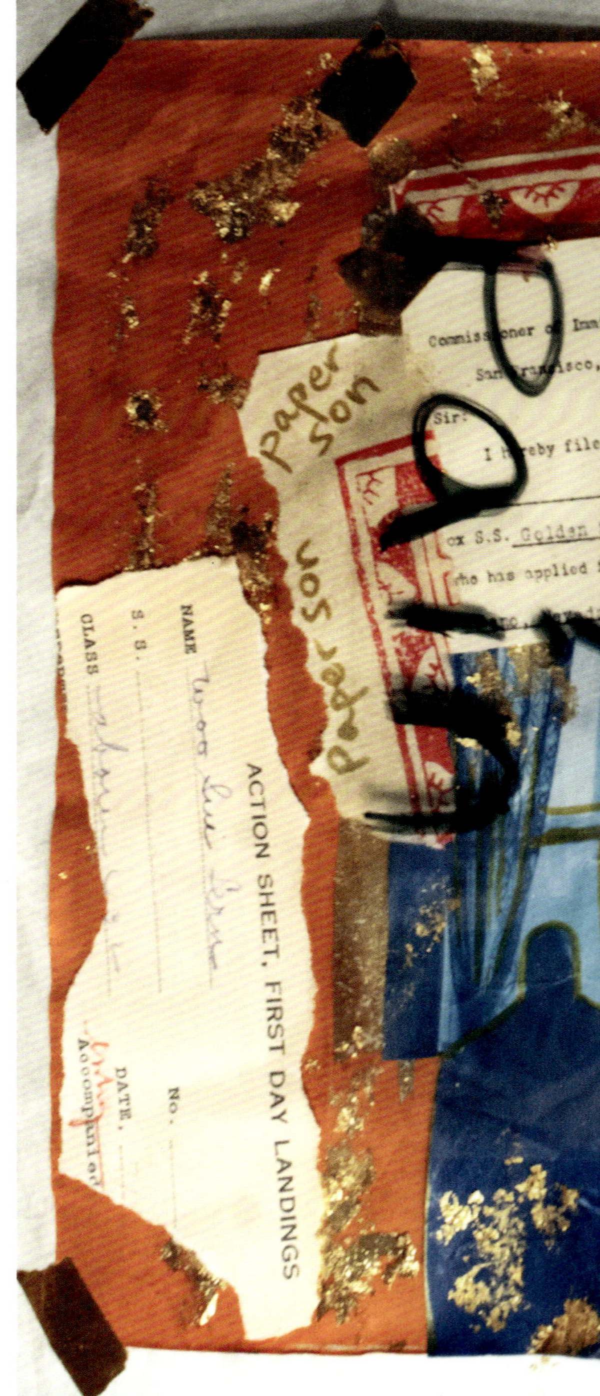

Above: "Son" of a merchant letter from 1922.

Right: *Your amnesia is my pain*, 2023. Mixed-media collage.

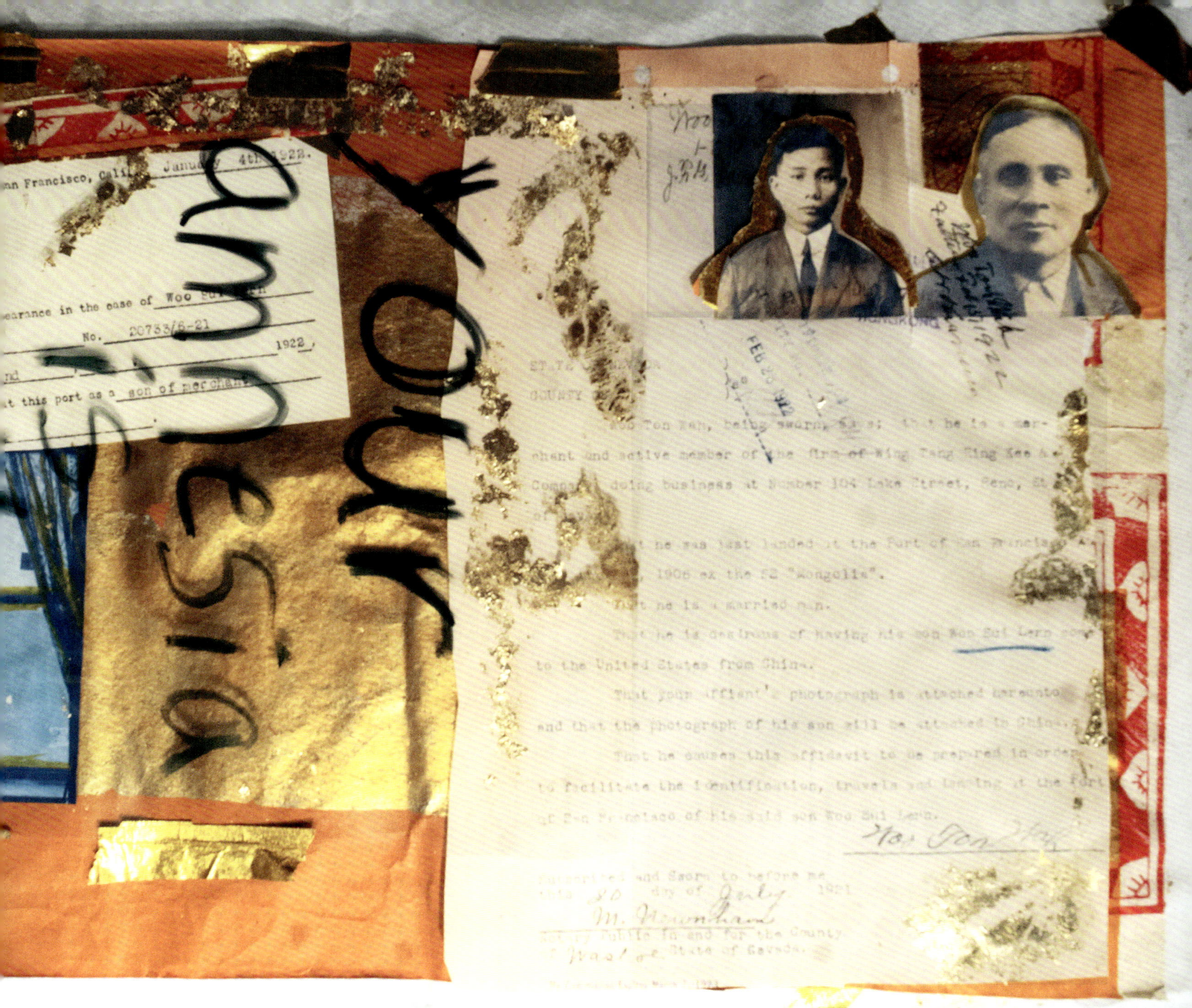

your
amnesia
No. 20733/6-21
1922
son of merchan
1906 ex the SS "Mongolia".
to the United States from China.
to facilitate the identification, travels and landing at the Port
State of Nevada.

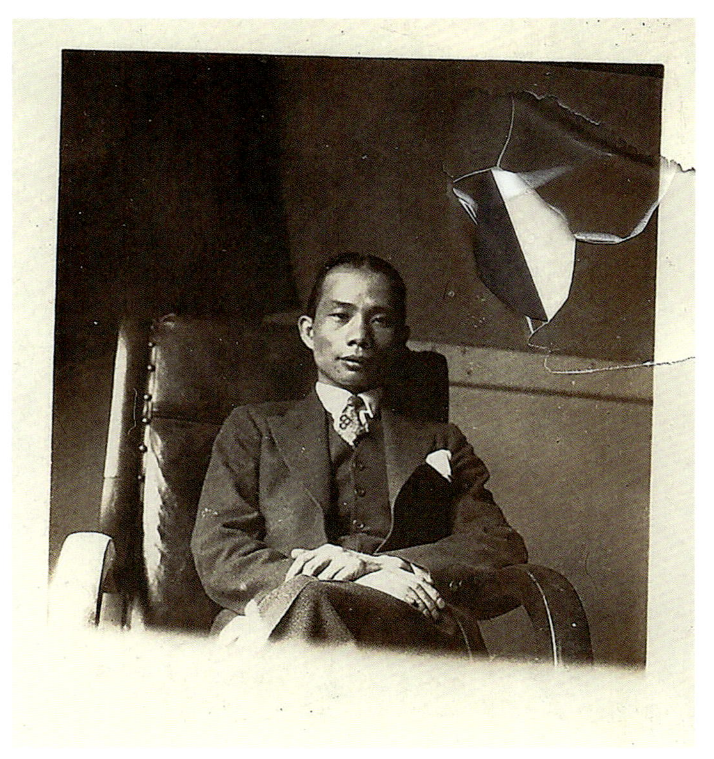

Above: Grandpa in Chicago, around 1925.

Right: Said Witness/Case is in Facto.

#20733/6-21 San Francisco, Cal., Jan. 24, 1922

Commissioner of Immigration,

Port of San Francisco

Dear Sir:

In Re: application to land at this Port of Woo Sui Lern from the SS "Golden State" of Jan. 2, 1922 as the minor son of a merchant of Reno, Nevada.

The identifying witness in this case resides in the lower part of the state and finds it impossible to take the time and defray the expense of a trip to Reno. We would ask permission that the testimony of the identifying witness be taken in Sacramento before your Inspector there. If this is granted the identifying witness will appear before your Inspector in Sacramento at his convenience.

Respectfully,

OPHedges

OPS/AW

Case is in facts

U. S. DEPARTMENT OF LABOR

IMMIGRATION SERVICE

[ANS]WERING REFER TO [N]O. 20733/6-21

Office of the Commissioner
Angel Island Station
Via Ferry Post Office
San Francisco, Calif.

6-21 Golden State

January 27, 1922.

Mr. C. H. Hannum,
Immigrant Inspector,
Sacramento, California.

The papers in the application of Woo Sui Lem for admission were referred to you for investigation on the 9th instant, the alleged father in the case being engaged as a merchant in Reno, Nevada. Since taking that action this office has been addressed by the attorney representing this case, copy of his letter being attached hereto. You will note that it is the desire of the attorney to have the supporting witness testify before you on relationship and it will be proper for you to correspond with the attorney in order that arrangements may be completed toward having the production of the said witness.

[...] WHITE

[M]ailed this day by ....

Commissioner.

FBJ:amt

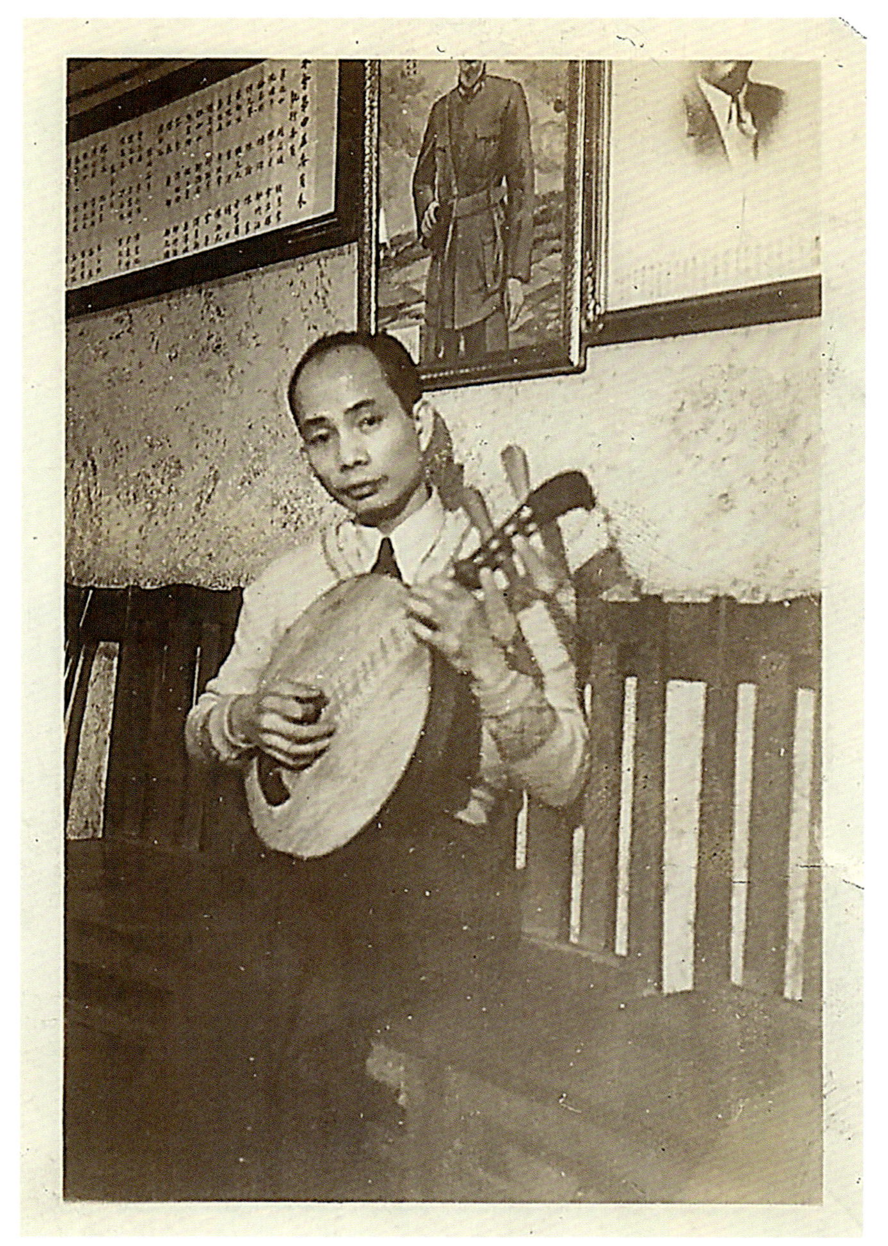

Grandpa playing the ruan (Chinese banjo) in New York City, 1930s (exact date unknown).

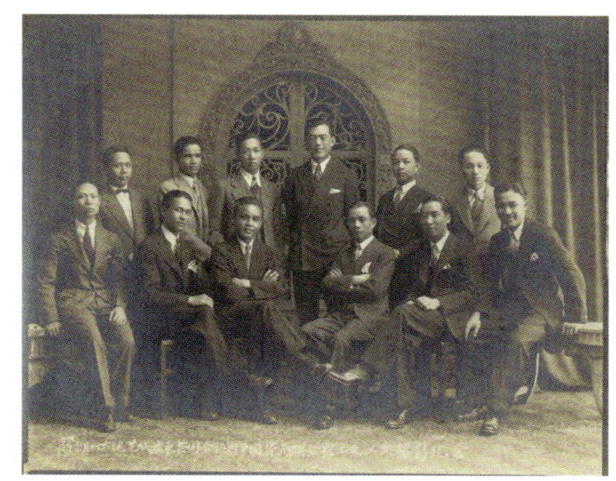

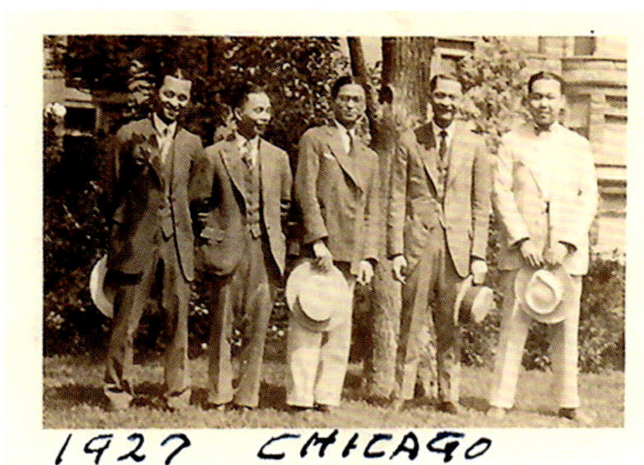

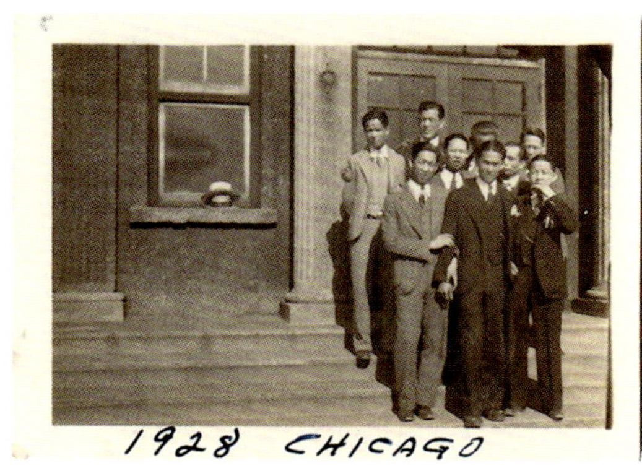

Grandpa with friends and coworkers in Chicago, late 1920s.

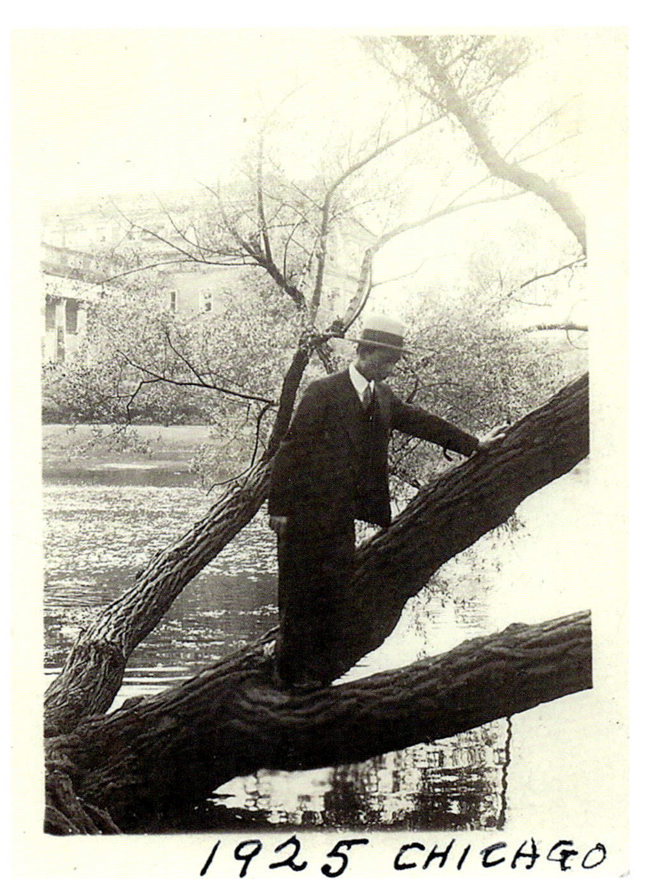

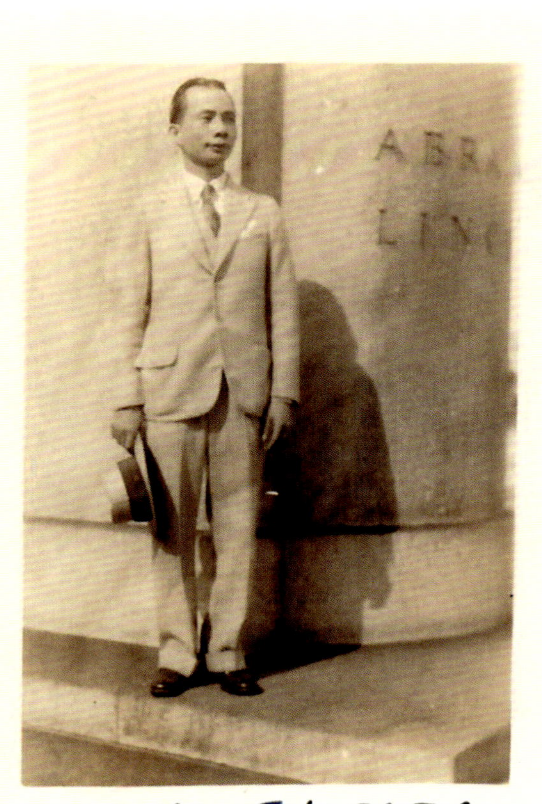

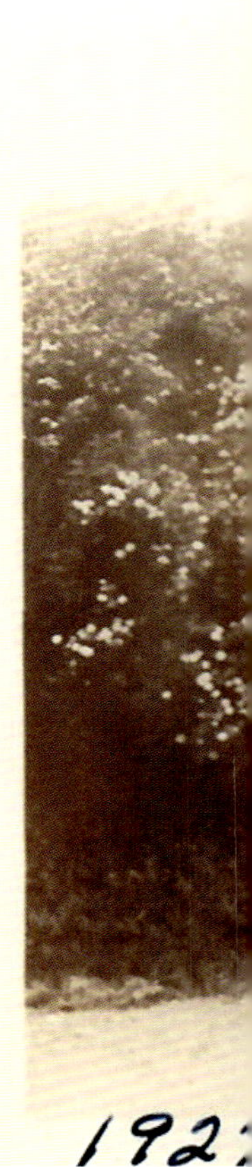

Grandpa in Chicago, late 1920s.

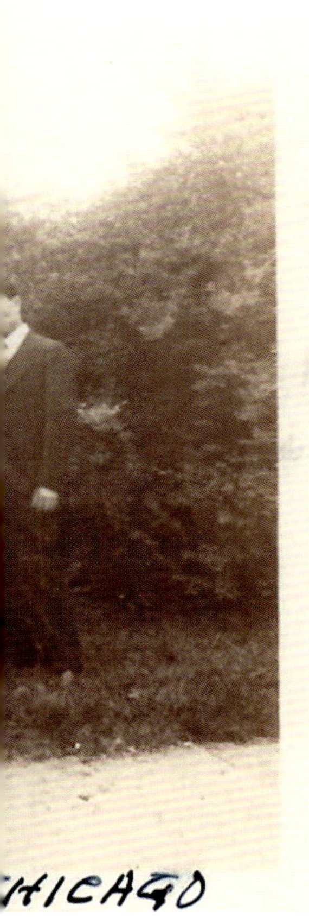

HICAGO

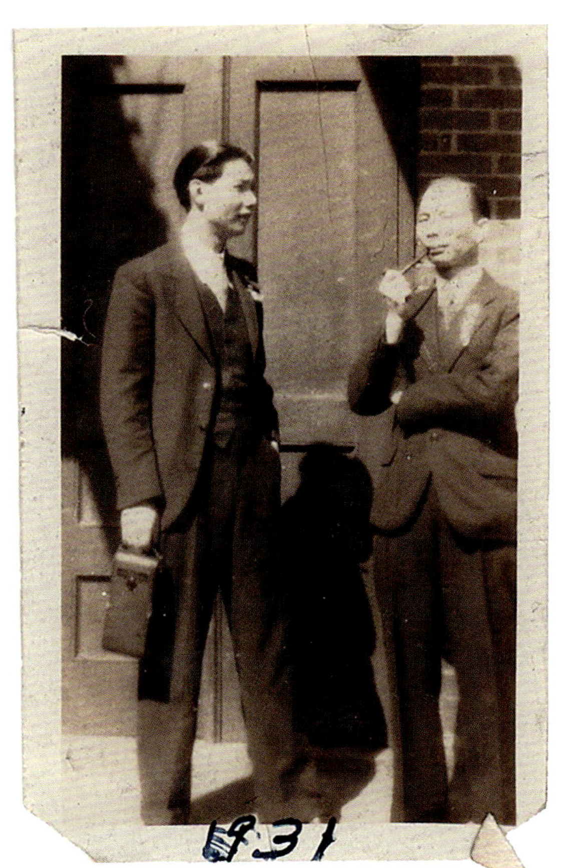

1931

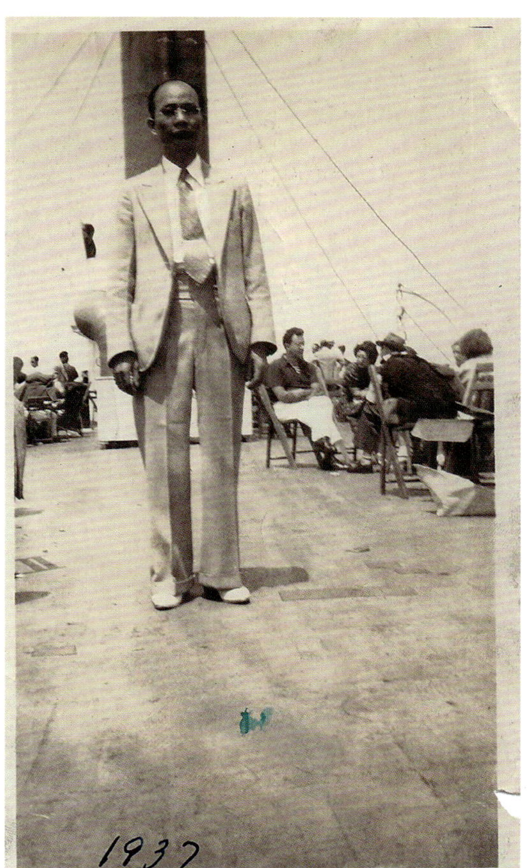

1937

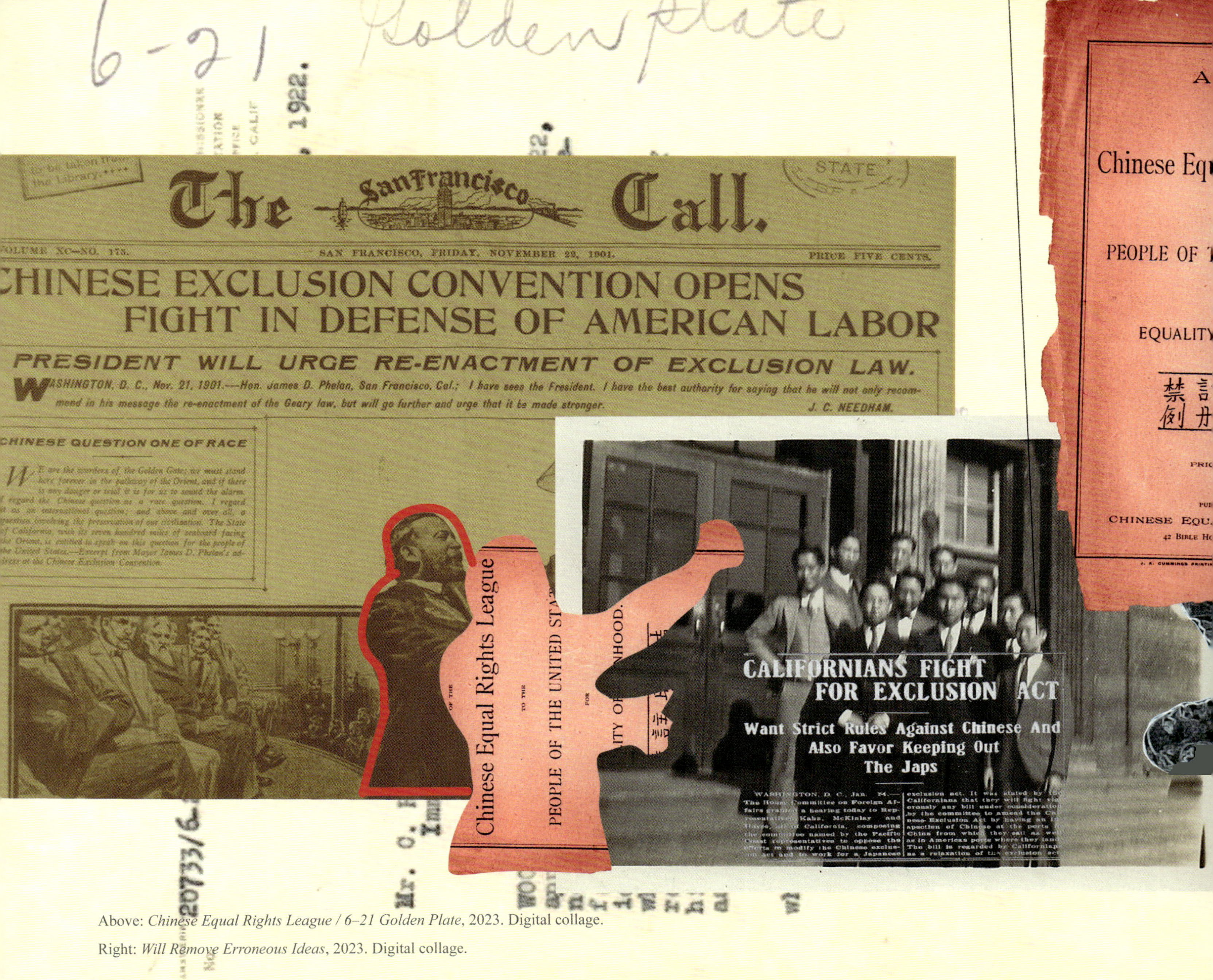

Above: *Chinese Equal Rights League / 6–21 Golden Plate*, 2023. Digital collage.

Right: *Will Remove Erroneous Ideas*, 2023. Digital collage.

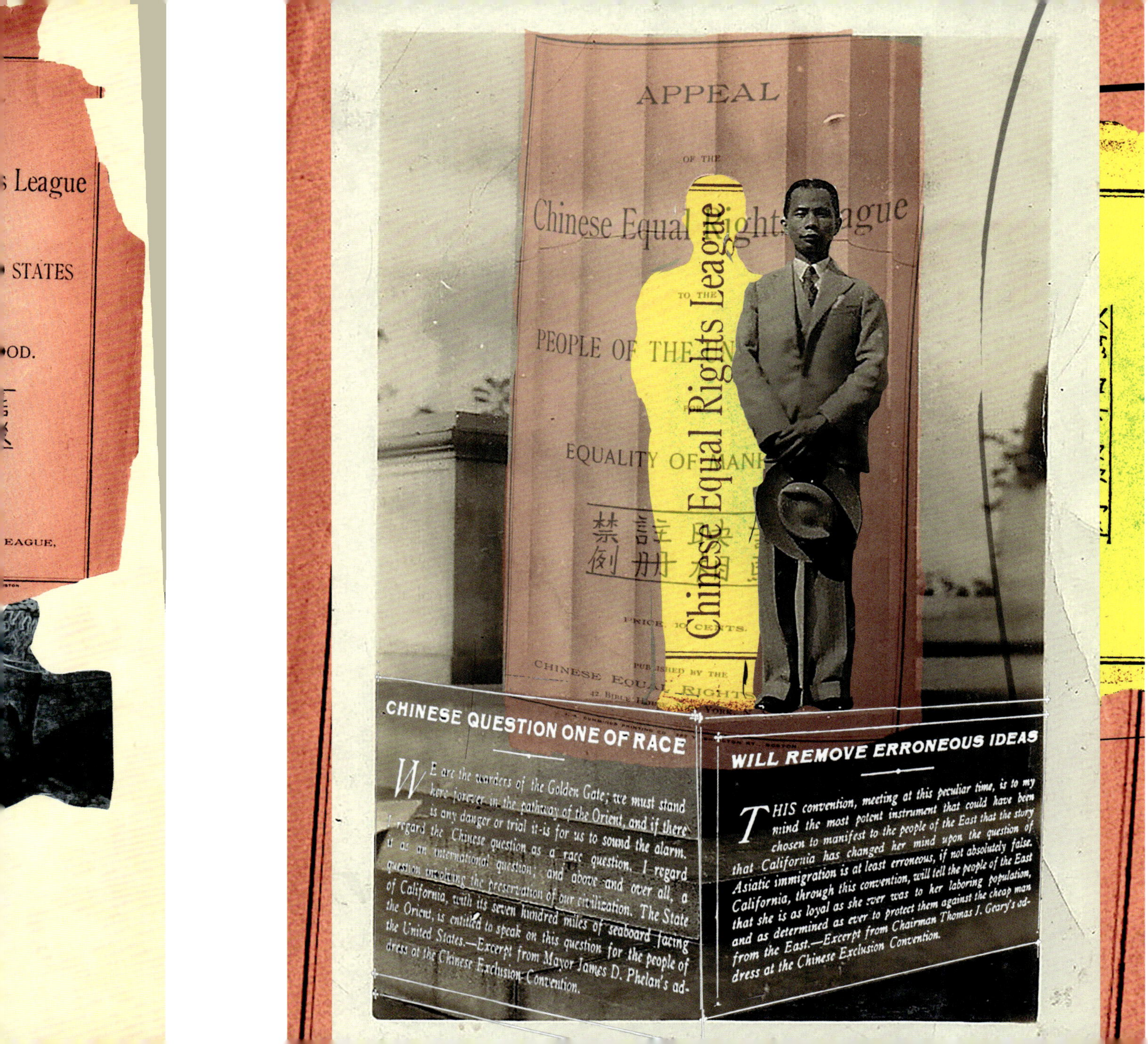

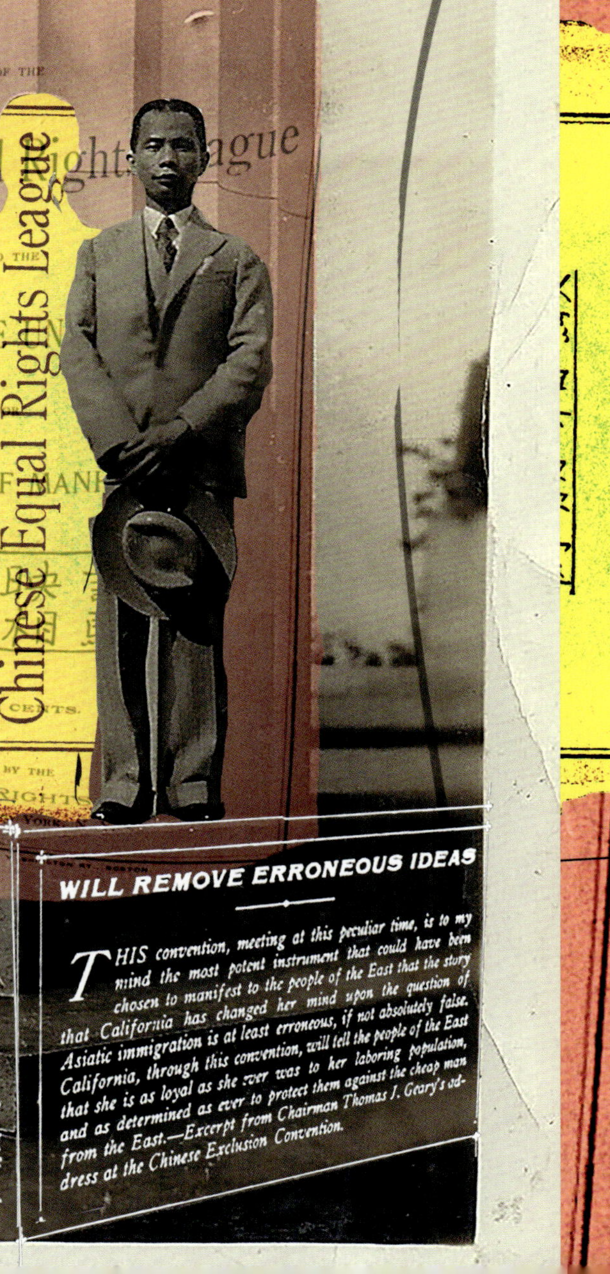
League
STATES
OD.
EAGUE.
APPEAL
OF THE
Chinese Equal
ague
TO THE
PEOPLE OF THE
EQUALITY OF MAN
禁 註
例 册
PRICE
CENTS.
PUBLISHED BY THE
CHINESE EQUAL RIGHTS
Chinese Equal Rights League
CHINESE QUESTION ONE OF RACE
WE are the warders of the Golden Gate; we must stand here forever in the pathway of the Orient, and if there is any danger or trial it is for us to sound the alarm. I regard the Chinese question as a race question. I regard it as an international question; and above and over all, a question involving the preservation of our civilization. The State of California, with its seven hundred miles of seaboard facing the Orient, is entitled to speak on this question for the people of the United States.—Excerpt from Mayor James D. Phelan's address at the Chinese Exclusion Convention.
WILL REMOVE ERRONEOUS IDEAS
THIS convention, meeting at this peculiar time, is to my mind the most potent instrument that could have been chosen to manifest to the people of the East that the story that California has changed her mind upon the question of Asiatic immigration is at least erroneous, if not absolutely false. California, through this convention, will tell the people of the East that she is as loyal as she ever was to her laboring population, and as determined as ever to protect them against the cheap man from the East.—Excerpt from Chairman Thomas J. Geary's address at the Chinese Exclusion Convention.

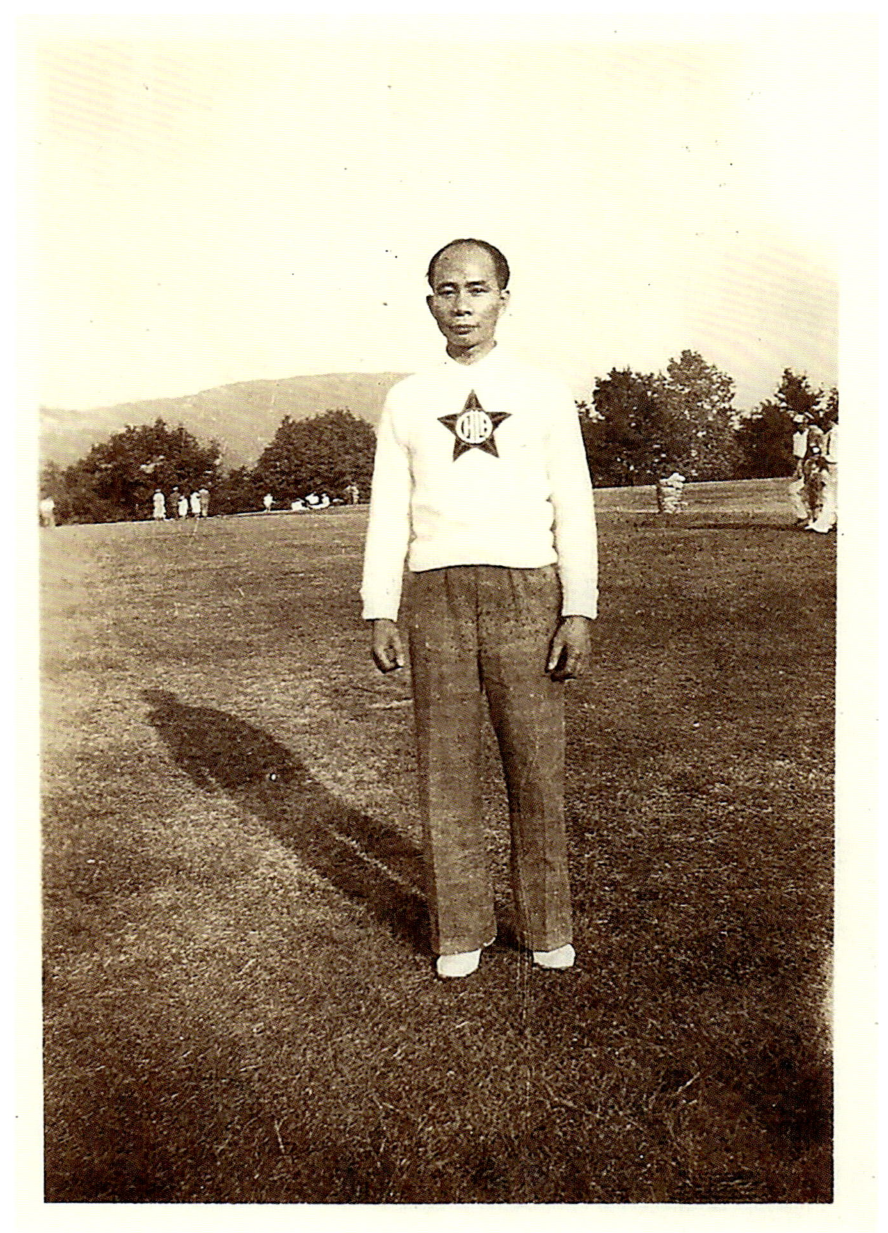

Grandpa in a Chinese Hand Laundry Alliance of NY sweatshirt at a CHLA retreat in Bear Mountain, sometime in the late 1930s.

IN THE ABSENCE OF MEMORIES ... THERE ARE FRAGMENTS

Family Amnesia is a love letter to my family and a visual tribute honoring the Chinese American experience in the United States. The book explores my family's multigenerational resilience and resistance through my mixed-media collages, my grandfather's photographs, my own captured images, and other archival material. Chinese Americans have been in the US since the mid-1850s, yet we are seldom represented in photographs or in the popular mainstream. When we are depicted, it's often through a Western gaze that feels reductive and stereotypical, and in caricatures that are racist. Images that show our full and complex humanity are often absent in mainstream narratives. This can often feel like cultural erasure. It is a painful part of our American history. I am reclaiming that narrative through my own family's story. *Family Amnesia* reflects on the incalculable and traumatic impact that historical events like the 1882 Chinese Exclusion Act continue to have on the Asian American experience. It recalls the anti-China and anti-Asian paranoia and hysteria that led to policies like the Exclusion Act. The collages draw visually on geopolitical history, recalling narratives that mocked China as the "sick man of Asia" and that demonized Chinese as the "yellow peril." This is particularly timely as the US government continues to vilify China as a global threat.

This book feels like a culmination of my work as an artist, community organizer, educator, and cultural worker over the past twenty-five years. It is deeply personal, political, and timely. The project reminds us that the rise of anti-Asian violence in the wake of the coronavirus pandemic is part of a larger history of systemic racism and ongoing xenophobia.

How do I preserve and pass on these stories of struggle that my ancestors wanted me to forget? For the four generations of my family, survival itself *was* and *is* an act of resistance. What was it like for my grandparents, my ancestors in the United States? What were their dreams? How did they stay resilient while facing racism on a daily basis?

Photographic archives have brought me closer to unpacking the Chinese diasporic experience through my family's personal lens. Ten years ago, I found hundreds of photographs belonging to my grandfather. They span his life, starting in the 1920s in Chicago to his military service during World War II to becoming a labor organizer, to the US reunification with my grandmother in the 1940s to the end of his life in the 1980s. His life is still an enigma to me. I was both surprised and excited to find photos of him as a leader with the New York Chinese Hand Laundry Alliance (CHLA)—a pivotal group fighting for the labor rights of hand-laundry workers—founded in 1933. The book also includes my mother's struggles as a garment worker who became an organizer, and my sister's legacy as a labor activist. My family story is not unique. It is part of the larger collective Asian American immigration experience.

Strangely, the meditative process of creating these collages has been healing medicine. These works aim to highlight joy and resilience in the face of adversity. They interweave the realities of displacement, dispossession, nativism, labor exploitation, and colonization (in Hong Kong) that have profoundly affected my family. The role of storytelling has never felt more palpable. It has allowed me to reconstruct the pieces, the fragments, and the stories, assembling a more holistic narrative of my family. These forgotten stories not only honor my ancestors' past, but also allow me to live in the present. Of course, these are my own reimagined memories. My grandparents are no longer alive to provide background on these old photographs. I have no idea who the other people are in the photos with my grandparents. I long to understand what life was like for Asian Americans from the 1920s to the 1960s.

From a young age I was obsessed with capturing what photographer Henri Cartier-Bresson called the "decisive moment." I remember running around with my film camera documenting my family members. I was only five when my grandfather passed away. But even after he passed, I would imagine him suddenly popping up and posing for my photographs.

I was always fascinated with the still image, especially when browsing through family albums, even as a child. I was the youngest of four girls, and by the time I came around, there were fewer and fewer photographs. I suppose my parents were working all the time. I remember poring over piles of photo albums hoping to get a glimpse of myself. I did find a few photos of myself as a baby. My parents dressed me as if I was a boy until I was five years old. Boys are still widely regarded as more important and valuable than girls in patriarchal Chinese society. But to be fair, my parents still loved me unconditionally.

This book is an open invitation to Chinese Americans, Asian Americans, and others to reflect on their own family photographs, ephemera, traditional artifacts, archival material, oral histories, and voices that defy the yellow-peril legacy while reclaiming our collective identity. I hope this book reminds us of the power of collective storytelling, generational survival, and creative resistance as medicine. This is a time of heightened anti-Asian xenophobia. Collective reflection is needed.

In the face of continuous attacks on Asian Americans, racial justice uprisings, and the Movement for Black Lives, there has never been a more critical moment for artists like me to connect to audiences through our work and to deepen our impact. I continue to challenge myself and to push the boundaries of how art can truly help shift the nation's consciousness and change hearts and minds. As a Chinese American, I hope this book is engaging and thought-provoking. I hope it inspires other Asian Americans and viewers to reflect on their own role in society and to see themselves as agents of change. I hope the book encourages and emboldens the Asian American community to speak out against anti-Asian racism and to support broader racial and social-justice movements.

Through the creation of these mixed-media collages I am reclaiming not only my family's narrative, but also our broader collective memory. Bringing our stories to the foreground is an act of resistance. This book is this act of resistance and love.

Discovering My Grandfather through Mao, a short documentary film about my personal journey as I uncover my grandfather's radical history as a labor organizer and cofounder of the Chinese Hand Laundry Alliance of New York (CHLA), 2011.

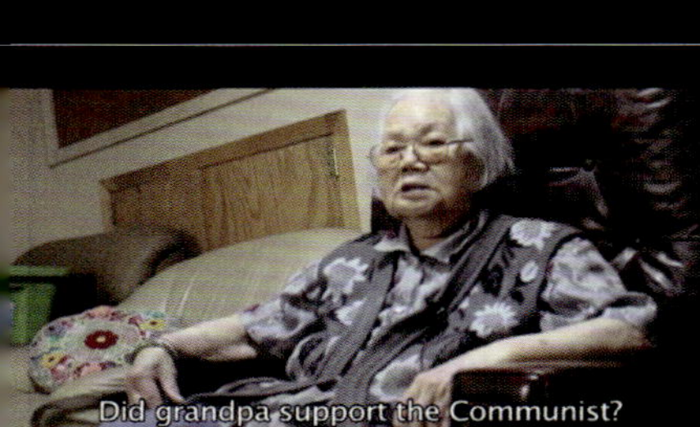

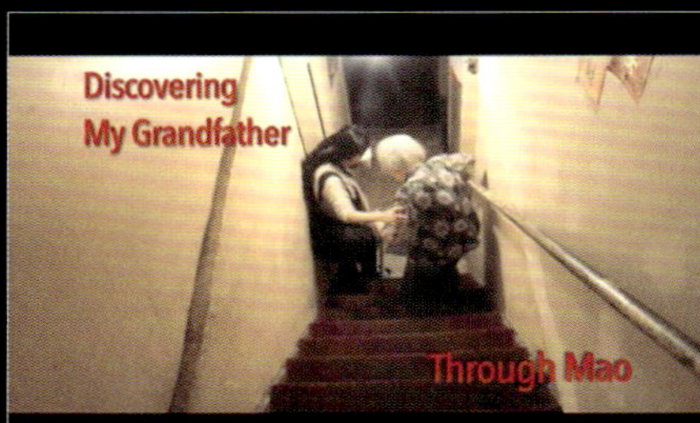

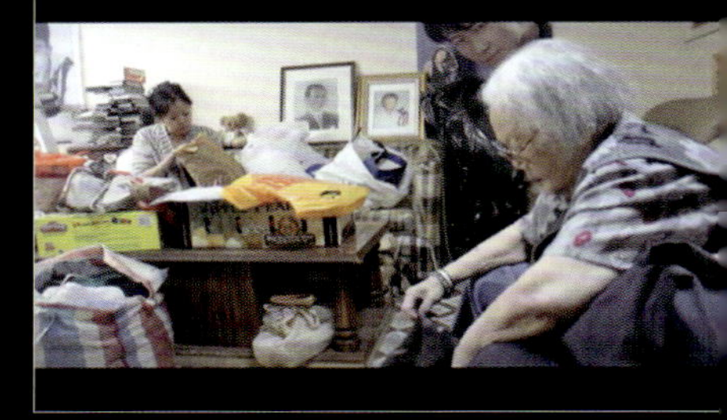

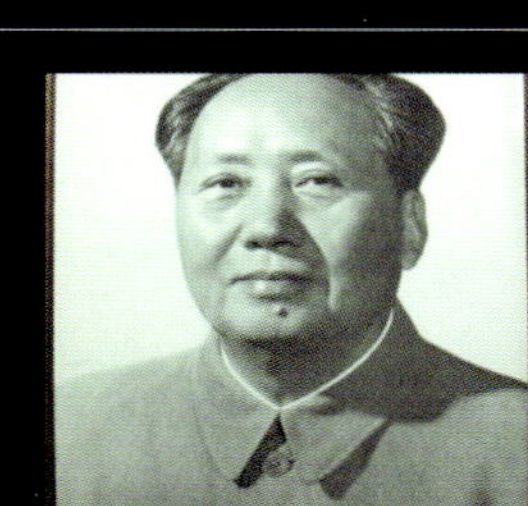

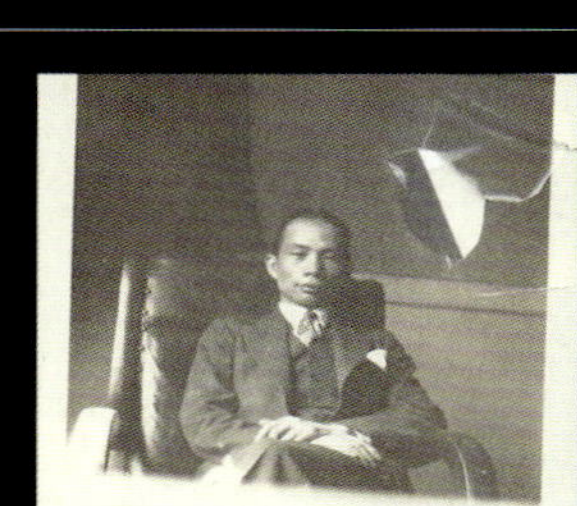

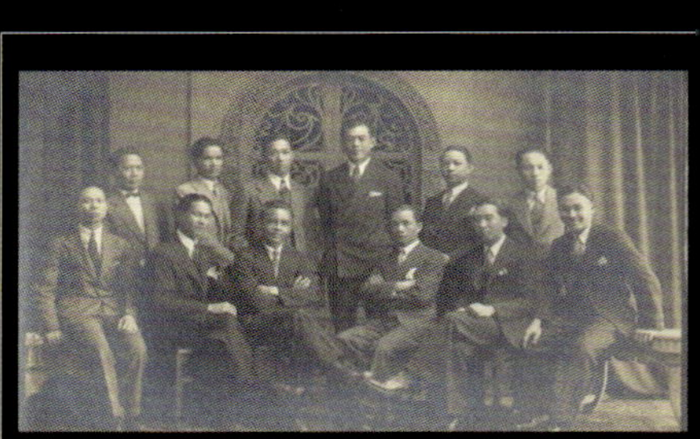

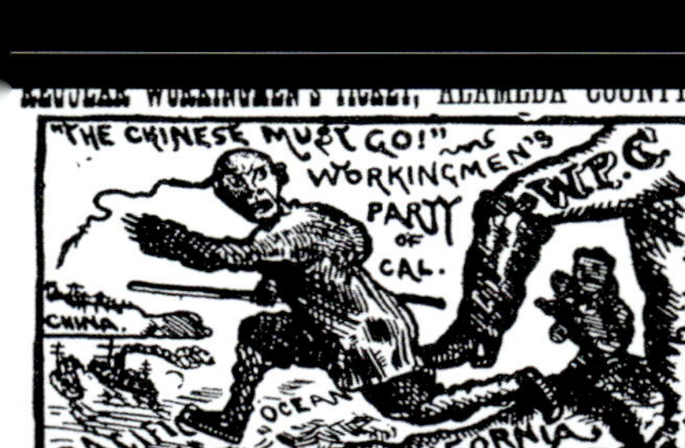

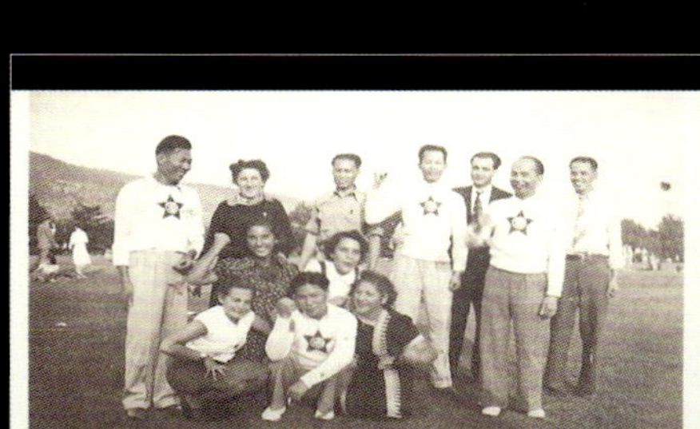

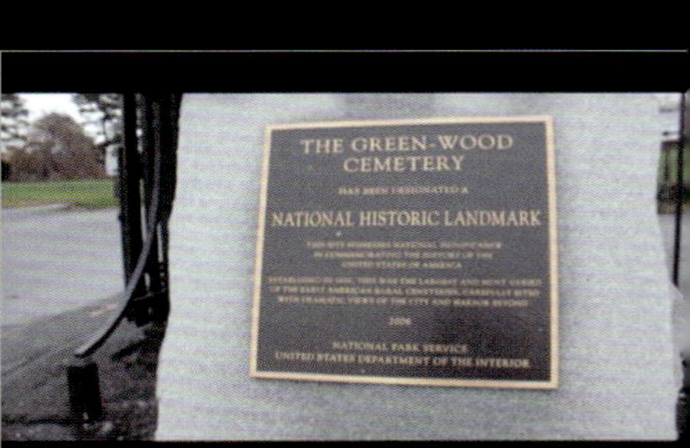

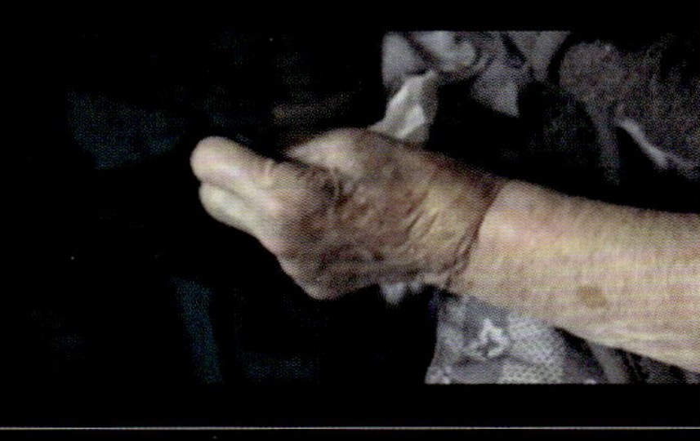

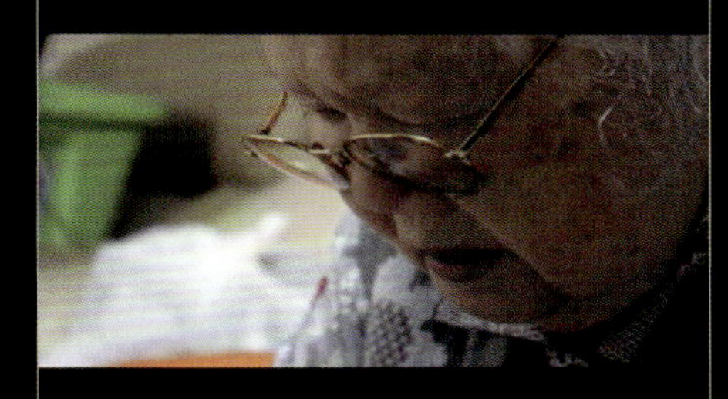

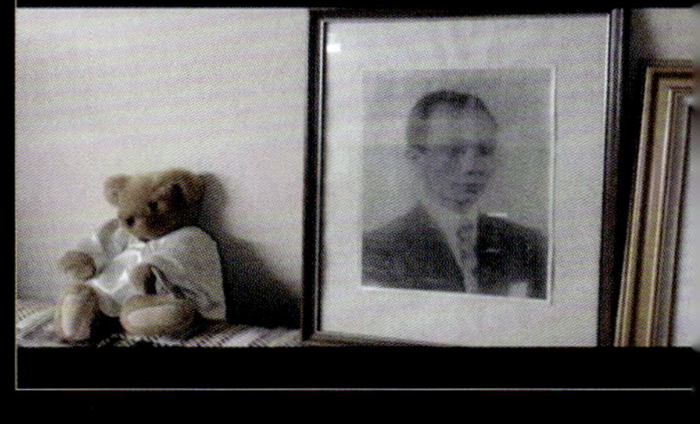

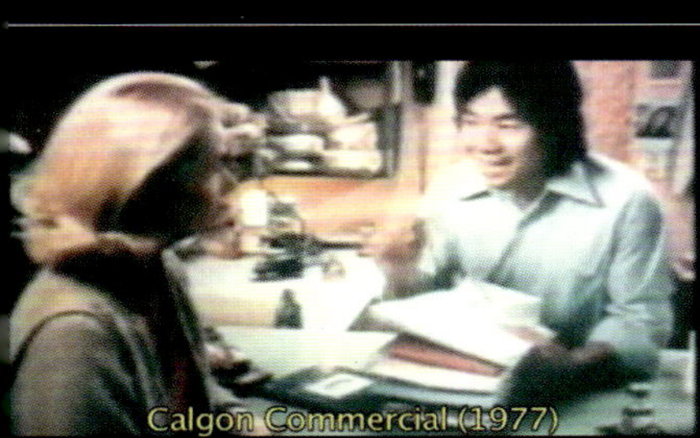
Calgon Commercial (1977)

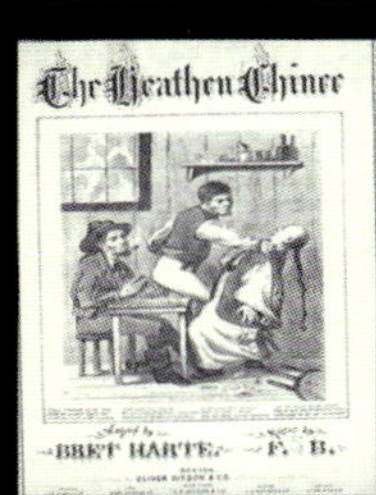
The Heathen Chinee
BRET HARTE
F. B.

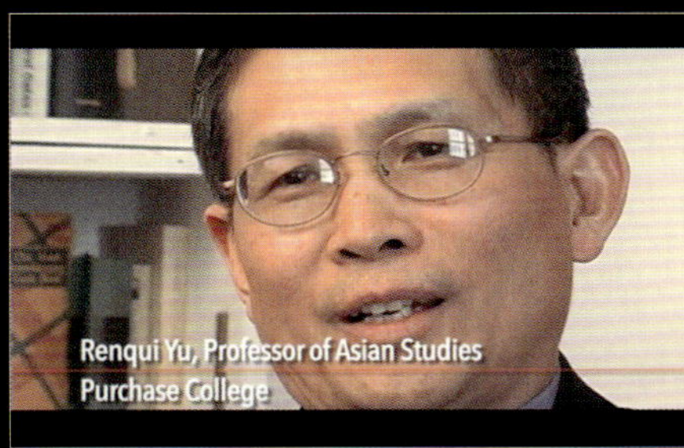
Renqui Yu, Professor of Asian Studies
Purchase College

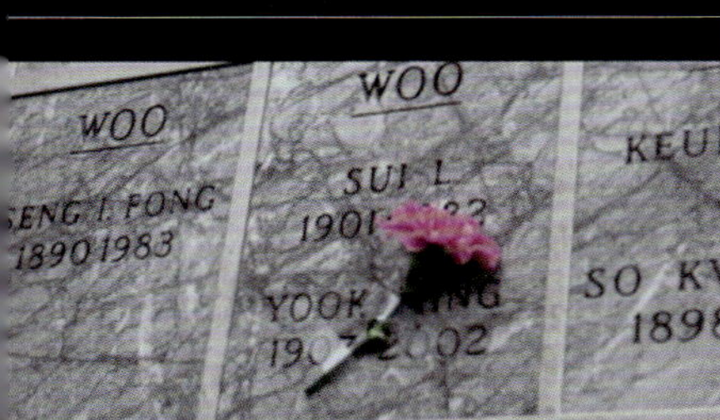
WOO
WOO
SUI L.
1890 1983

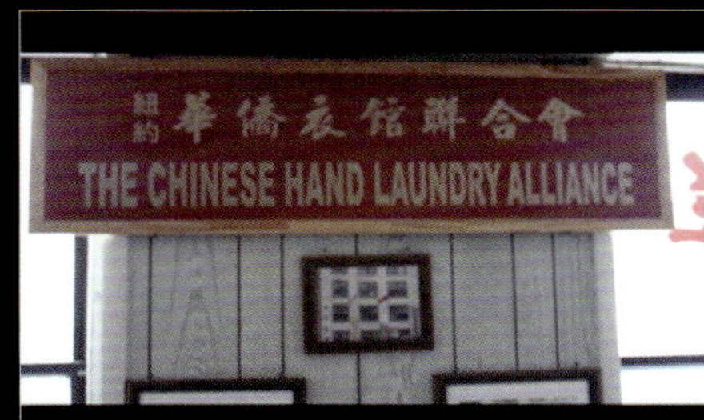
紐約華僑衣館聯合會
THE CHINESE HAND LAUNDRY ALLIANCE

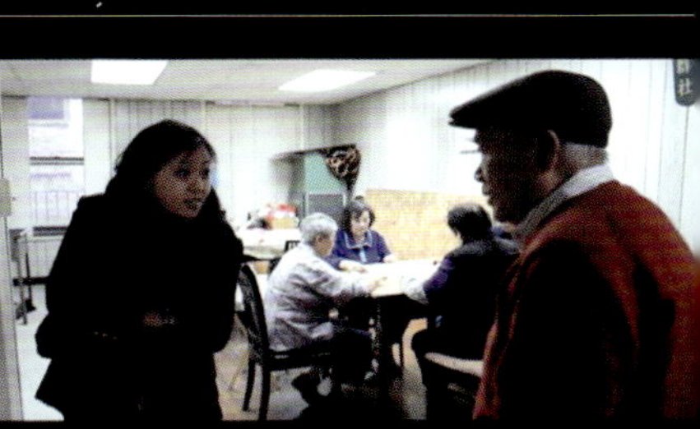

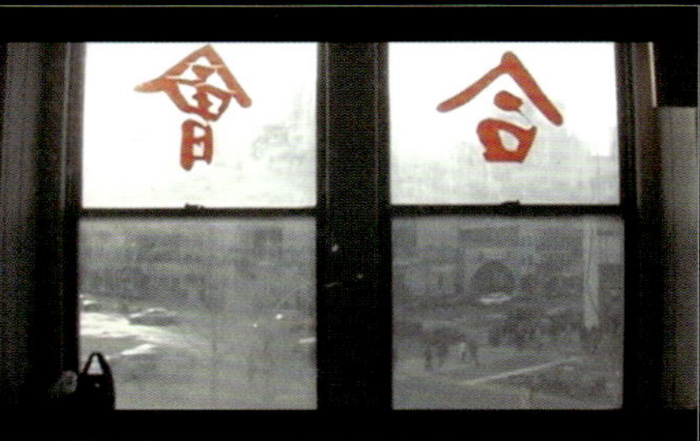

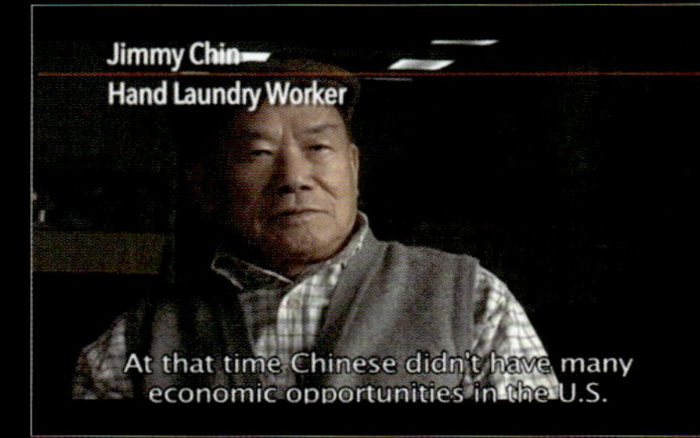

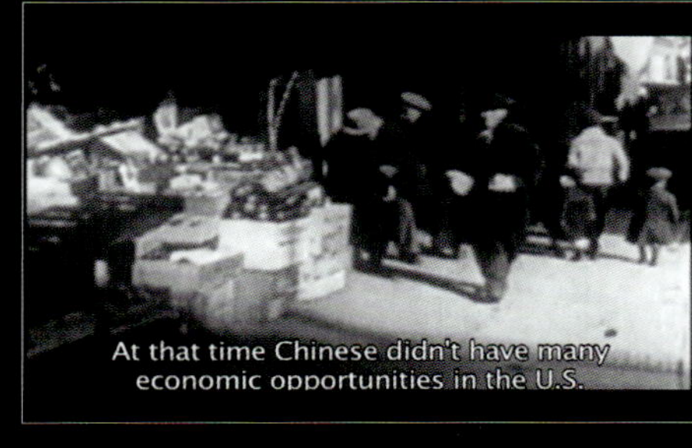

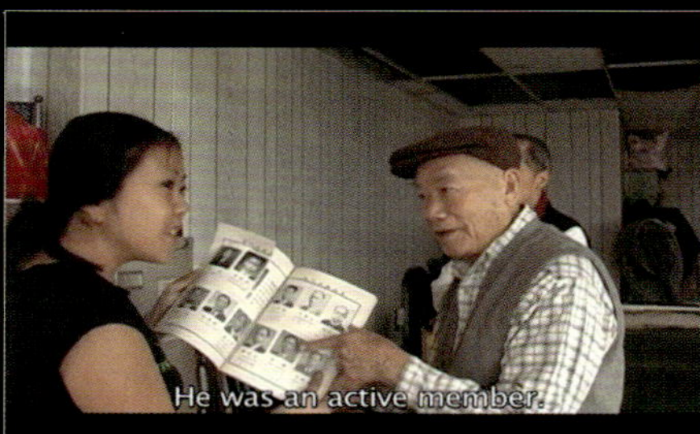

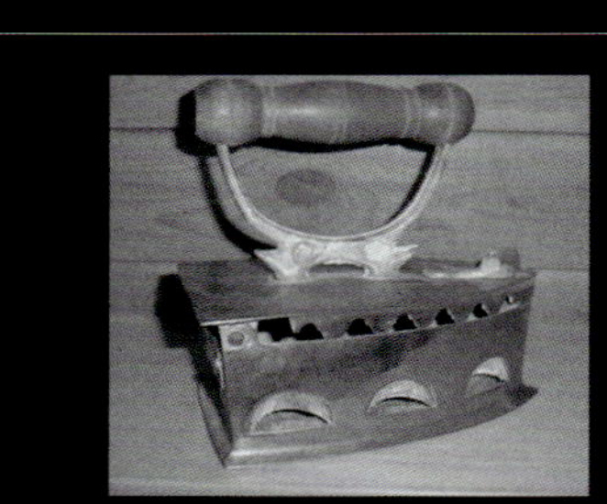

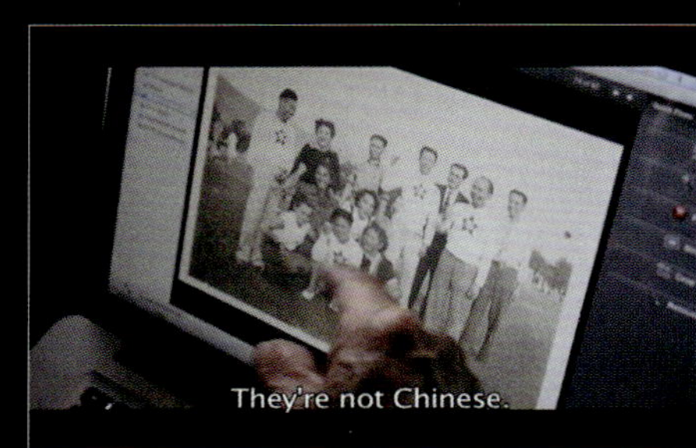

$500 Raised Here for China

After several hours of anti-Japanese oratory, 150 New York Chinese laundrymen contributed nearly $500 yesterday to a new national defense fund. The meeting, sponsored by the Chinese Hand Laundry Alliance, Inc., was held at 191 Canal Street.

The New York Times
Published: August 23, 1937

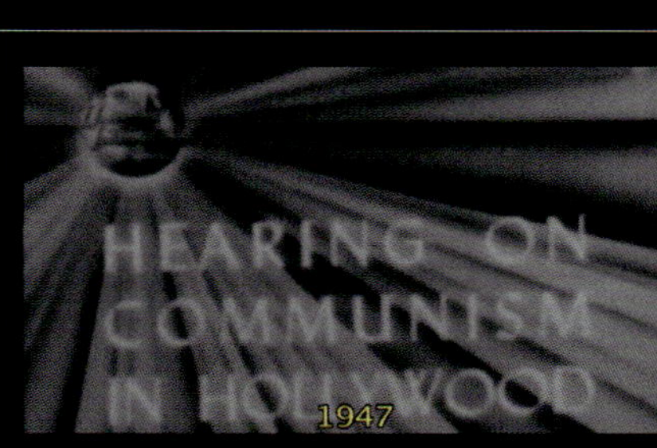

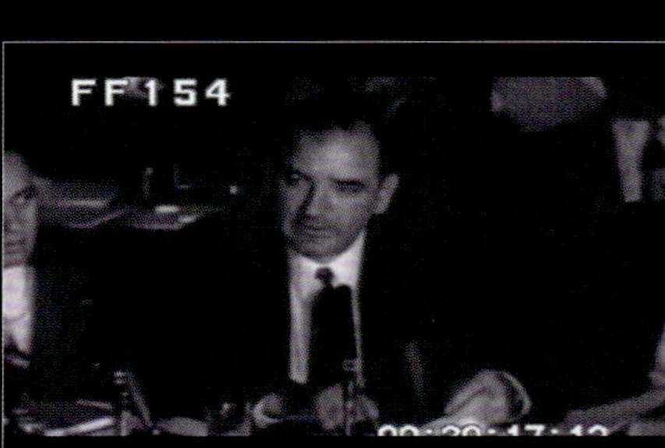

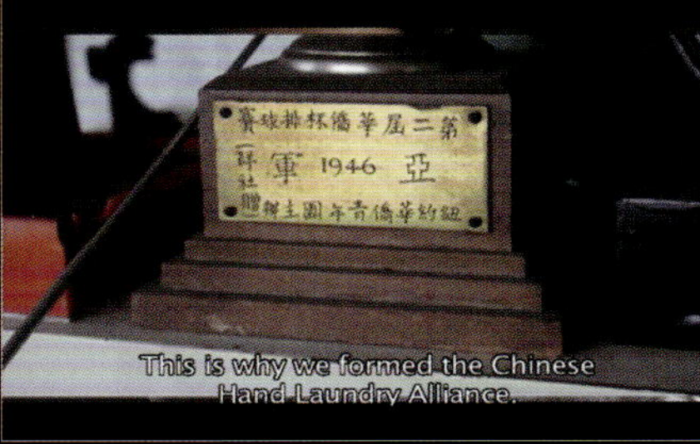
1946
This is why we formed the Chinese
Hand Laundry Alliance.

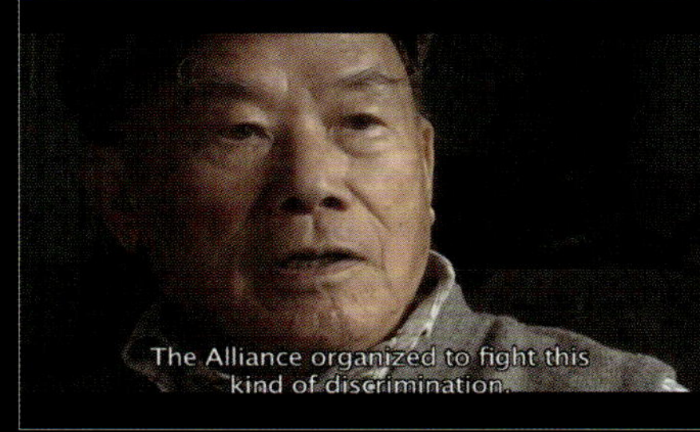
The Alliance organized to fight this
kind of discrimination.

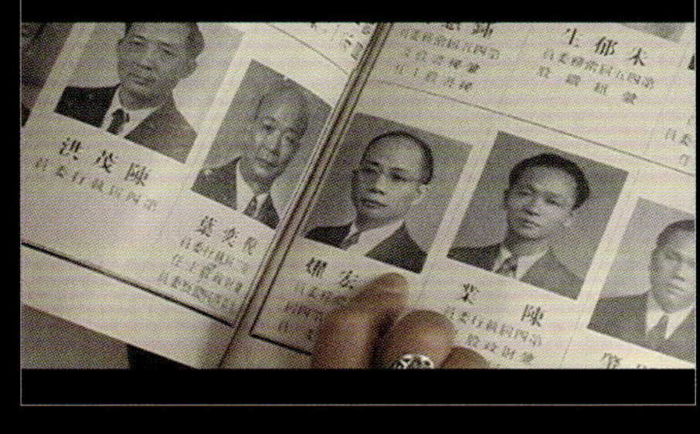

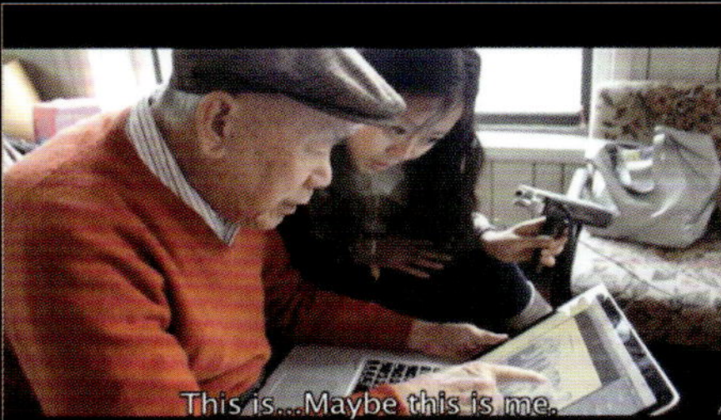
This is...Maybe this is me.

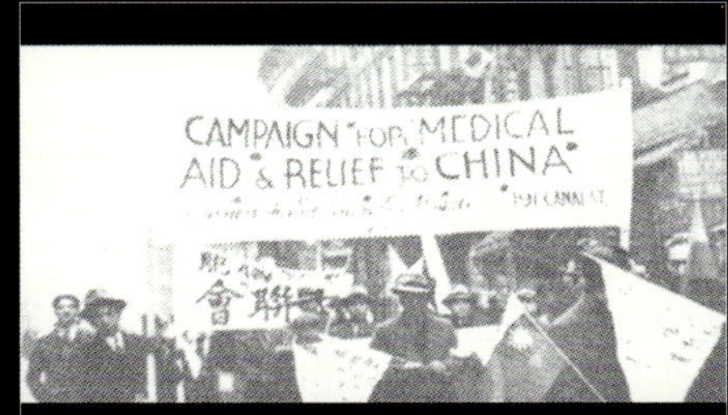
CAMPAIGN FOR MEDICAL
AID & RELIEF TO CHINA

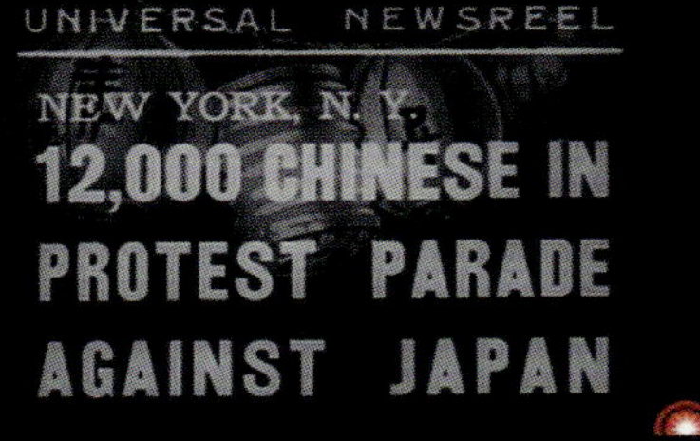
UNIVERSAL NEWSREEL
NEW YORK, N.Y.
12,000 CHINESE IN
PROTEST PARADE
AGAINST JAPAN

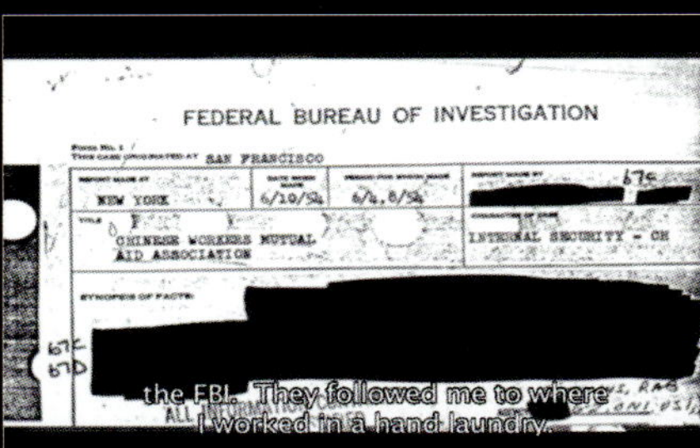
FEDERAL BUREAU OF INVESTIGATION
SAN FRANCISCO
NEW YORK
6/10/54
CHINESE WORKERS MUTUAL
AID ASSOCIATION
INTERNAL SECURITY - CH
the FBI. They followed me to where
I worked in a hand laundry.

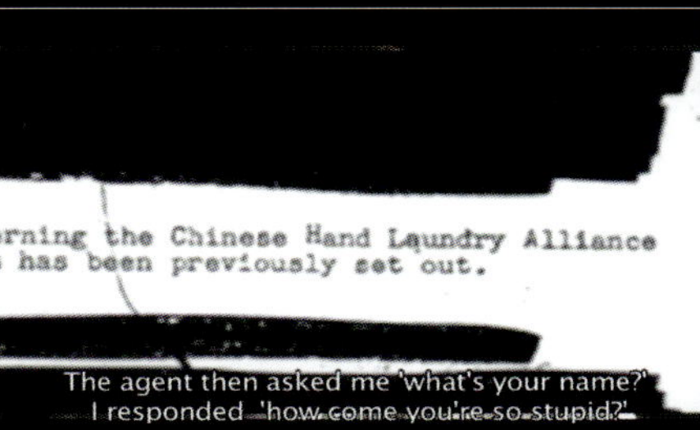
rning the Chinese Hand Laundry Alliance
s has been previously set out.
The agent then asked me 'what's your name?'
I responded 'how come you're so stupid?'

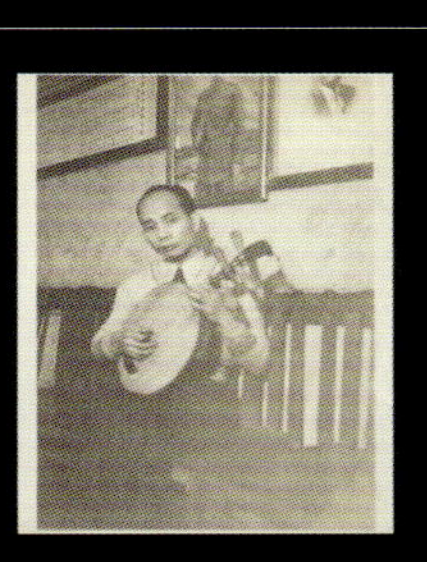

Chinese Laundrymen to Close in Protest As Power Washers Raise Rates a Third

NYT 12/9/46

Hundreds of thousands of New Yorkers will have to find some other way to get the family wash done when 4,000 Chinese hand laundries stop accepting soiled clothing today, though they will keep their shops open until next Monday.

The laundrymen are protesting a price increase of one third imposed on them by the eleven laundries of the Chinese Power Laundries Association, the group that does all the washing for the individual operators. In a series of bitter charges leveled at the power laundries, the hand laundrymen, members of the Chinese Hand Laundry Alliance and the Chinese Hand Laundry Association, contended that it would be "unpatriotic" for them to pass on the increase, which went into effect Nov. 30, to their customers.

Jamming the small auditorium of the New York Chinese Public School on Mott Street and overflowing into the street, 500 members of the hand laundry organizations agreed to follow the strike action planned by their action committee. In addition to closing down next Monday, they mapped plans to picket the power laundries and uncooperative individual shops.

Among the charges made by Eng York Shu, chairman of the meeting and an executive of the Hand Laundry Alliance, was that the power group had made an agree-

It also was pointed out that many customers would not receive their laundry back because, when some of the laundrymen refused to pay the new increase, the power laundries retained the wash.

On Nov. 28 the power laundries placed advertisements in the local Chinese papers announcing the price increase beginning Nov. 30. No individual laundry was ... of the new rate, it was said ... two hand organizations ... cided to hold ... Thursday, and ... the power associ... to attend.

Chu Tong, adv... committee, said ... had refused to ... last week, bu... fort would ... them wi...

Benjam... power g... at his ... to answ... he met ... power g...

"We ... to nego... ly sent ... we could ...

Mr. Jaffe said the increase was necessitated by an increase in labor costs and "up to a 200 per cent increase in soap."

Among other charges made by the hand laundrymen, who conducted the meeting in Chinese

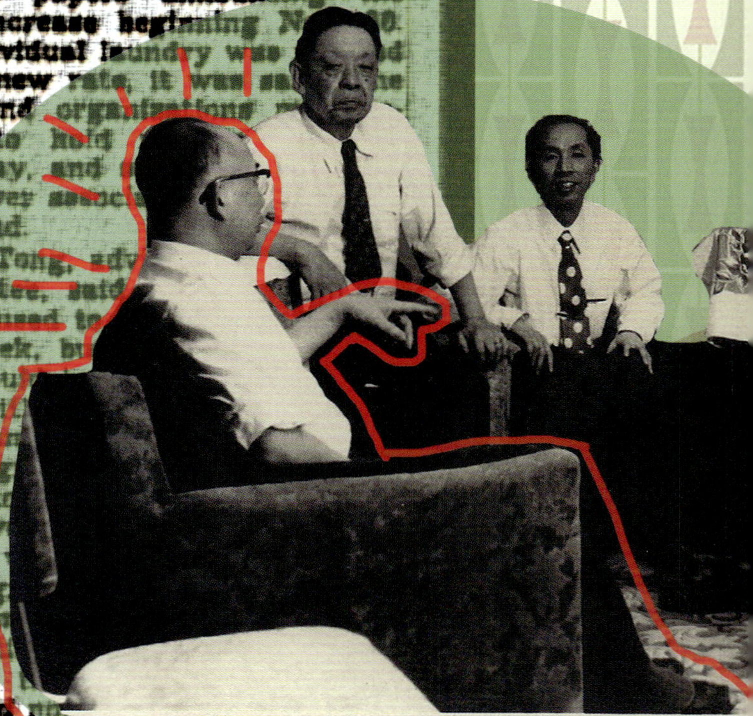

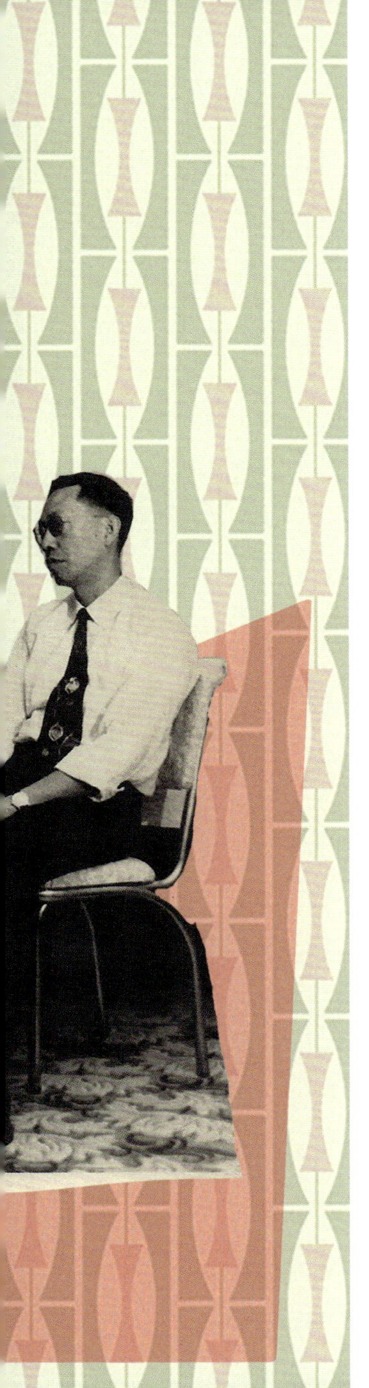

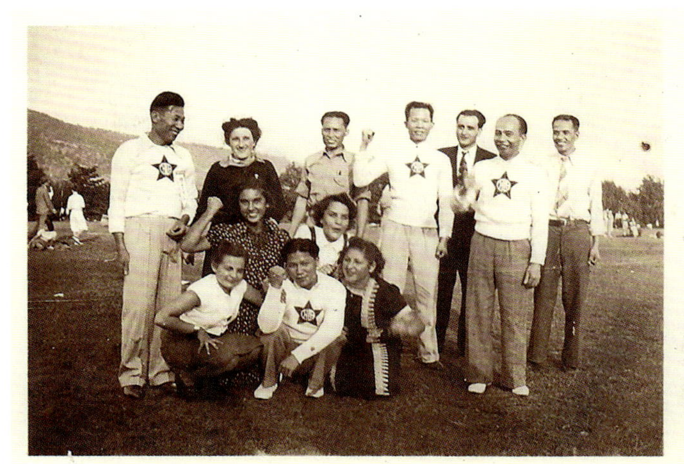

My grandpa with CHLA members and other comrades in Bear Mountain, north of New York City. The person in a suit standing next to my grandpa is most likely Julius Bezozo, a well-known progressive lawyer for the CHLA and other causes. The group photo includes Jewish and Italian immigrant workers, representing the multiracial solidarity that was prevalent on the left at the time. Sometime in the late 1930s.

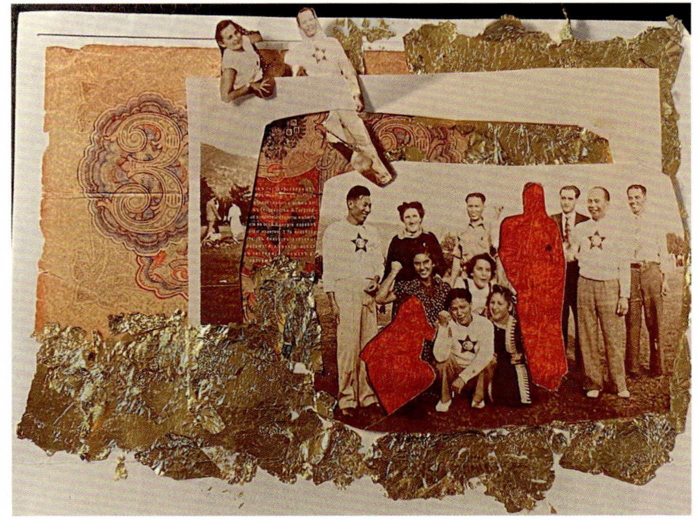

My grandpa with the Chinese Hand Laundry Alliance and Allies in Red + Gold, 2021. Mixed-media collage.

Left: *CHLA gets organized*, 2024. Digital collage.

My grandfather, Sui Woo, came to the US in the late 1920s as a "paper son." A "paper son" refers to a person who bought false papers proving that his dad was living in the country. My grandpa went on to own and operate small hand laundries, one of the only industries that Chinese could work in because of rampant discrimination. In 1933, he joined together with other hand-laundry workers to form the Chinese Hand Laundry Alliance (CHLA) of New York, an organization that would challenge racist and anti-Chinese policies. The group organized in response to a New York City Board of Aldermen policy that imposed large increases for hand-laundry licensing fees and required citizenship. Many Chinese workers who were residents were denied citizenship under Chinese Exclusion laws. Because of their organizing, the city dropped the citizenship requirements. The CHLA grew to over 3,000 members, which made up half of the city's Chinese laundry workers. CHLA helped members apply for laundry licenses while also fighting the city's unjust discrimination. They also provided mutual aid and recreational activities from their headquarters in Chinatown, located at 191 Canal Street.

衣聯會組織會員遊行，號召僑胞及各界人士支持祖國抗日戰爭。（一九三八年）

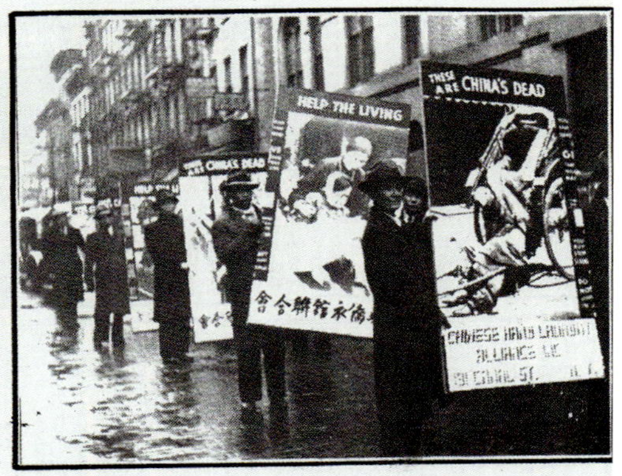

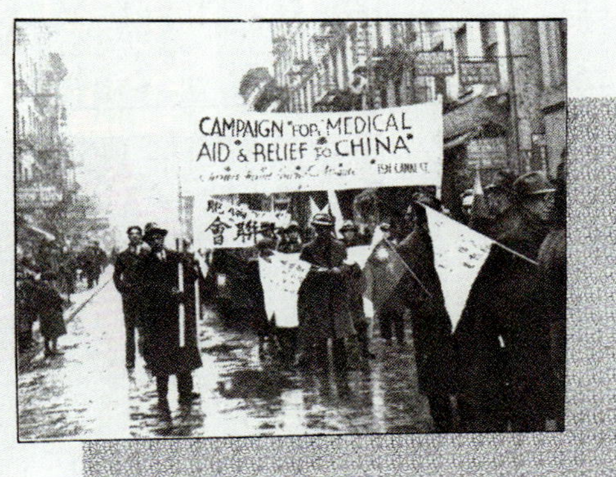

Above and to the right:
Images from CHLA's 50th-anniversary booklet.

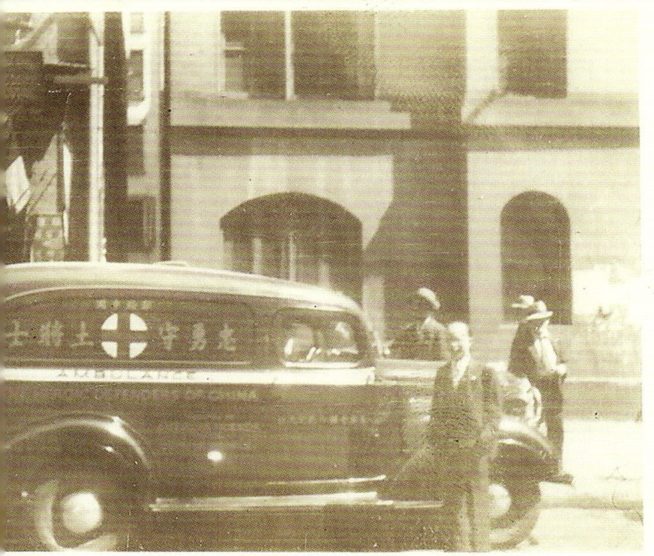

5 AMBULANCES FOR CHINA

Cost, $10,000, Subscribed by Laundrymen in New York

The New York Chinese Hand Laundry Alliance will ship to China today five ambulances, valued at $10,000, according to an announcement yesterday by James Lee, president of the alliance. The money for the ambulances was donated by 1,500 Chinese laundrymen in the metropolitan area.

Dr. Co Tui of the American Bureau for Medical Aid to China announced the shipment to China on another vessel today of more than $15,000 worth of medical and surgical supplies. For this shipment $5,500 was donated by the Chinese Patriotic Association of Port Lewis on the Island of Mauritius off the coast of India. The remainder was contributed by American and Chinese groups in the United States.

The New York Times
Published: April 23, 1938

贈送前方將士之救護車
四架於運送回國之前在碼頭攝影 (1938)

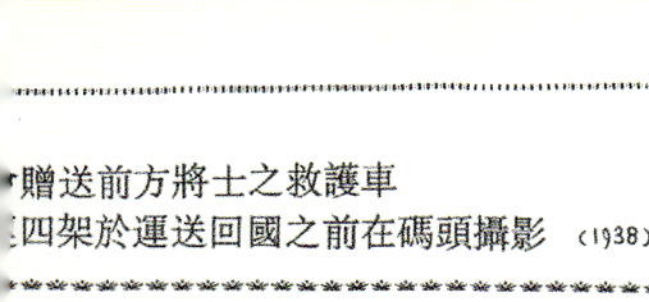

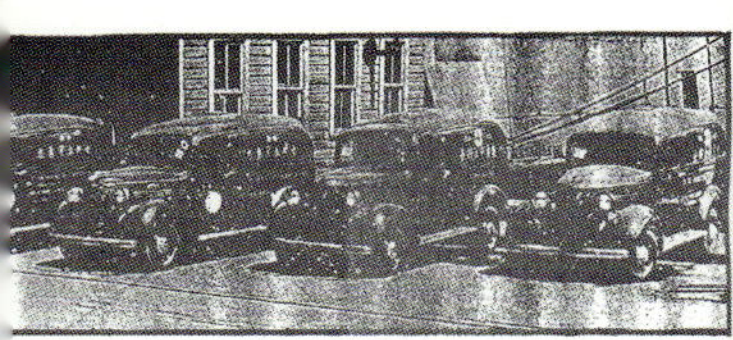

車内的部份設備。
(一九三八年)

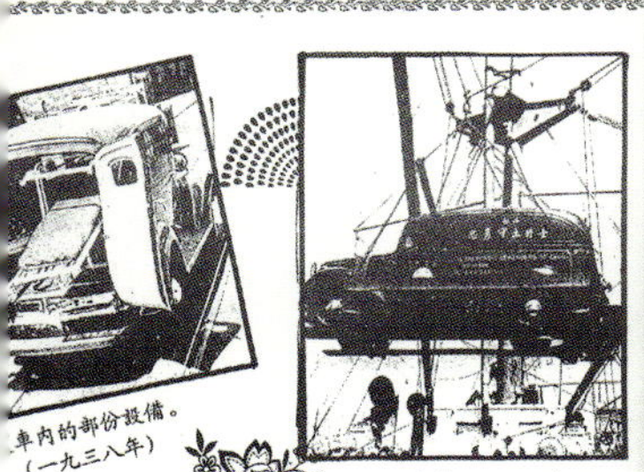

救護車裝運回祖國時的
情形。(一九三八年)

35

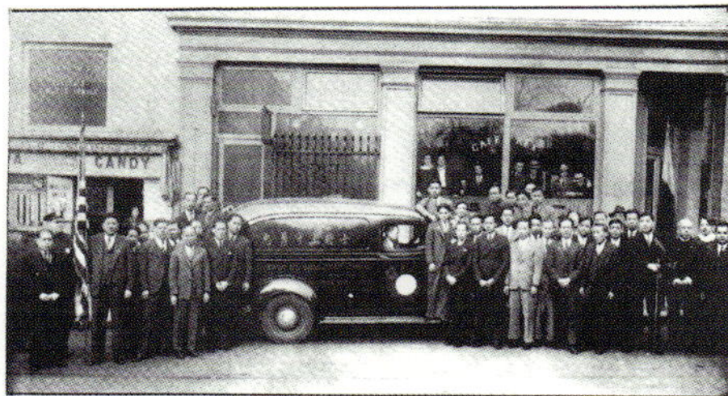

衣聯會贈送前方將士之救護車

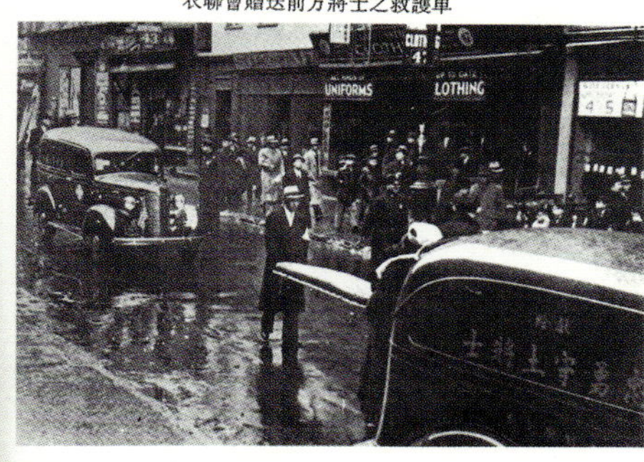

34

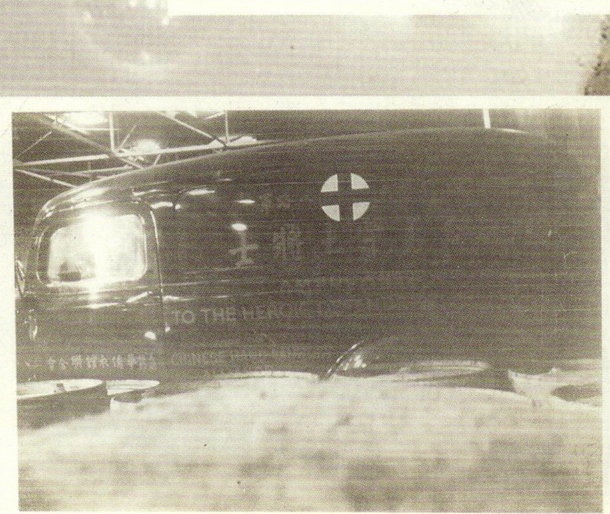

SF:100-15018

CONFIDENTIAL

Information concerning the Chinese Hand Laundry Alliance and the China Daily News has been previously set out.

b2
b7C
b7D

The Communist Party has been designated by the Attorney General of the United States pursuant to Executive Order 10450.

CONFIDENTIAL

- 5 -

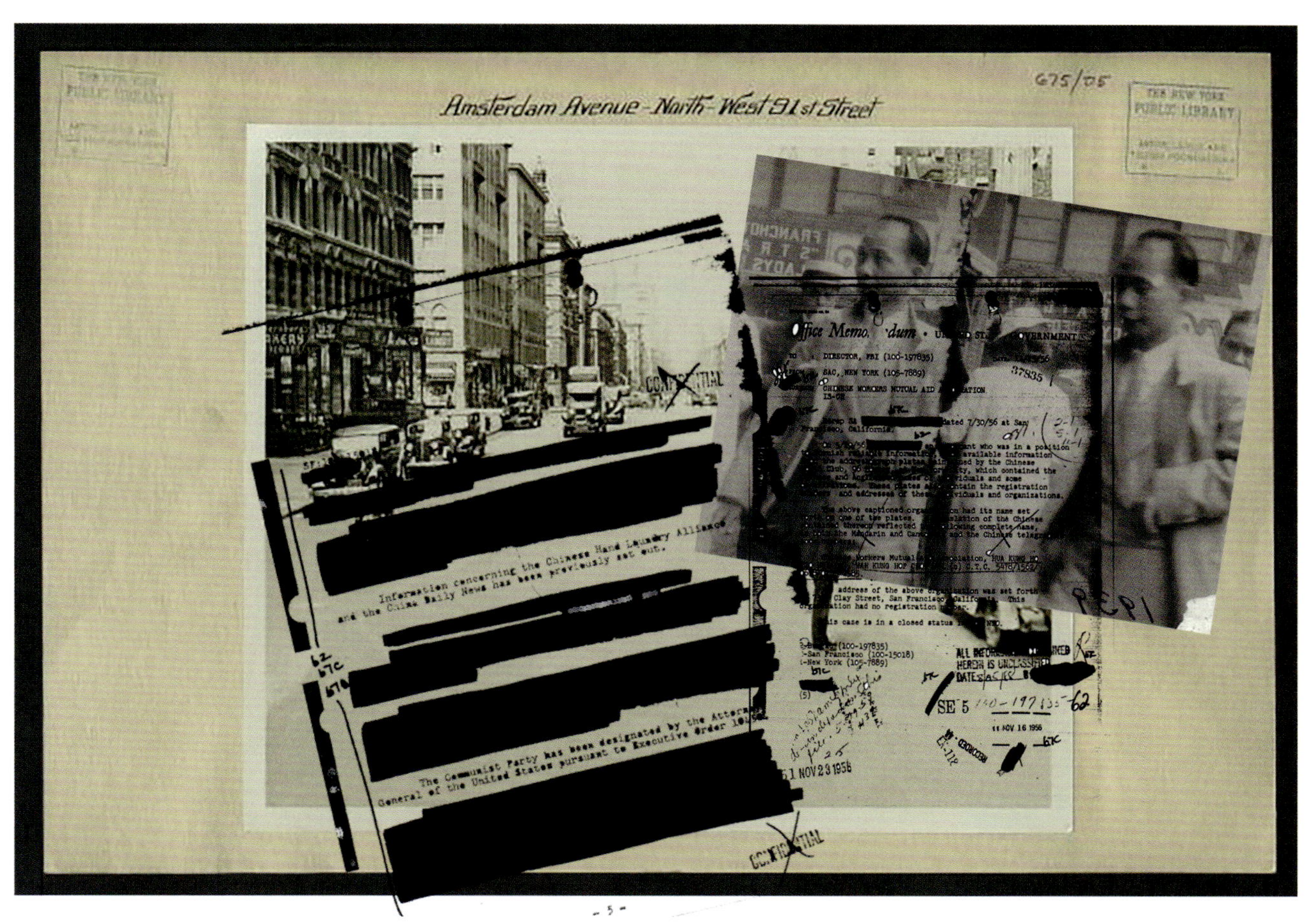

Above: *Grandpa lived in NYC's Upper West Side, FBI Targeted Him Labor Organizing*, 2021. Digital collage.

Left: *Redacted FBI files targeting CHLA during the second red scare*, 2021. Digital collage.

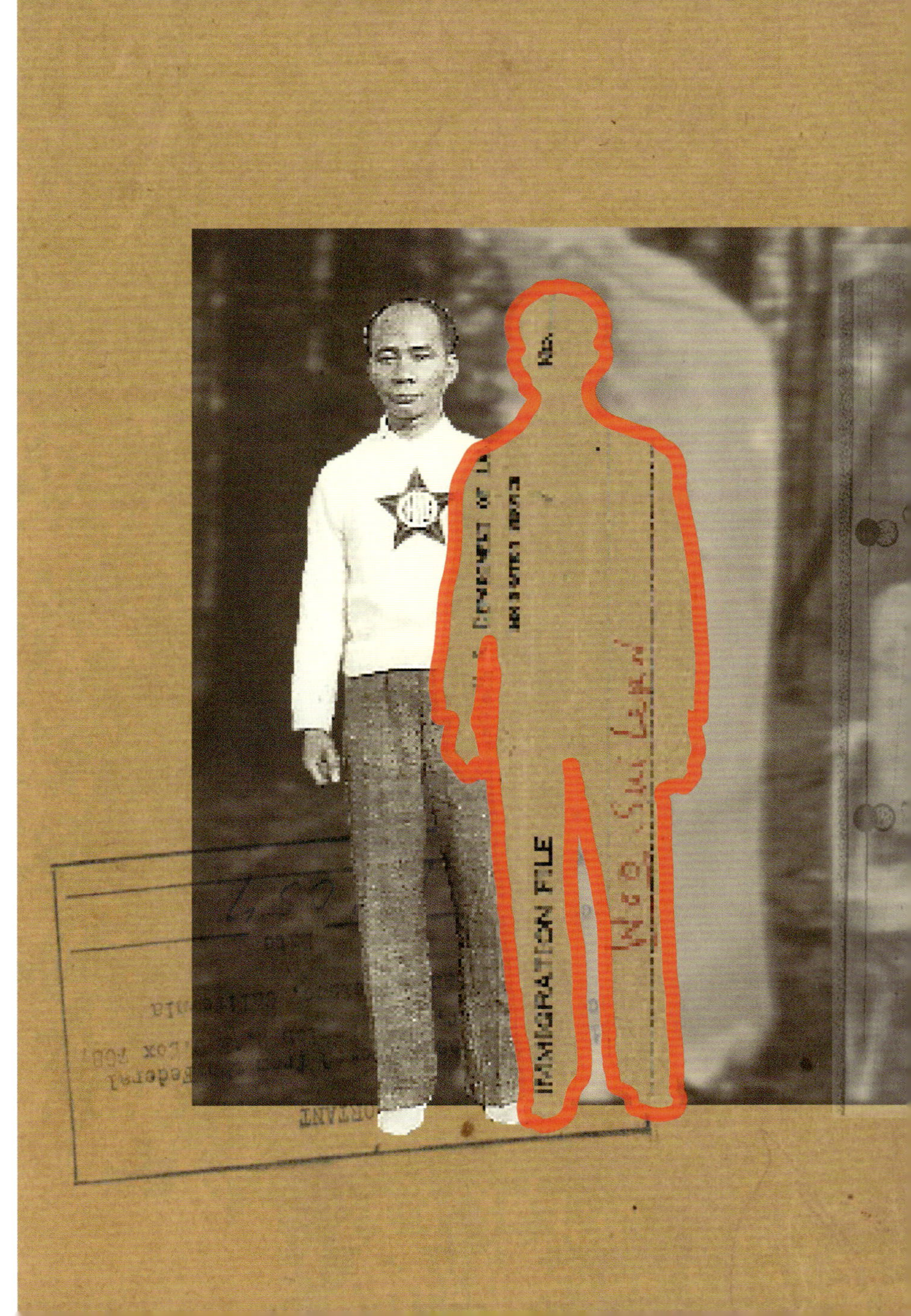

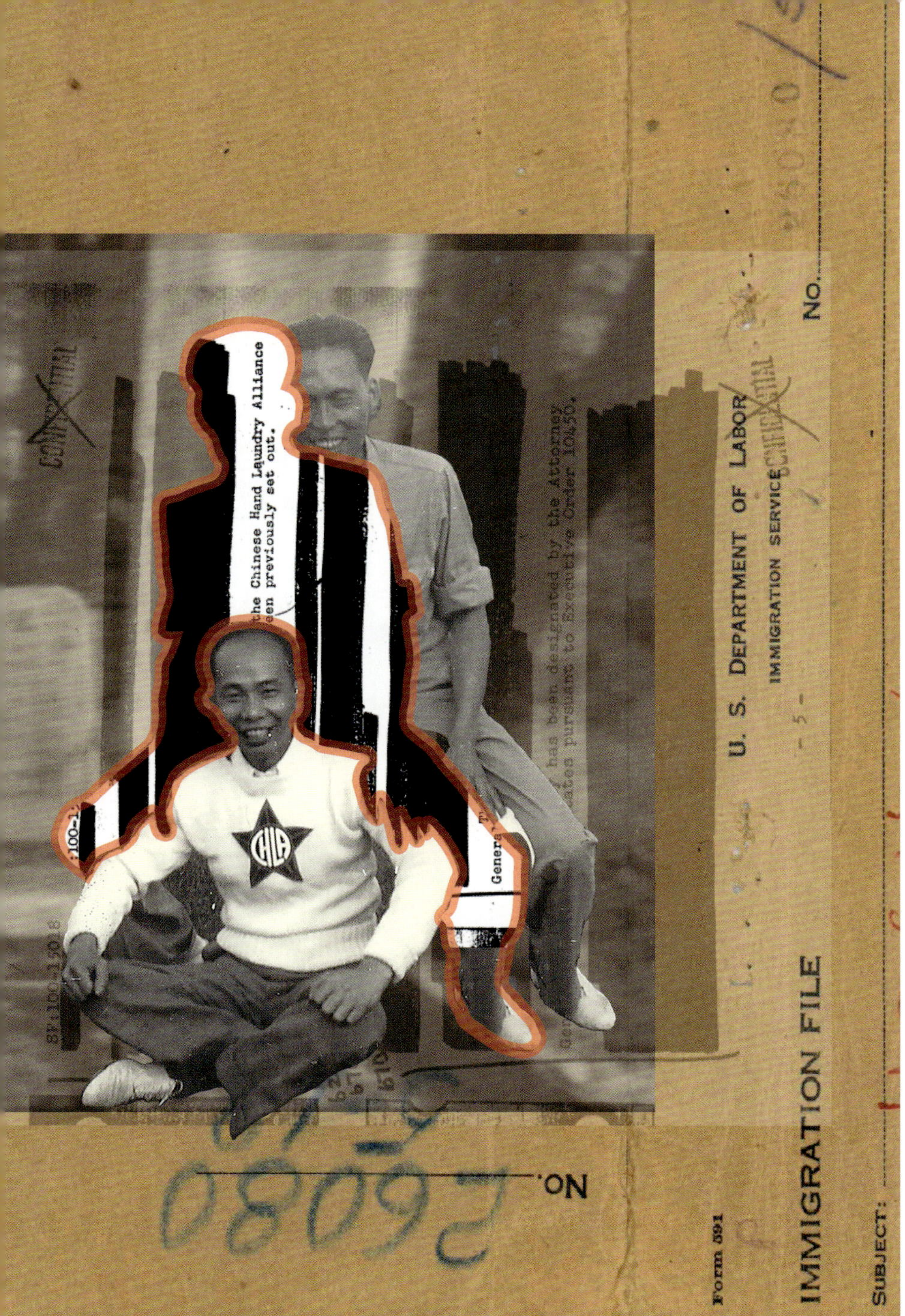

Grandpa's immigration file No. 26080,
2024. Digital collage.

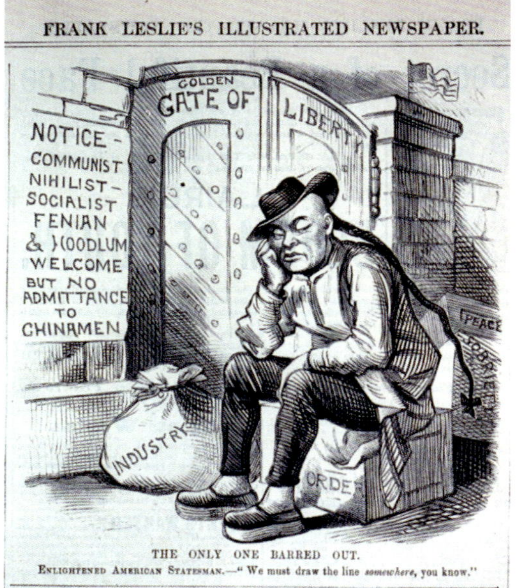

The only one barred out. Enlightened American statesman—"We must draw the line somewhere, you know." Frank Leslie's Illustrated Newspaper, vol. 54, April 1, 1882. Library of Congress, 1882.

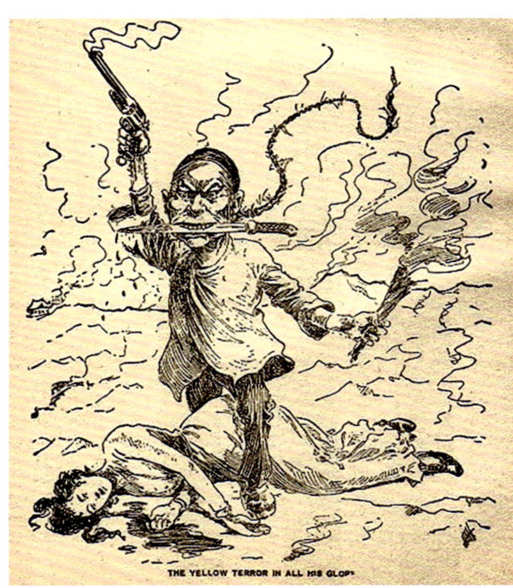

The Yellow Terror in all His Glory, an 1899 editorial cartoon depicting a Chinese man standing over a fallen white woman. Wikimedia Commons, 1899.

The Magic Washer, manufactured by Geo. Dee, Dixon, Illinois. The Chinese Must Go. Cartoon showing Uncle Sam, with proclamation and can of Magic Washer, kicking Chinese out of the United States. Chicago: Shober & Carqueville Lith Co., 1886.

Right: *The coming man—John Chinaman.* The Miriam and Ira D. Wallach Division of Art, Prints and Photographs: Picture Collection, The New York Public Library Digital Collections. 1869.

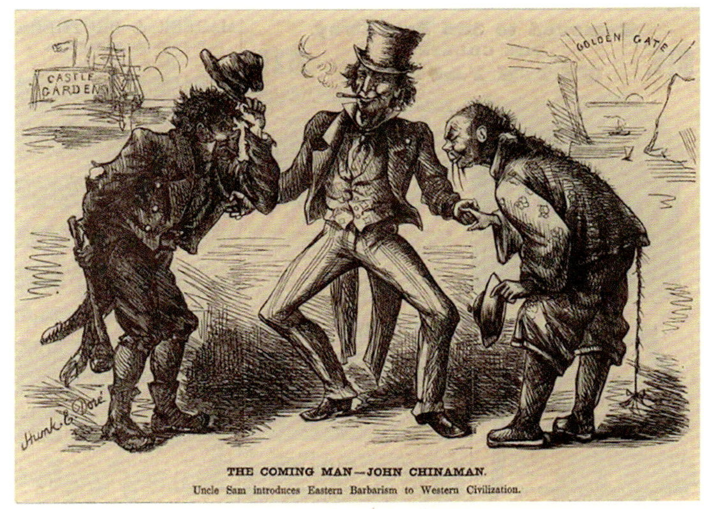

Below: *They are pretty safe there.* The Miriam and Ira D. Wallach Division of Art, Prints and Photographs: Picture Collection, The New York Public Library Digital Collections. 1869.

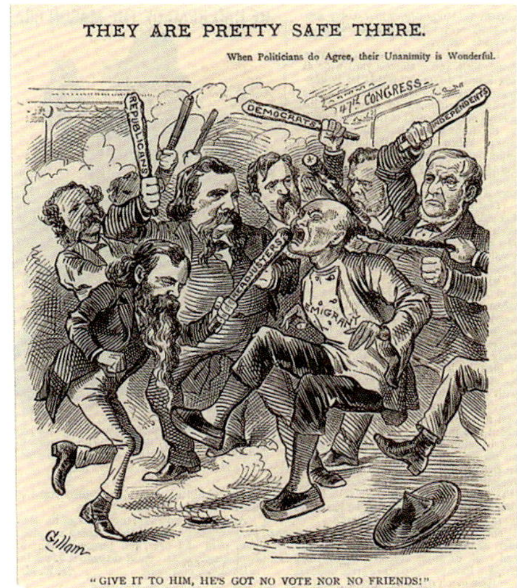

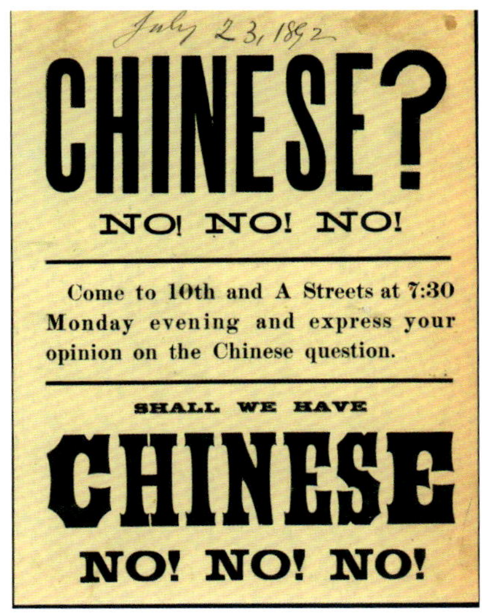

July 23, 1892

CHINESE?

NO! NO! NO!

Come to 10th and A Streets at 7:30 Monday evening and express your opinion on the Chinese question.

SHALL WE HAVE

CHINESE

NO! NO! NO!

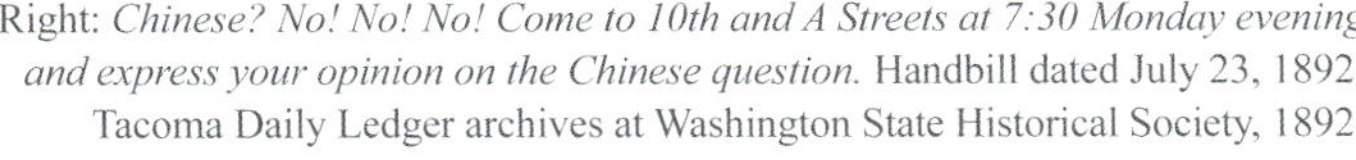

Right: *Chinese? No! No! No! Come to 10th and A Streets at 7:30 Monday evening and express your opinion on the Chinese question.* Handbill dated July 23, 1892. Tacoma Daily Ledger archives at Washington State Historical Society, 1892.

Despite the contributions of Chinese people in the US, anti-Chinese sentiment grew rampant, reaching its peak from the 1870s through the 1880s.

Anti-Chinese propaganda in periodicals, newspapers, and other magazines was widespread, depicting people of Chinese descent as heathens and cowards, deceitful, filthy, and intellectually inferior. In racist caricatures and illustrations, Chinese laborers were often portrayed as rat-eating dirty people who accepted lower wages, which created an "unfair labor competition" for whites; their yellow skin and different beliefs and culture made them unassimilable. This level of dehumanization had real-life consequences, leading to Chinese folks being harassed, beaten, and even murdered. It was so commonplace that newspapers seldom reported these events. On the West Coast, hundreds of Chinese people were lynched. Angry white mobs chased away and burned down towns with Chinese residents. This xenophobia was deeply felt throughout the country, leading to the passage of the 1882 Chinese Exclusion Act, federal legislation that prohibited Chinese people from coming to the US. This remains the only law that prevented members of a specific ethnic or national group from immigrating to the country.

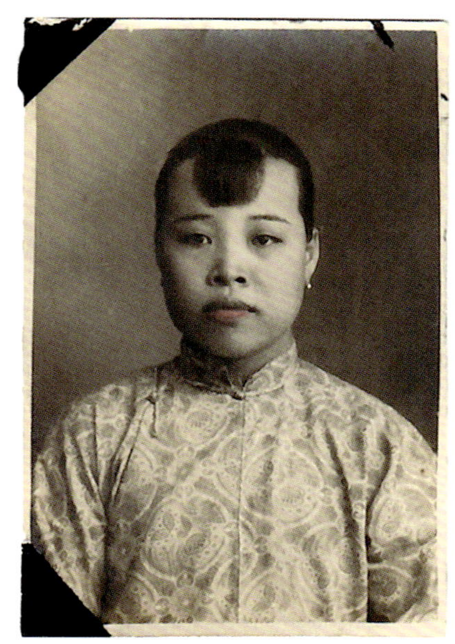

Grandma as a young woman, 1920s or '30s (exact date unknown).

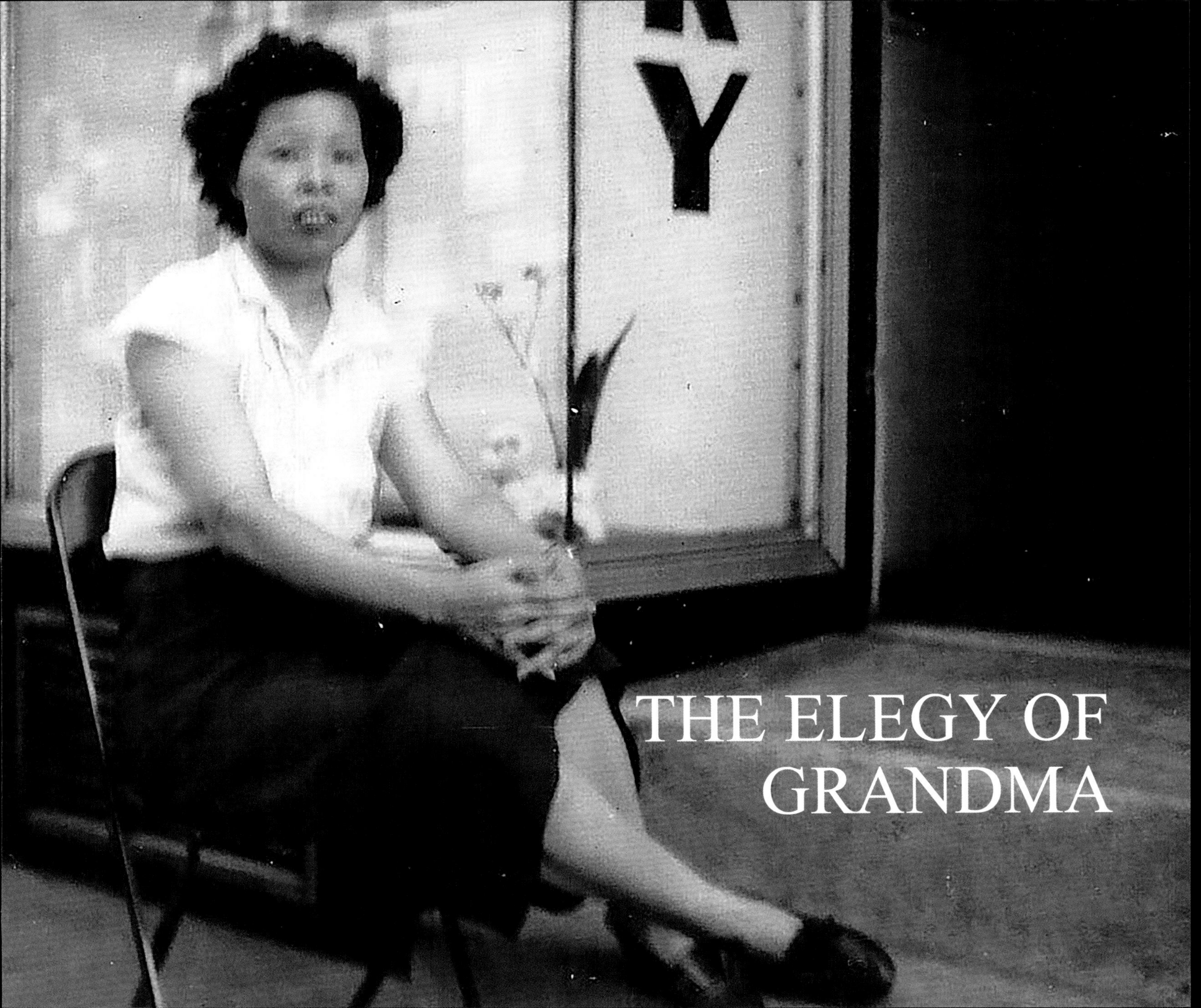

THE ELEGY OF GRANDMA

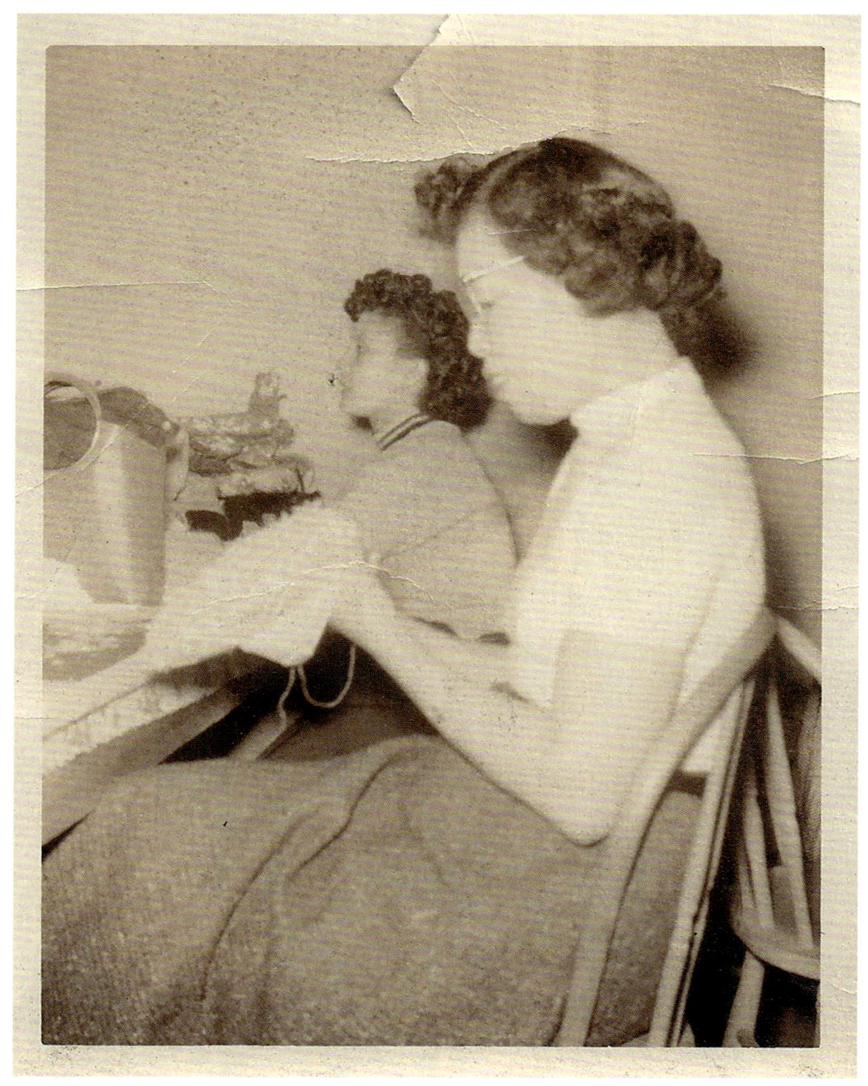

In 1942, at the age of thirty-nine, my grandfather enlisted in the US Army to fight fascism during World War II. He was motivated to join because of his distress over the Japanese invasion of China in the late 1930s. By 1938, Japan had taken over much of the Guangdong Province and his hometown of Taishan. Years later, it was because of his veteran status that he was able to bring his wife, my grandmother, to the US through the 1945 War Brides Act. My grandmother worked in the family-owned hand-laundry business, as well as in food and garment factories.

Grandma sewing, 1950s (exact date unknown).

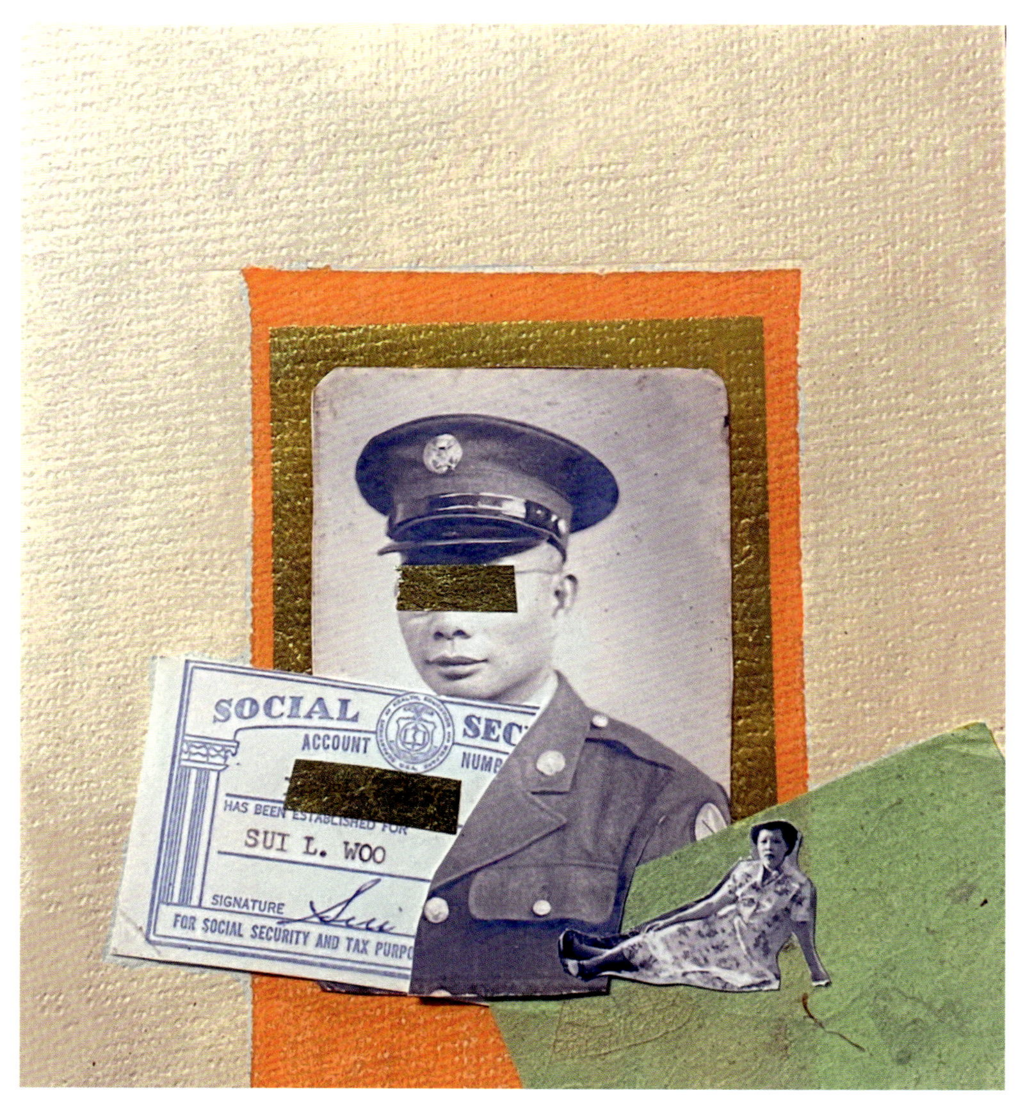

My grandpa served in the US military during World War II, while the Chinese Exclusion Act was still in place; my grandma came later, 2021. Mixed-media collage.

Grandma in Central Park,
New York City, 1940s.

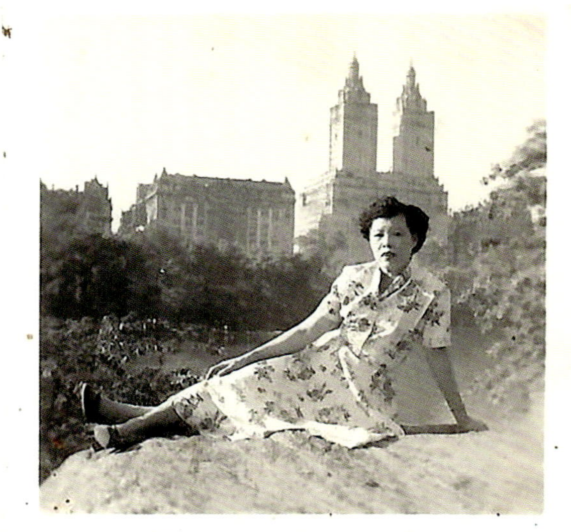

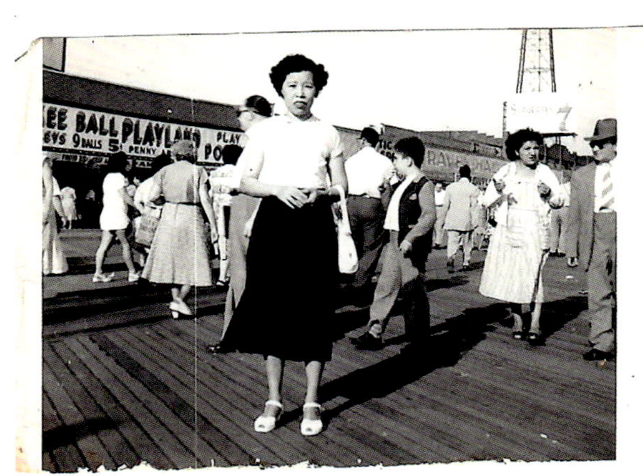

Grandma in Coney Island,
Brooklyn, 1940s.

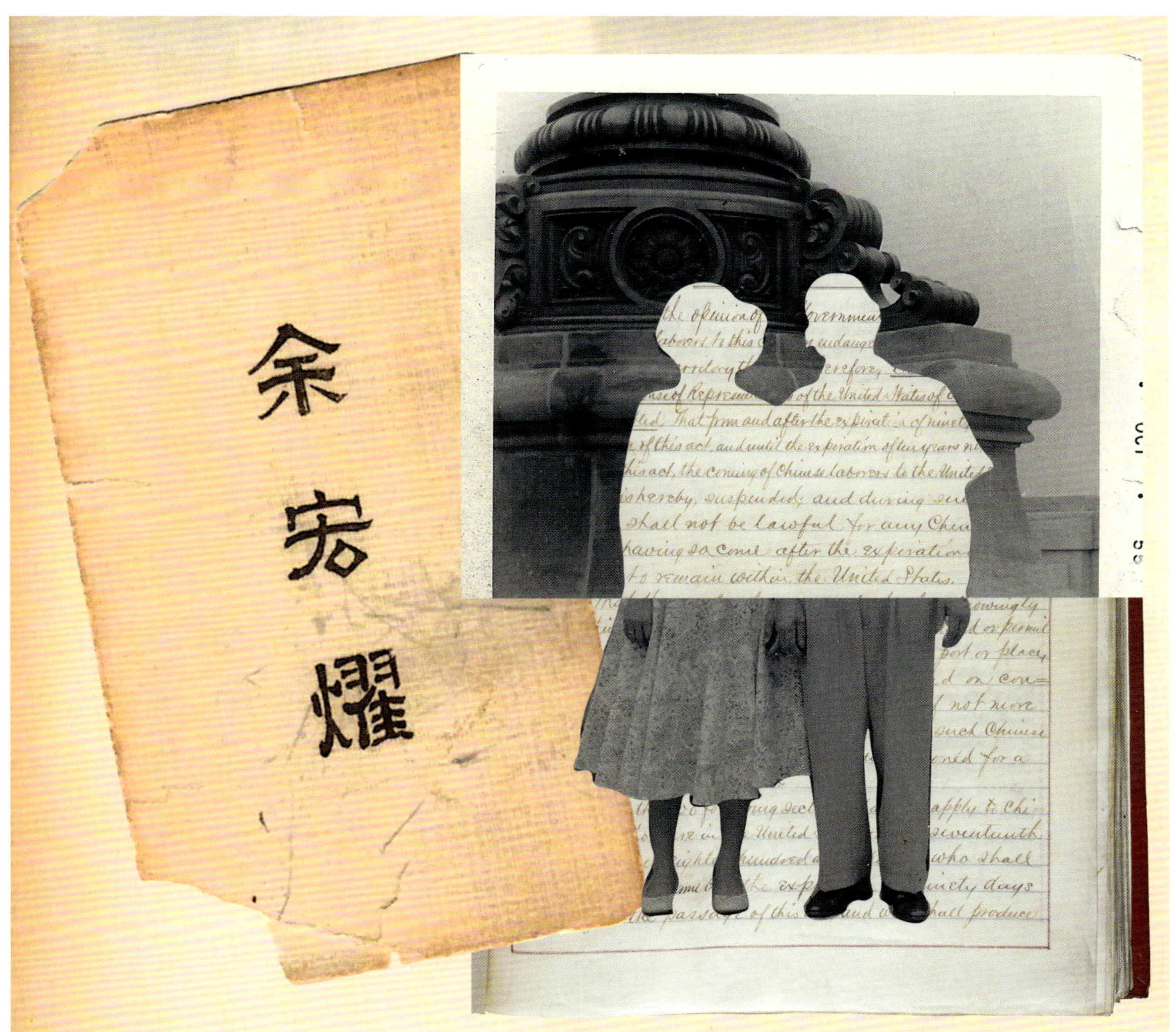

My grandparents in New York City in the 1950s with the cutout of 1882 Chinese Exclusion Act in the background, 2020. Mixed-media collage.

These are documents and photos that my grandpa carried with him in his wallet and belongings between the 1920s and 1950s. He and my grandma were fearful and ready to prove their immigration status when their "American allegiance" was questioned, especially during the height of the anti-Communist political climate in the US.

127-24-4168

(SOCIAL SECURITY ACCOUNT NUMBER)

YOOK MING WOO
c/o Temple Frosted Foods
454 Berry Street
Brooklyn 11, New York

WORKER'S SIGNATURE

FOR SOCIAL SECURITY PURPOSES • NOT FOR IDENTIFICATION

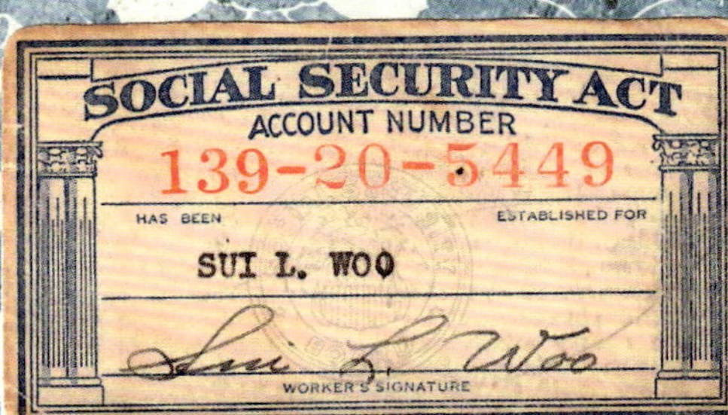
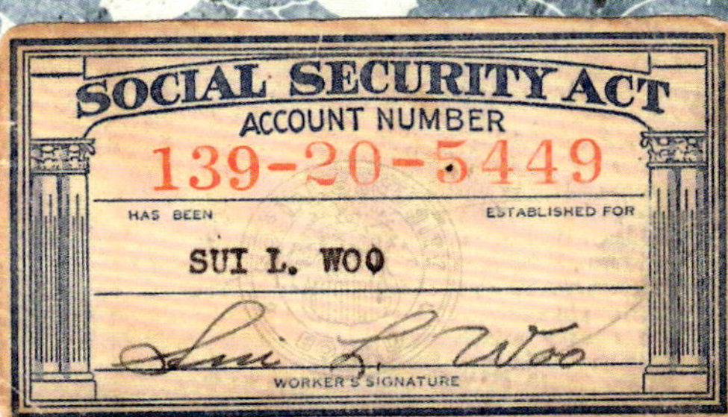
SOCIAL SECURITY ACT
ACCOUNT NUMBER
139-20-5449
HAS BEEN ESTABLISHED FOR
SUI L. WOO
Sui L. Woo
WORKER'S SIGNATURE

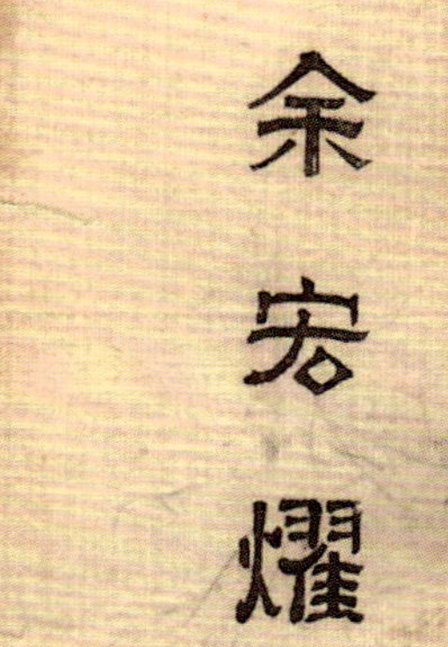

DETACH THIS PORTION from the upper half of the card and keep it in a safe place. Your Name and Social Security Account Number appear on the other side. If you lose the upper portion take this lower part to any field office of the Social Security Administration, where a duplicate account number card will be issued to you immediately. Unless you present half of the card, you may have to wait several days for your duplicate.

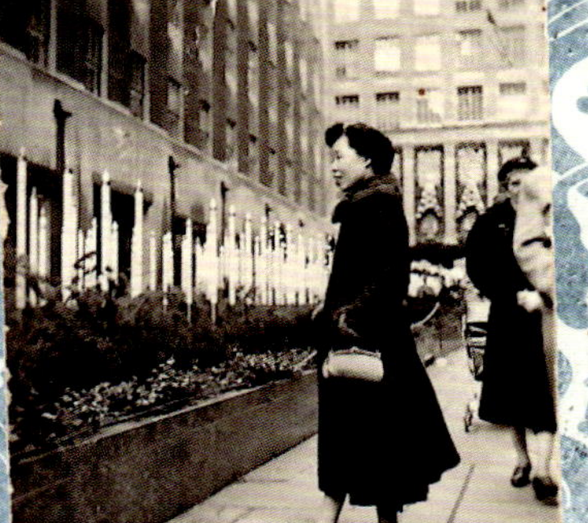

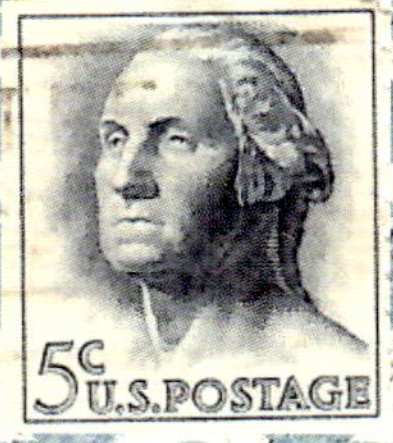

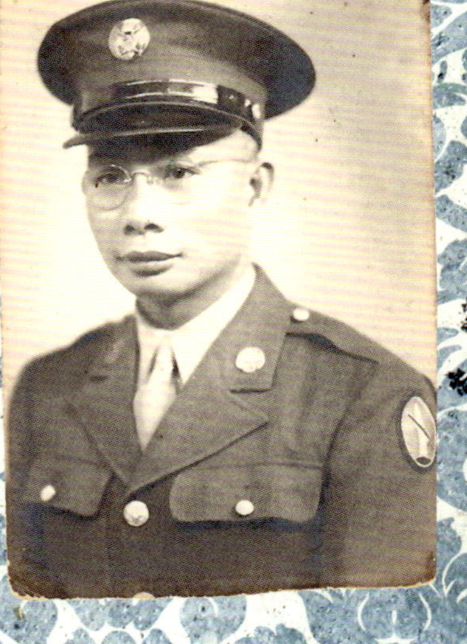

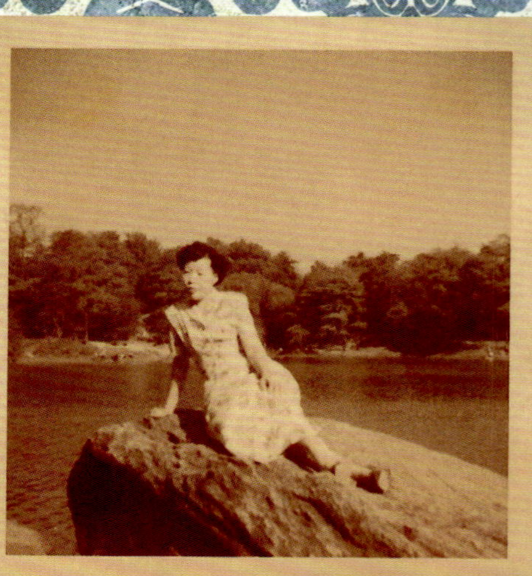

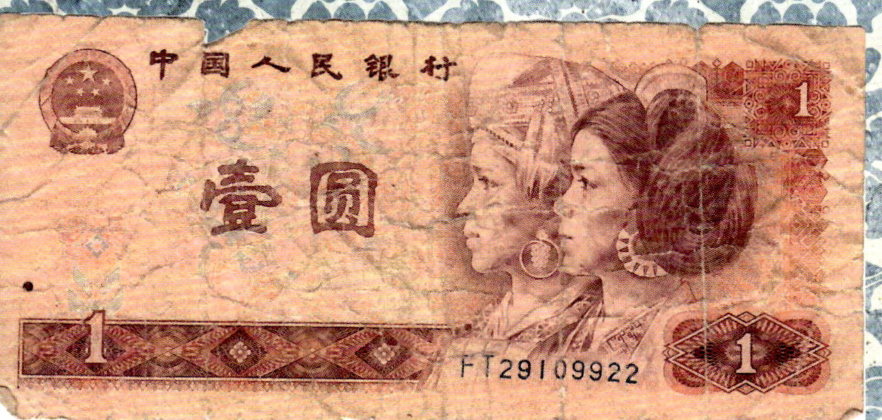
中國人民銀行
壹圓
1
FT29109922

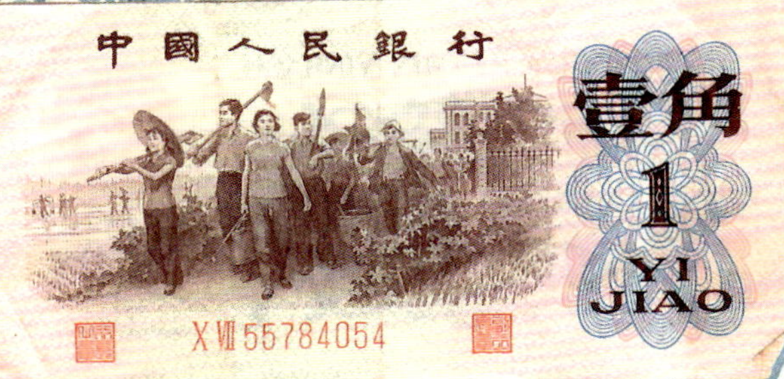
中國人民銀行
壹角
1
YI
JIAO
XⅦ55784054

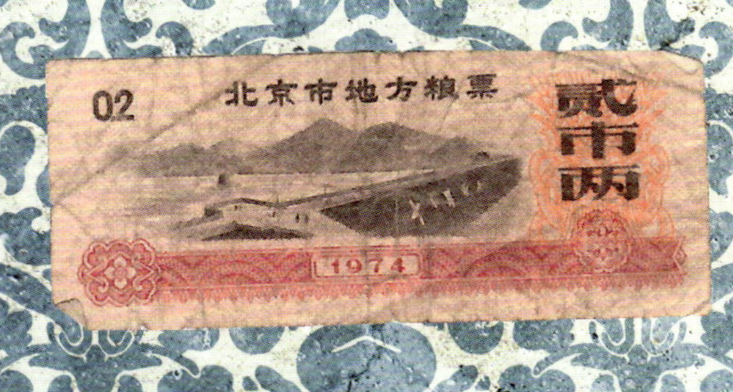
02
北京市地方粮票
贰市两
1974

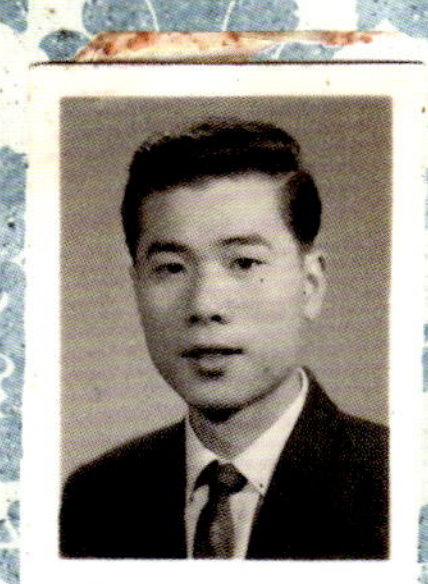

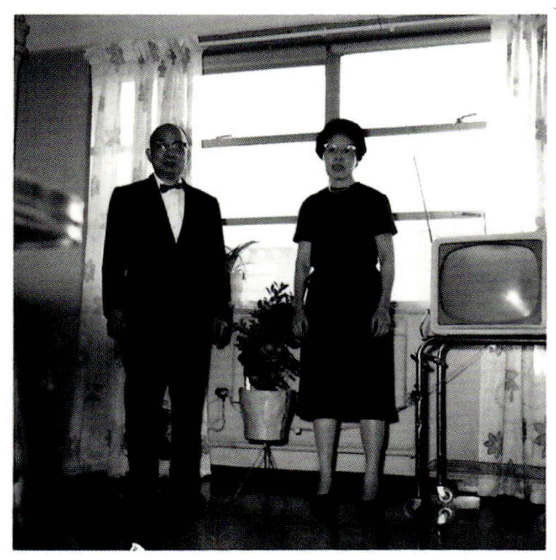
FEB • 63

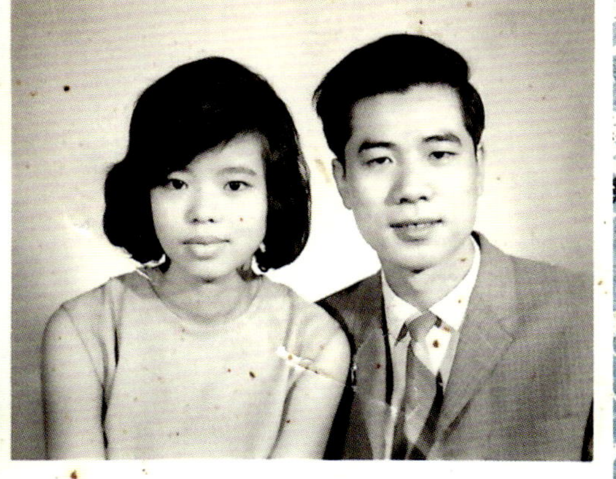

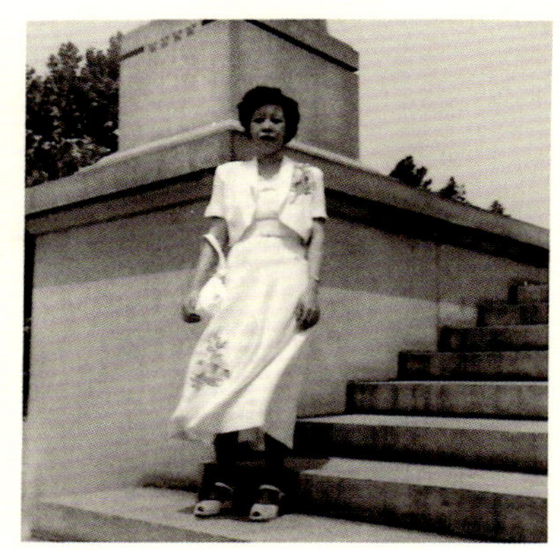

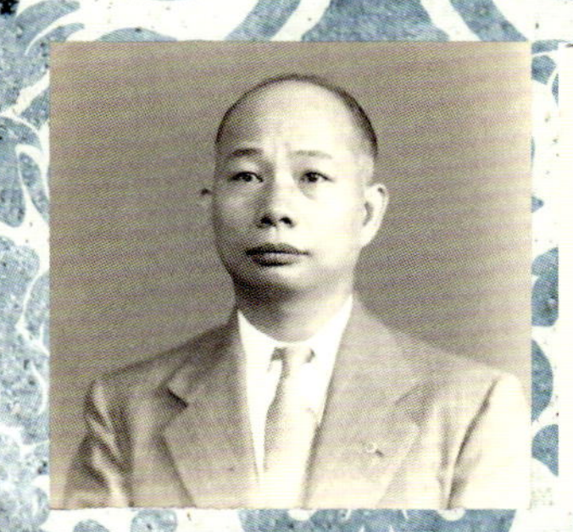

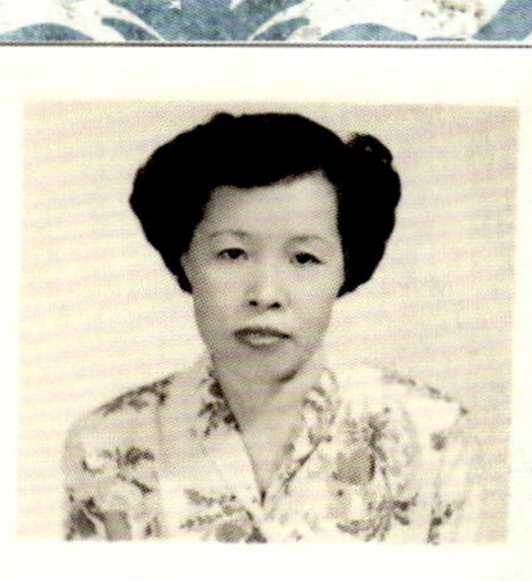

Left:
Grandma was a war bride, 2024.
Digital collage.

Right:
My family in fragments, 2023.
Digital collage.

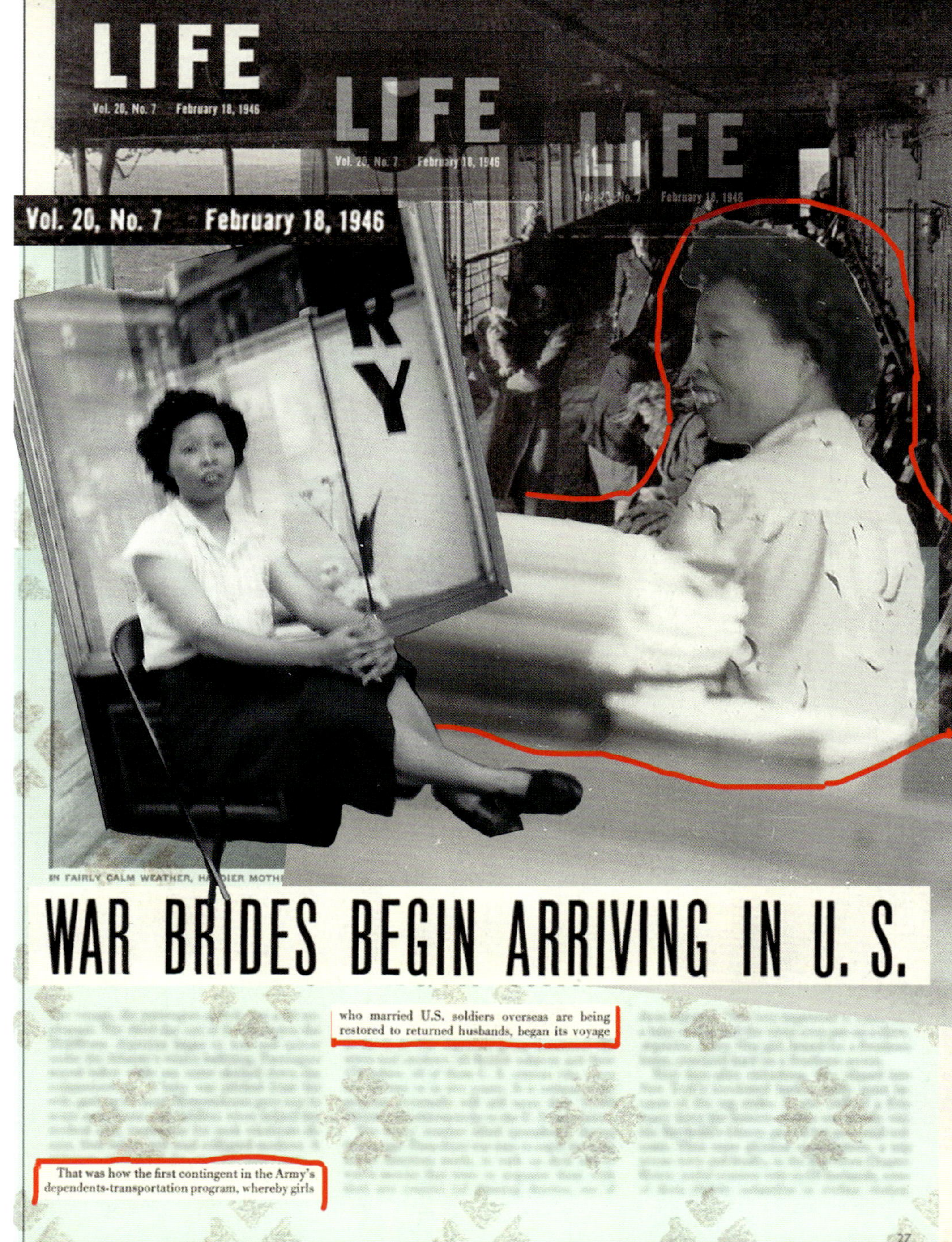

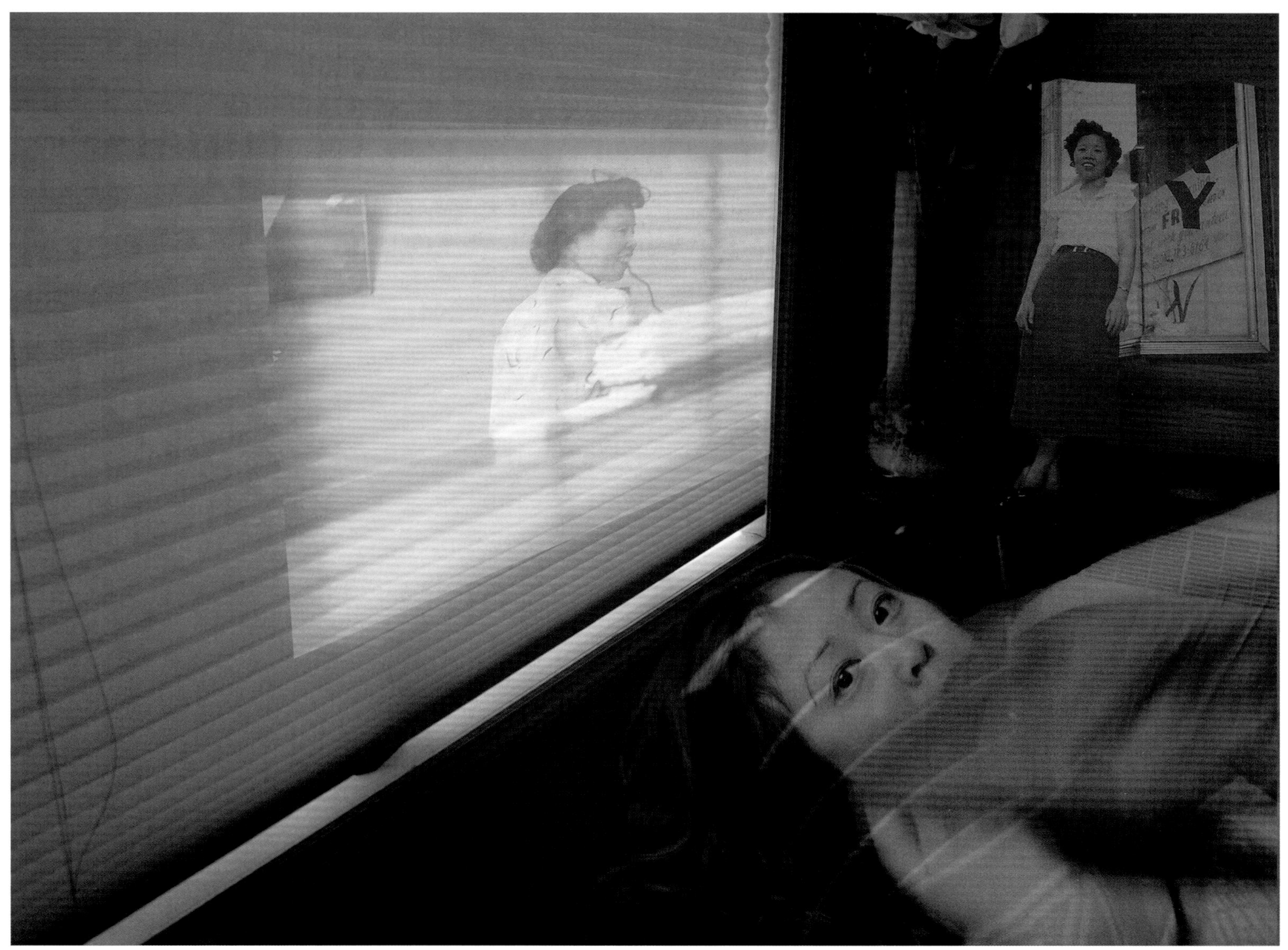

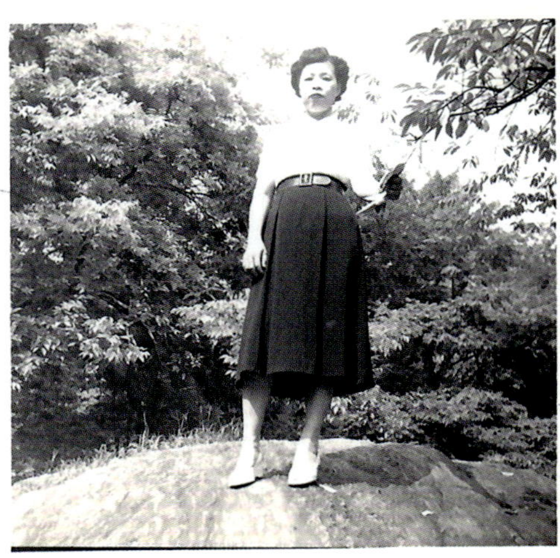

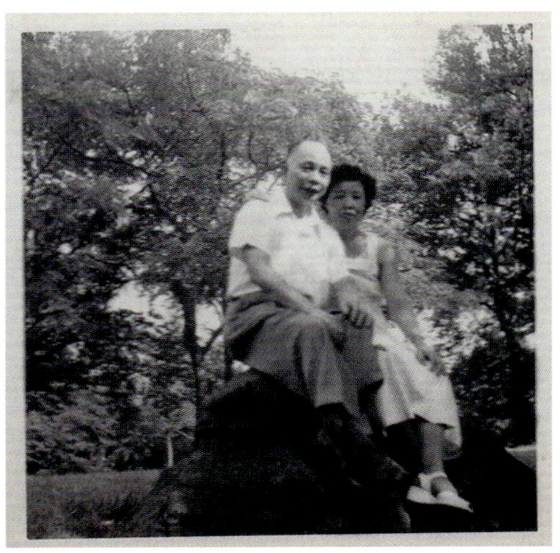

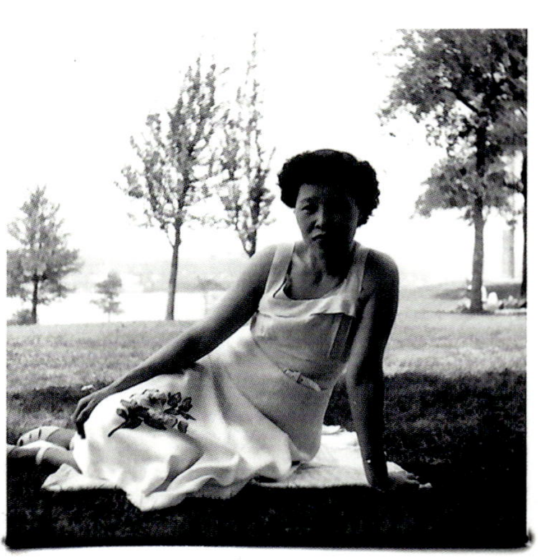

Above: My grandparents during one of several Central Park photo shoots, late 1940s.

Right: *Cut out, paste, repeat: reimagining is an act of resistance*, 2024. Mixed-media collage.

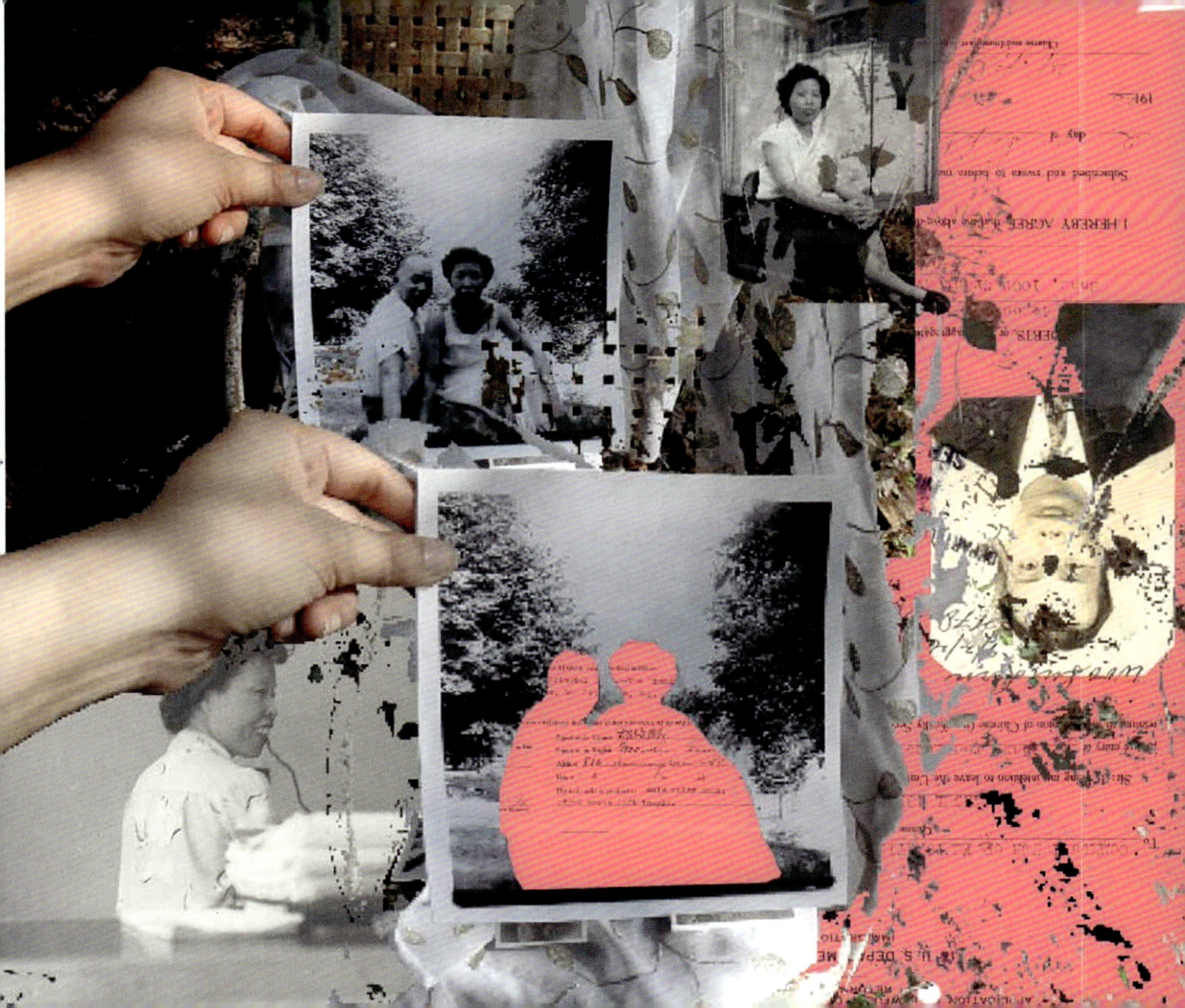

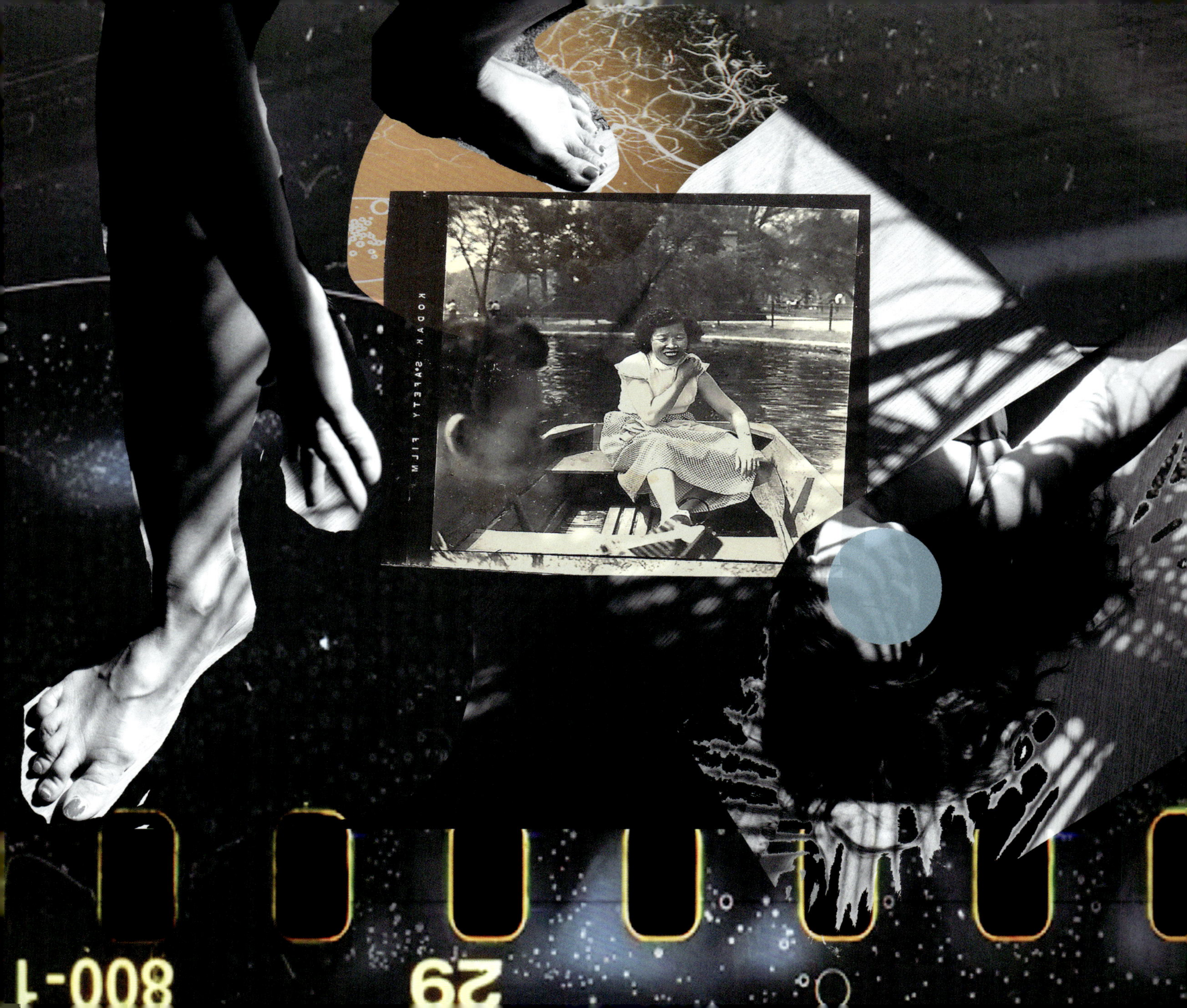
KODAK SAFETY FILM

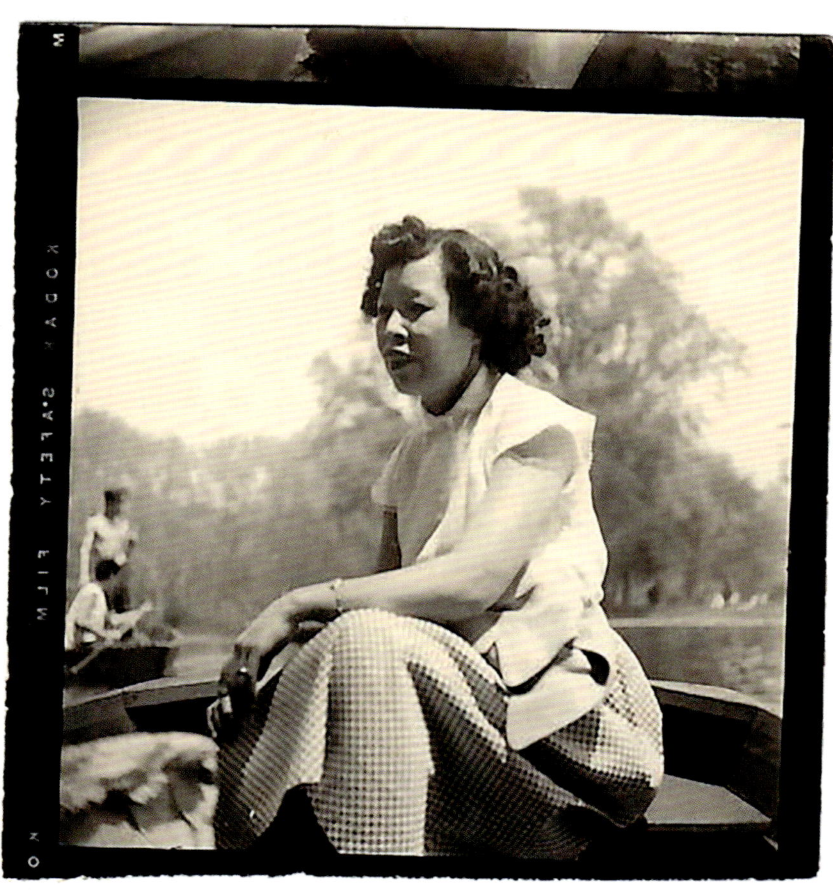

Above: Grandma on a rowboat in Central Park, New York City, late 1940s.

Left: *Grandma and the unknown*, 2024. Digital collage.

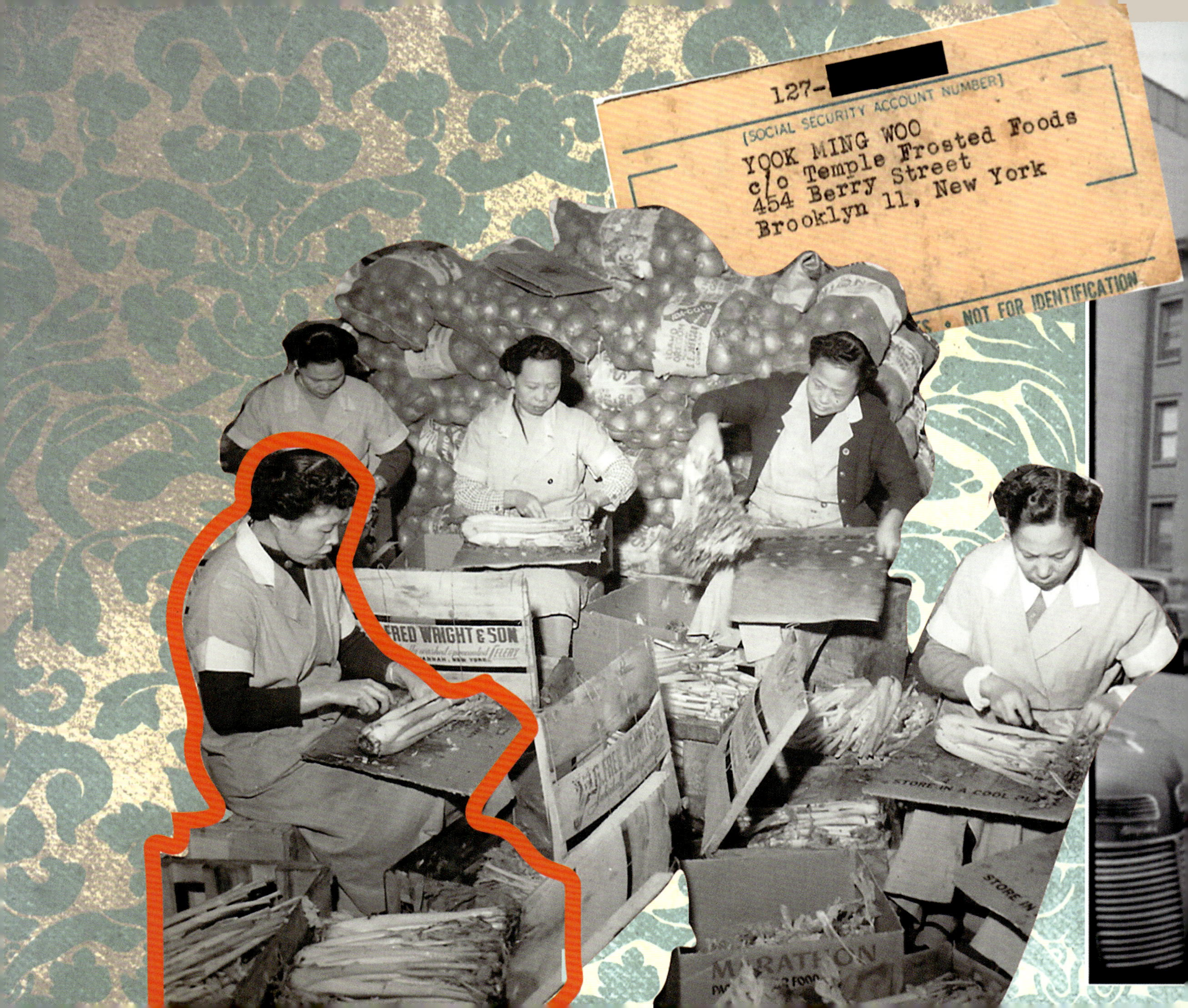
127-
(SOCIAL SECURITY ACCOUNT NUMBER)
YOOK MING WOO
c/o Temple Frosted Foods
454 Berry Street
Brooklyn 11, New York
NOT FOR IDENTIFICATION
FRED WRIGHT & SON
MARATHON

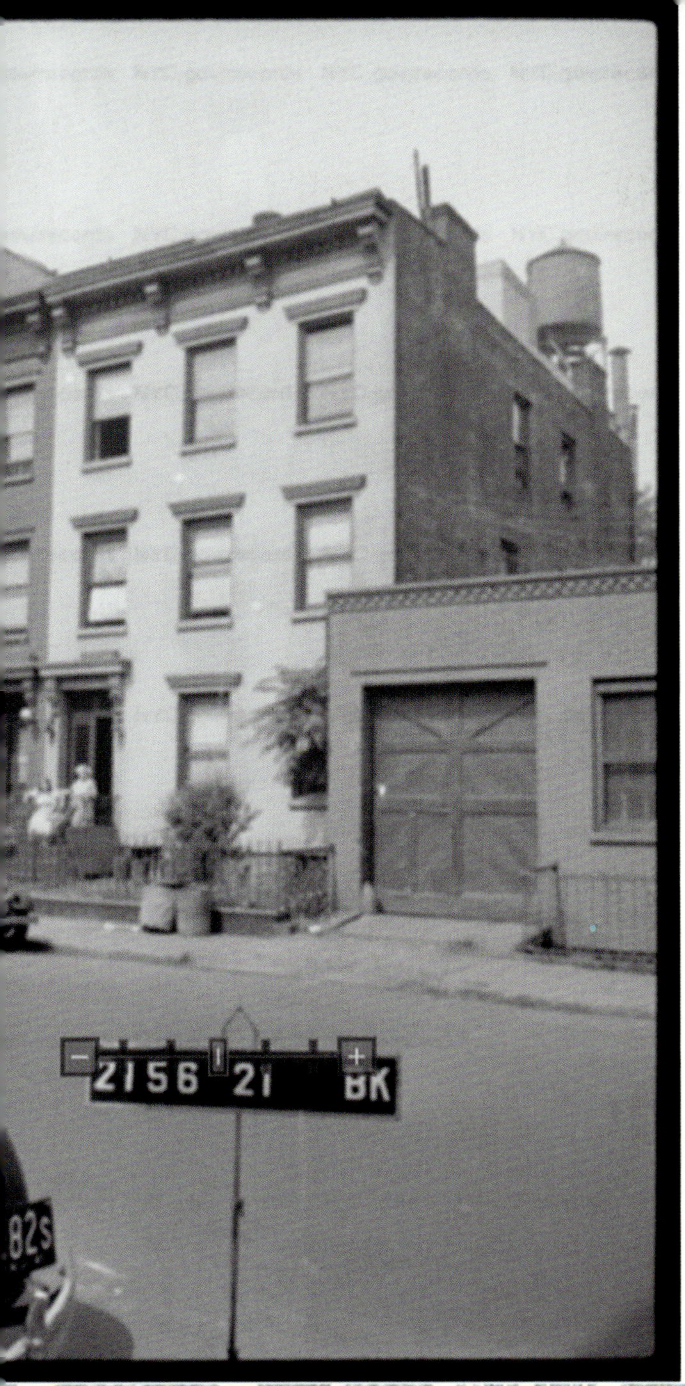

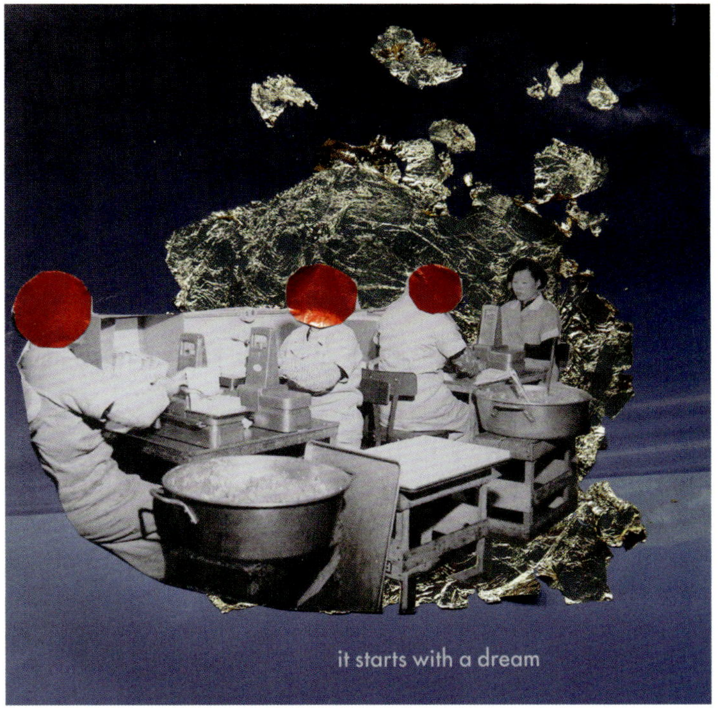

Above: *The dream of golden mountains that never was*, 2021. Mixed-media collage.

Right: *My grandma working at a food factory in Williamsburg, Brooklyn, 1950s*, 2021. Mixed-media collage.

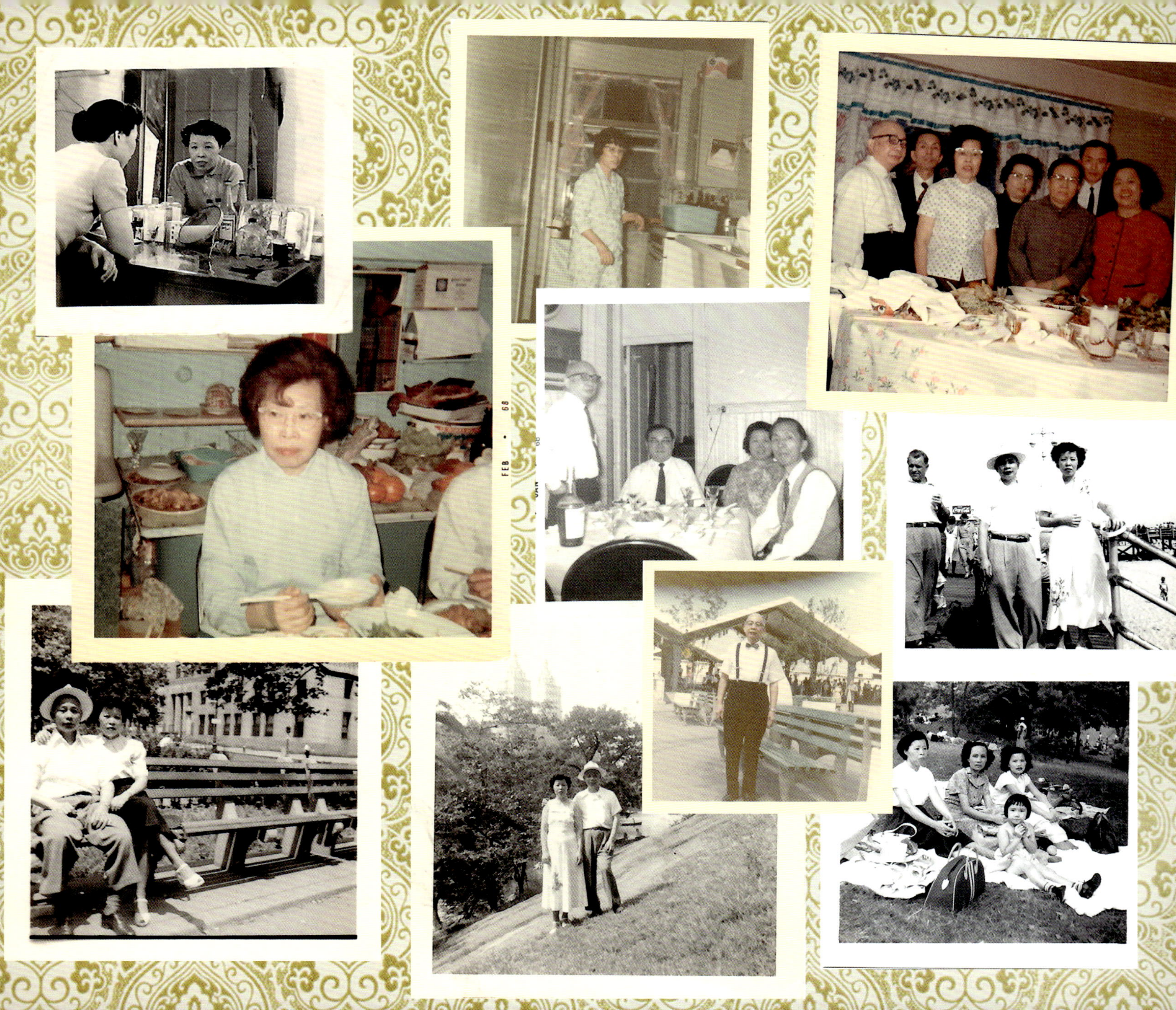
FEB • 68

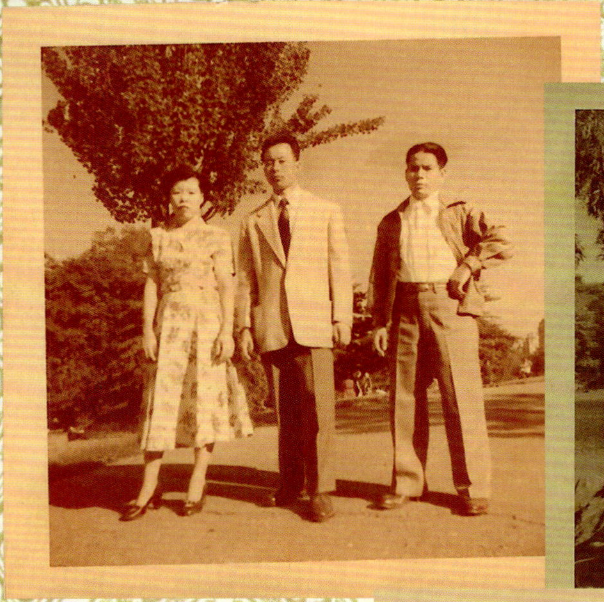

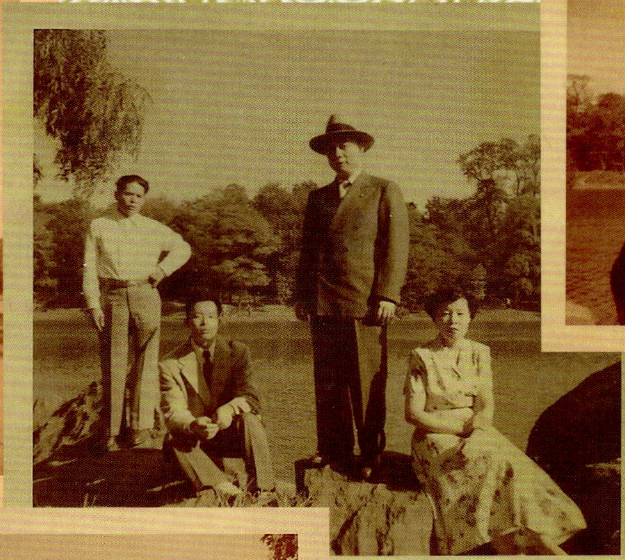

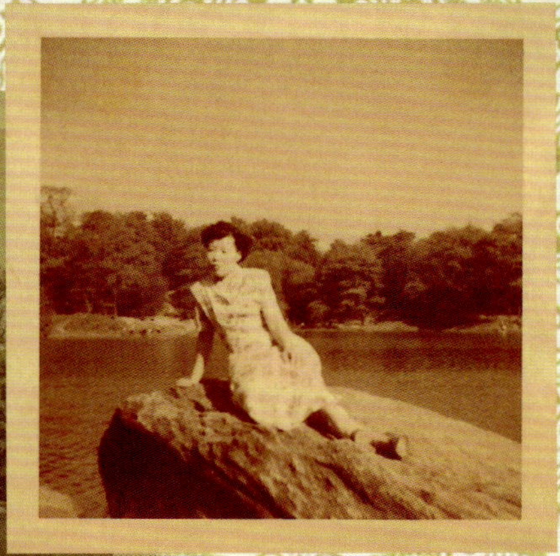

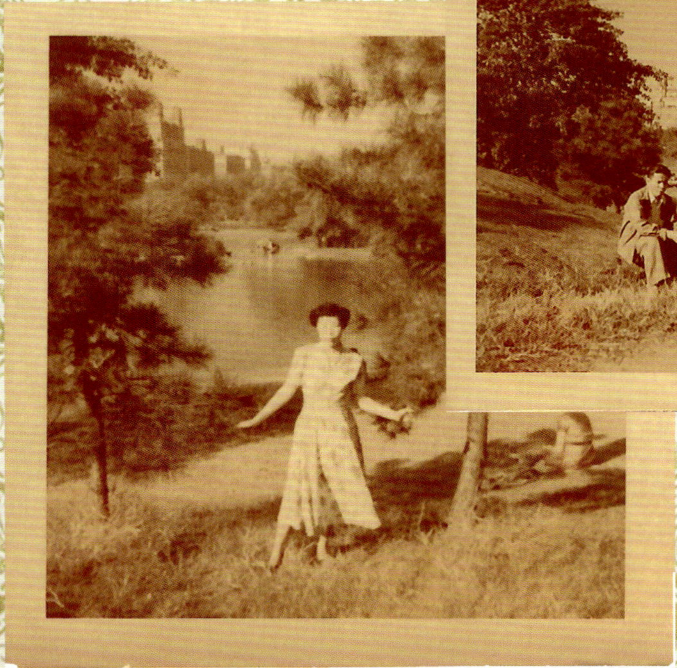

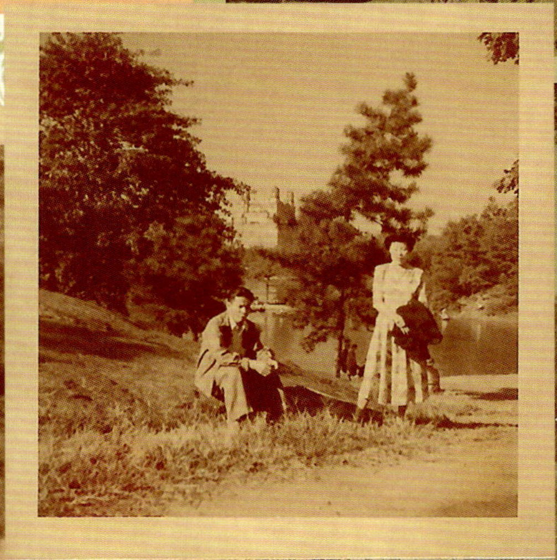

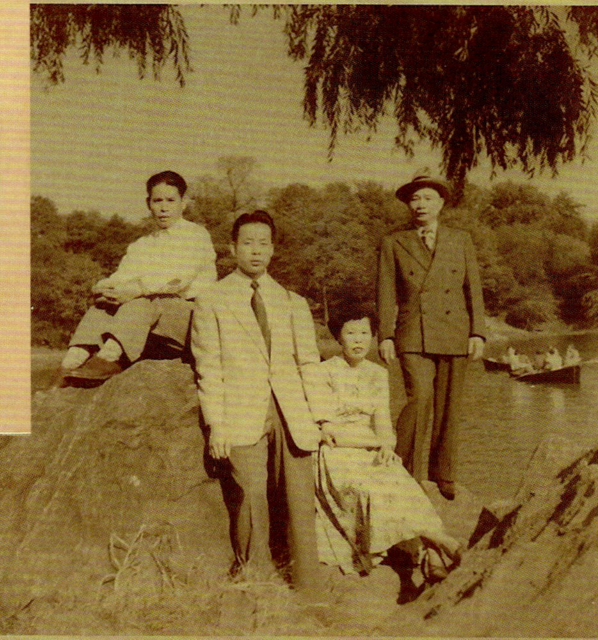

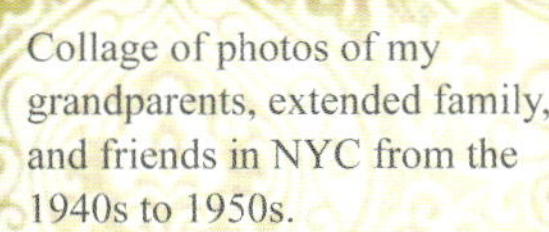

Collage of photos of my grandparents, extended family, and friends in NYC from the 1940s to 1950s.

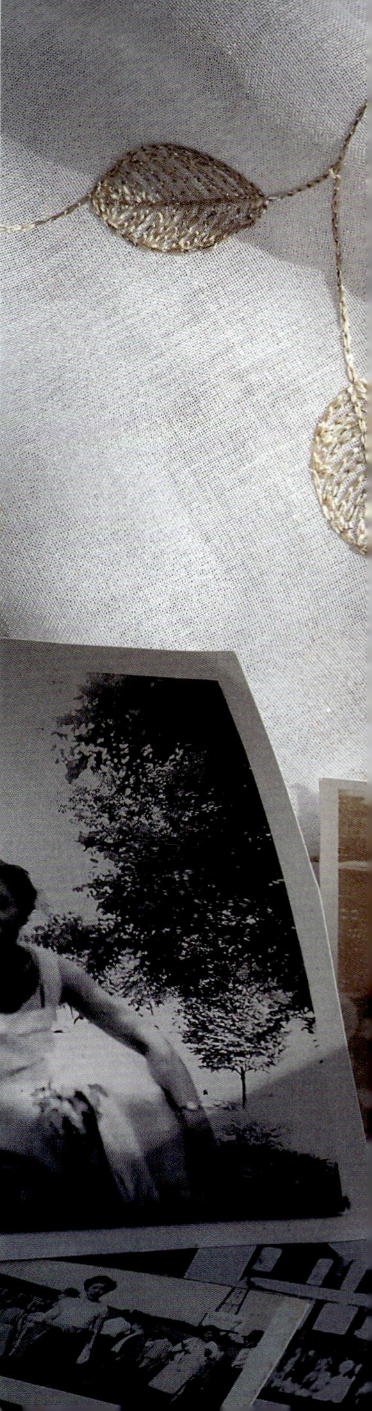

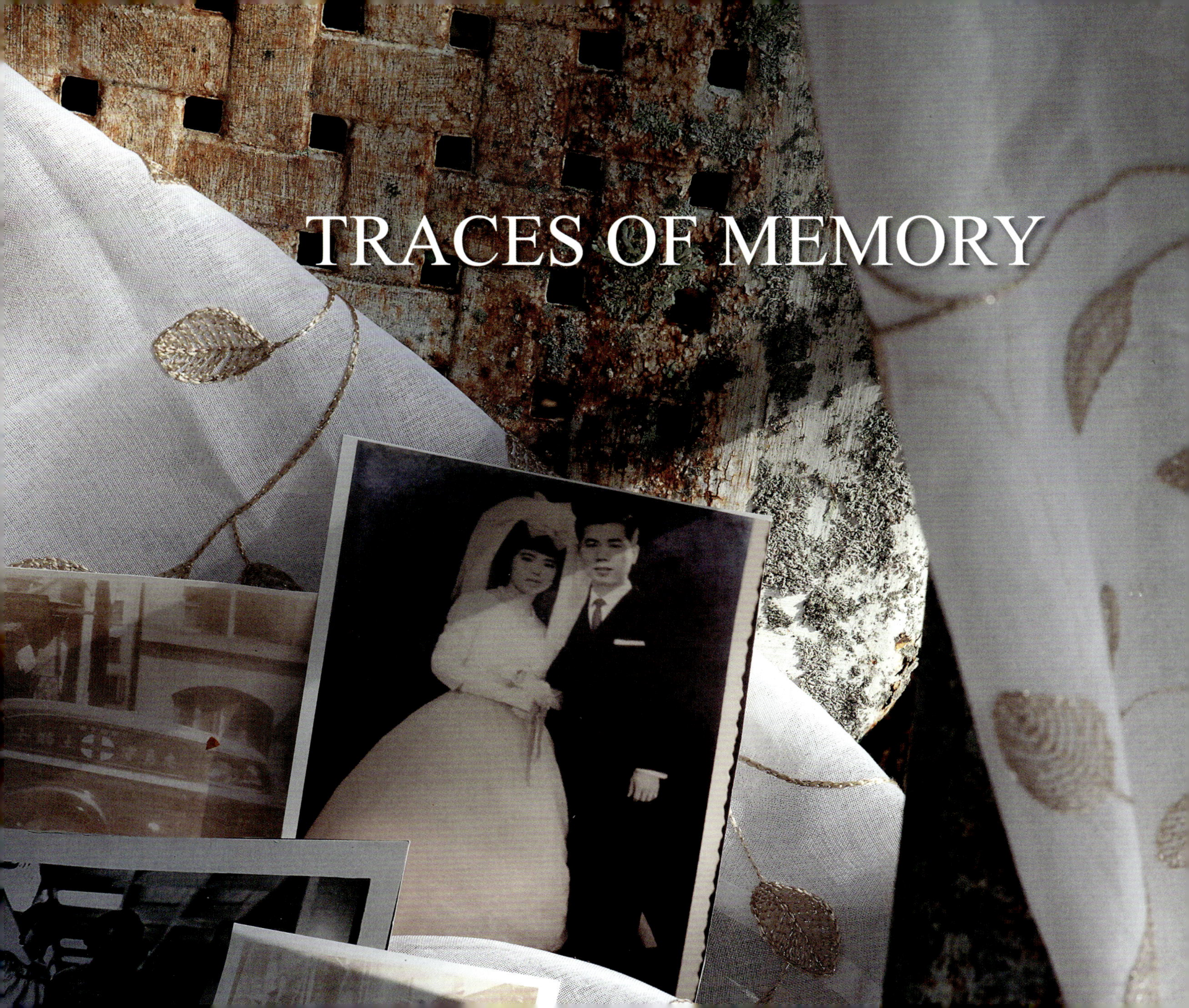

TRACES OF MEMORY

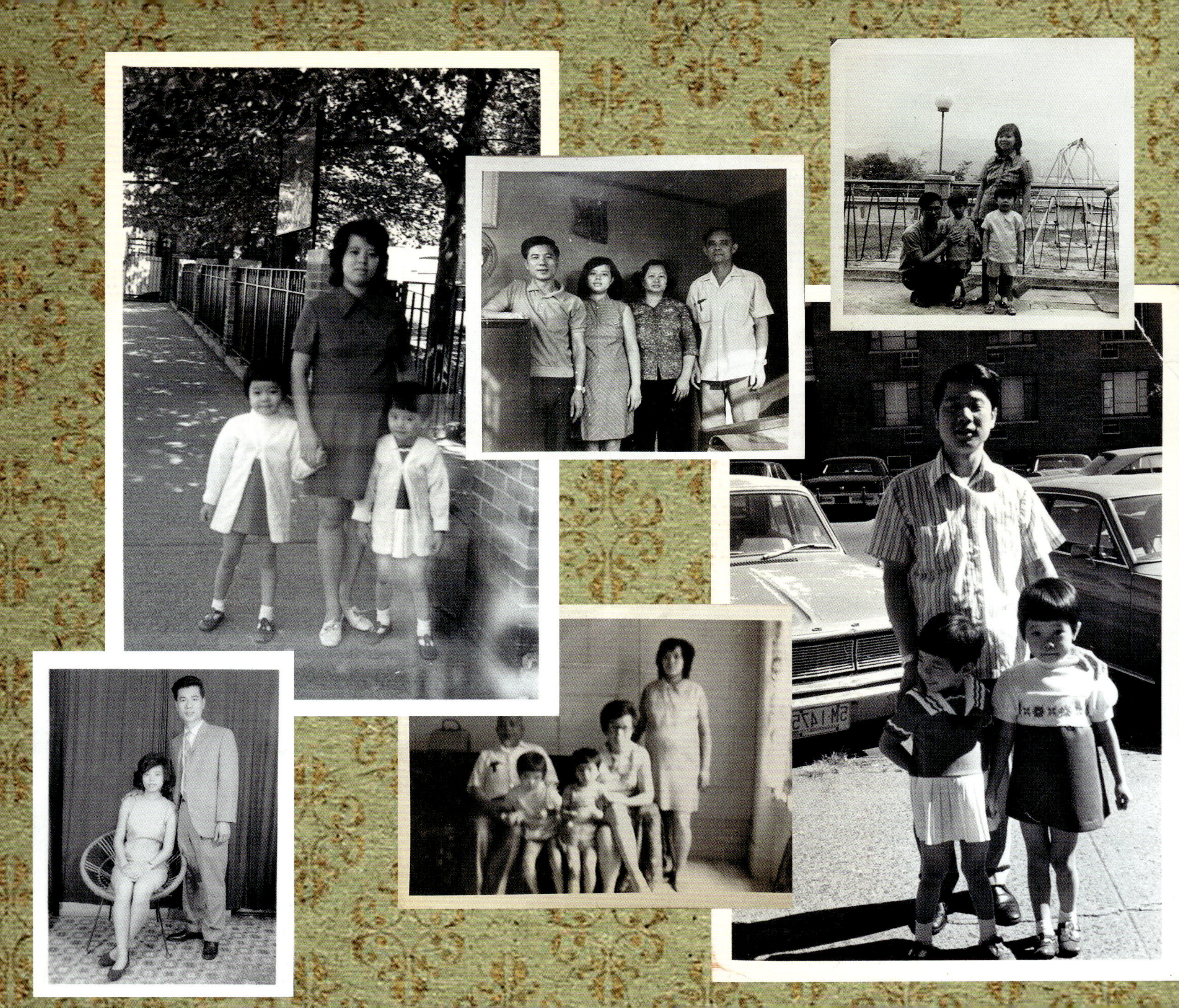

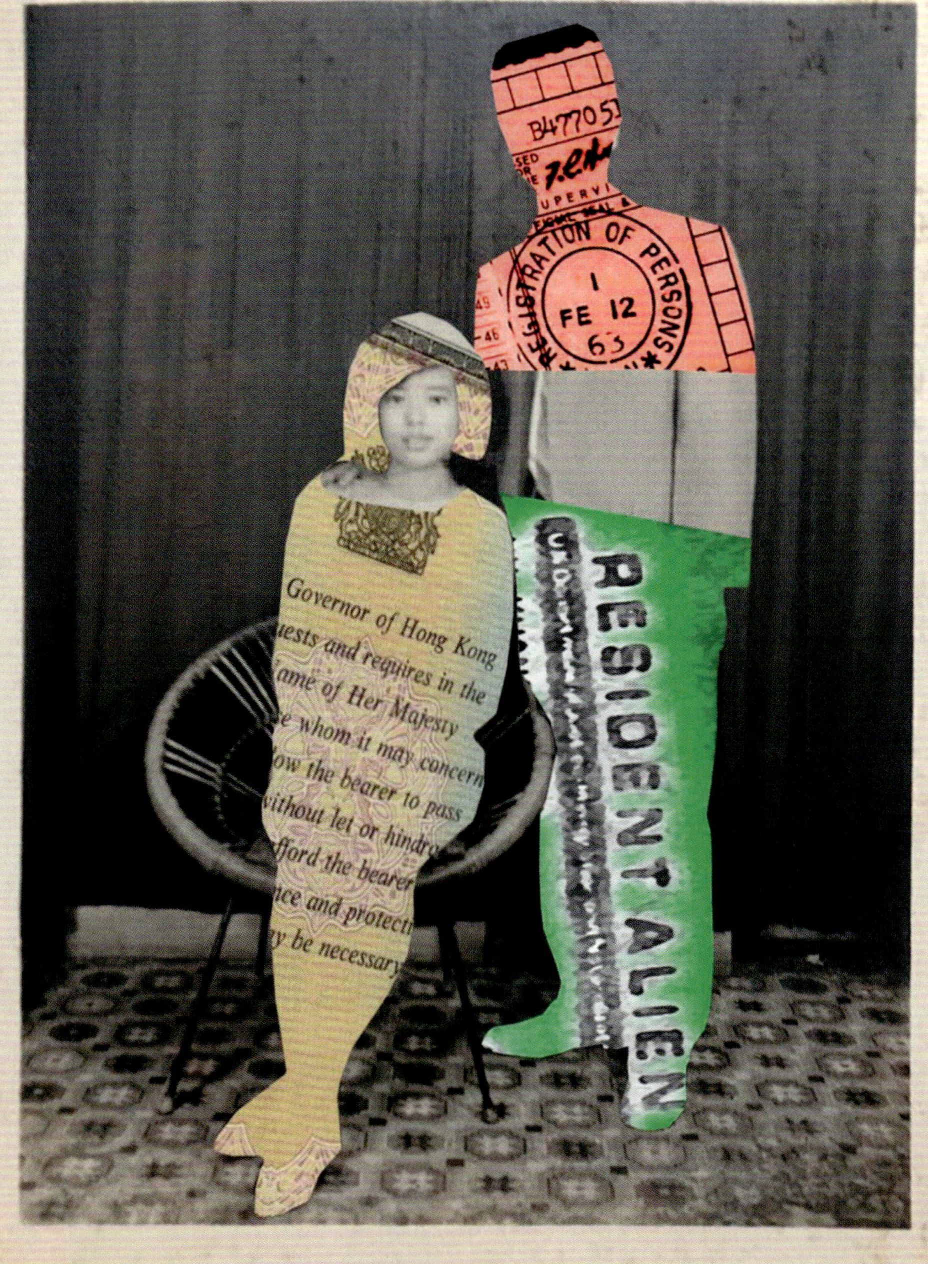

Left: Collage of photos from my parents and sisters in Hong Kong and in New York City from 1967 to the early 1970s.

Right: *Multiple identities, never a citizen*, 2022. Digital collage.

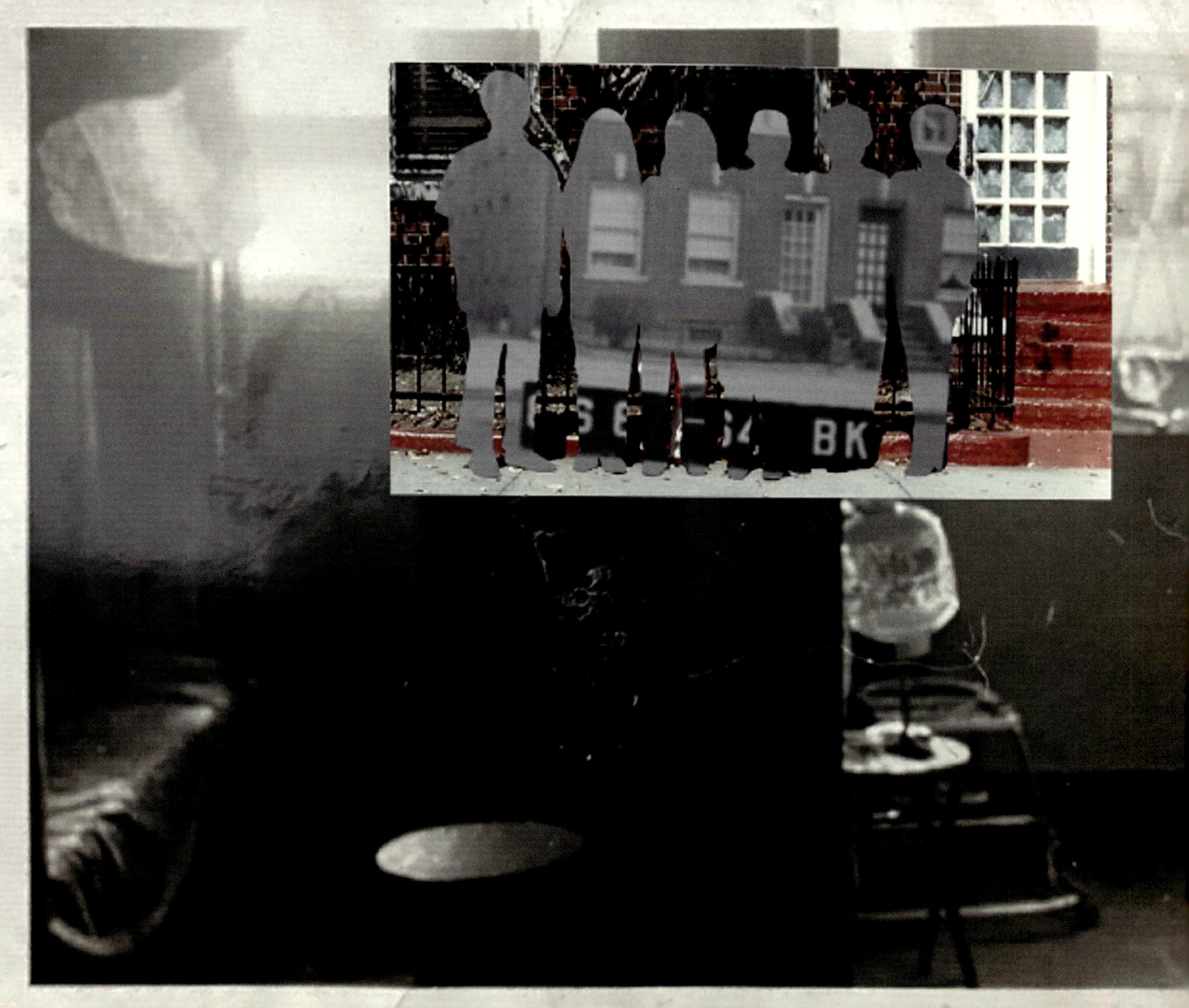

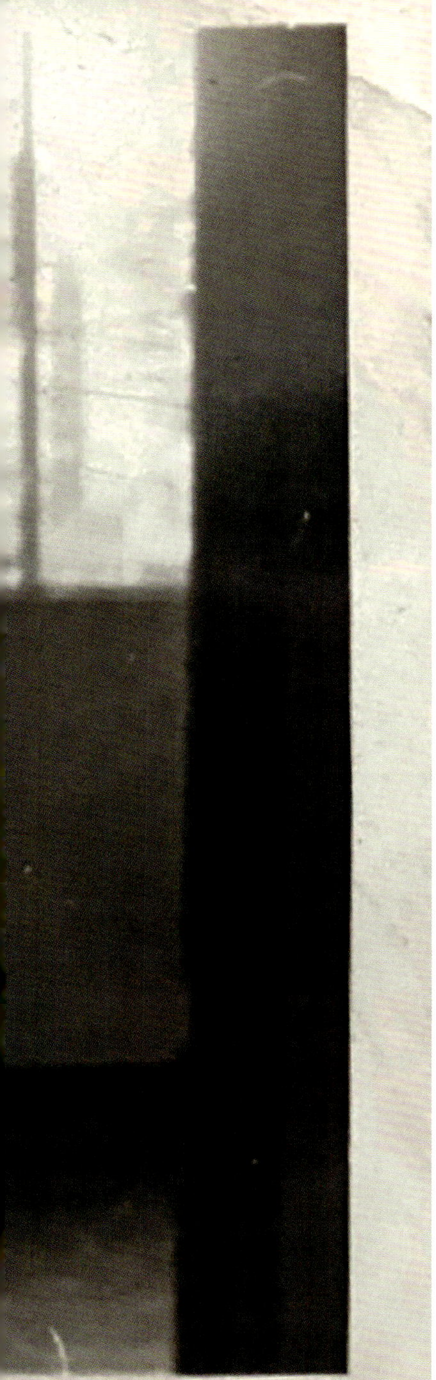

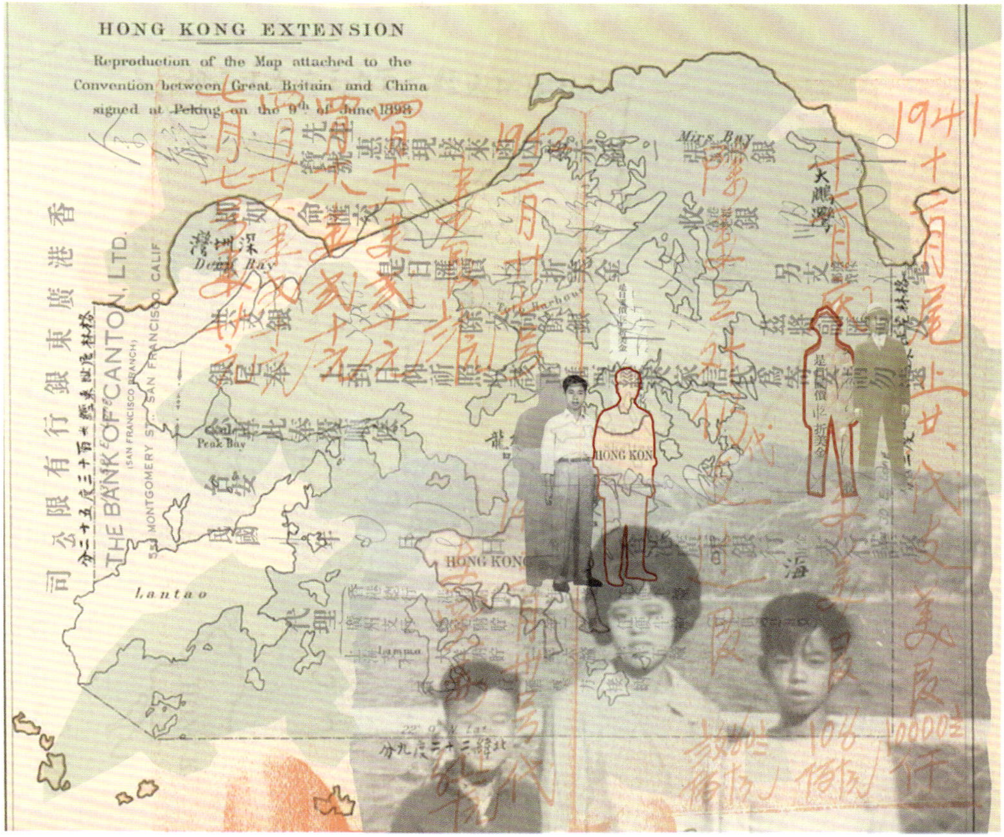

Above: *Hong Kong Extension, colonized by Britain*, 2024. Digital collage.

Left: *Dis/Relocation - from Hong Kong to Brooklyn*, 2020. Mixed-media collage.

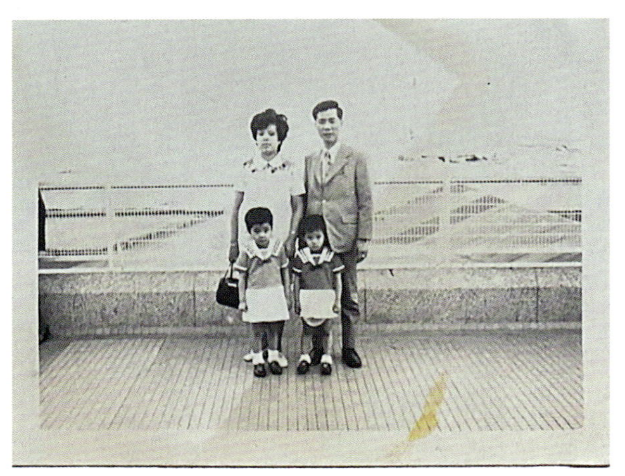

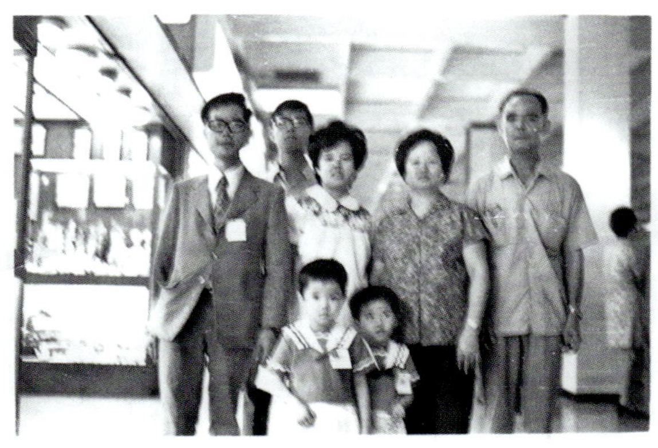

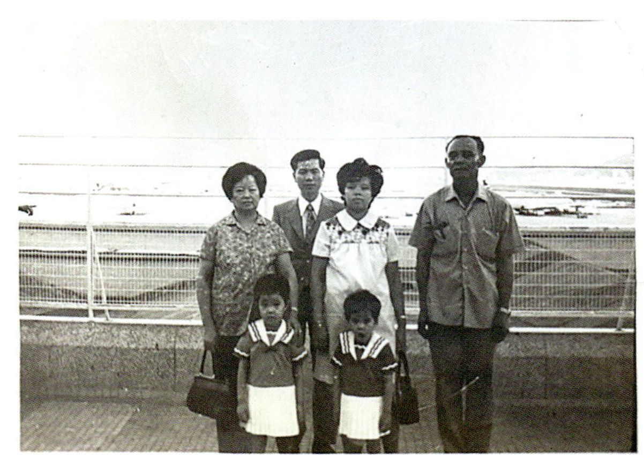

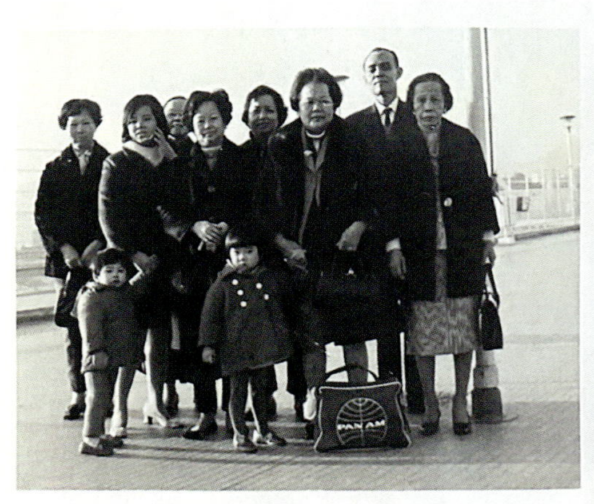

Above: Leaving the airport in Hong Kong to immigrate to the US, 1972.

Right: *My dad's arrival to his second home country, Hong Kong*, 2021. Digital collage.

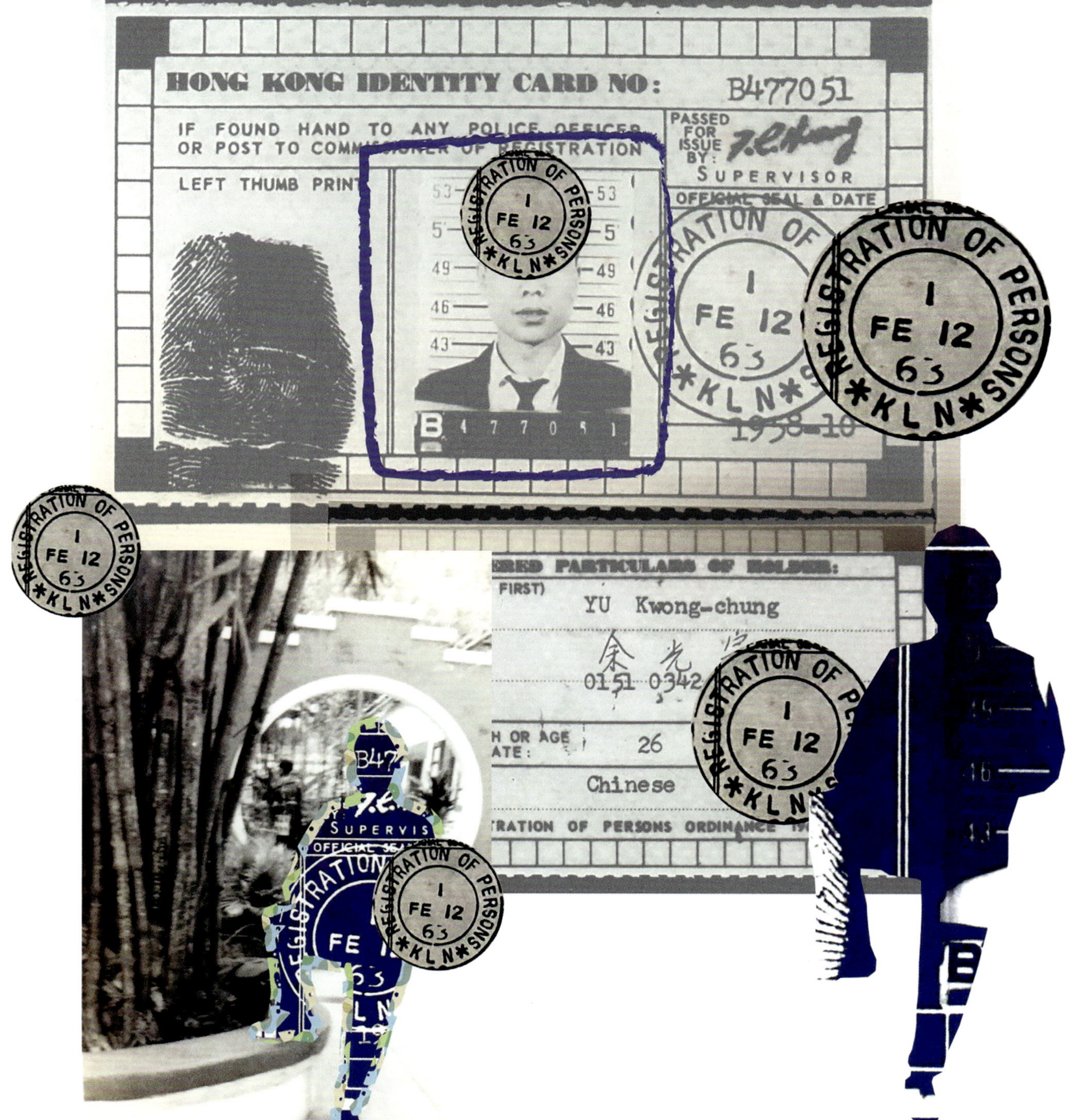
HONG KONG IDENTITY CARD NO:
B477051
IF FOUND HAND TO ANY
OR POST TO
LEFT THUMB
PASSED FOR ISSUE BY:
SUPERVISOR
REGISTRATION OF PERSONS
1
FE 12
63
KLN
B 477051
1958-10
YU Kwong-chung
0151 0342
26
Chinese
OF PERSONS ORDINANCE

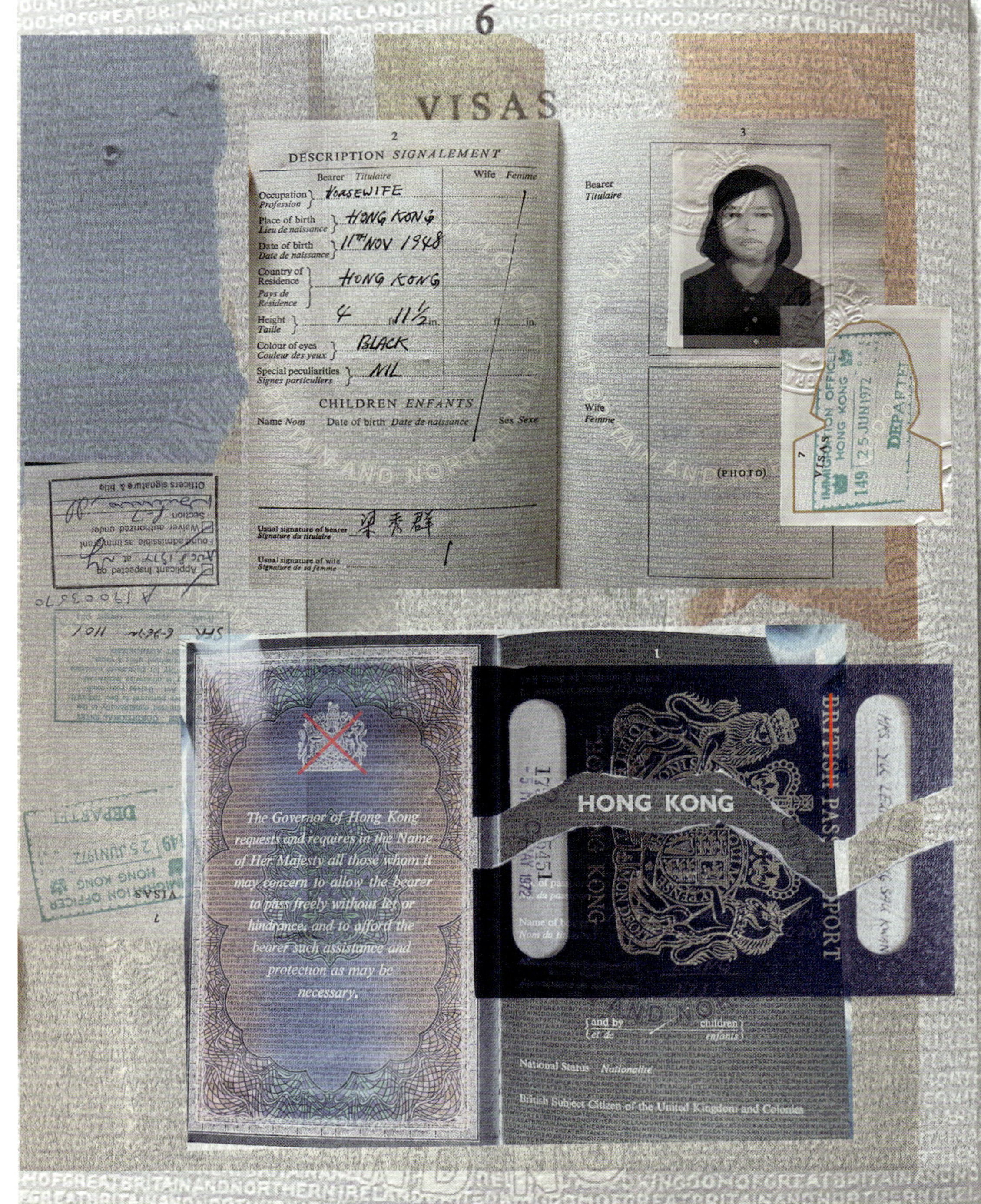
6
VISAS
2
DESCRIPTION SIGNALEMENT
Bearer Titulaire
Wife Femme
Occupation Profession HOUSEWIFE
Place of birth Lieu de naissance HONG KONG
Date of birth Date de naissance 11TH NOV 1948
Country of Residence Pays de Résidence HONG KONG
Height Taille 4 ft. 11½ in.
Colour of eyes Couleur des yeux BLACK
Special peculiarities Signes particuliers NIL
CHILDREN ENFANTS
Name Nom Date of birth Date de naissance Sex Sexe
Usual signature of bearer Signature du titulaire 梁秀群
Usual signature of wife Signature de sa femme
3
Bearer Titulaire
Wife Femme
(PHOTO)
VISAS
IMMIGRATION OFFICER HONG KONG
149 25 JUN 1972
DEPARTED
1
HONG KONG
BRITISH PASSPORT
The Governor of Hong Kong requests and requires in the Name of Her Majesty all those whom it may concern to allow the bearer to pass freely without let or hindrance, and to afford the bearer such assistance and protection as may be necessary.
and by et de
children enfants
National Status Nationalité
British Subject Citizen of the United Kingdom and Colonies

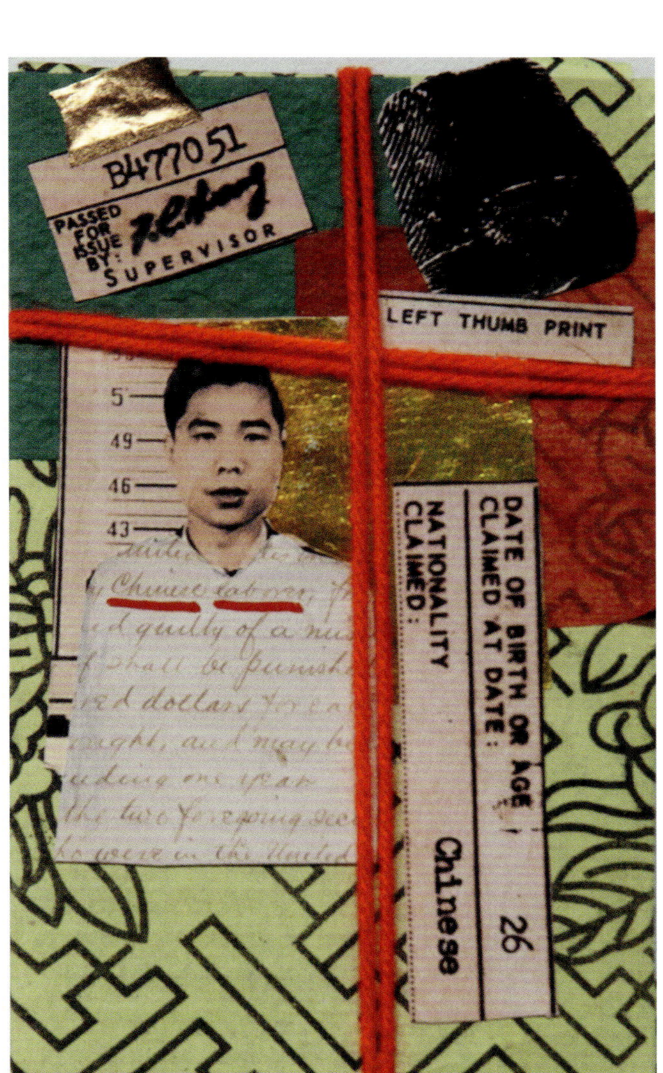

Left: *My mom: a citizen of her majesty*, 2024. Digital collage.

Right: *Dad, a Chinese Laborer in the US, No. B477051*, 2021. Mixed-media collage.

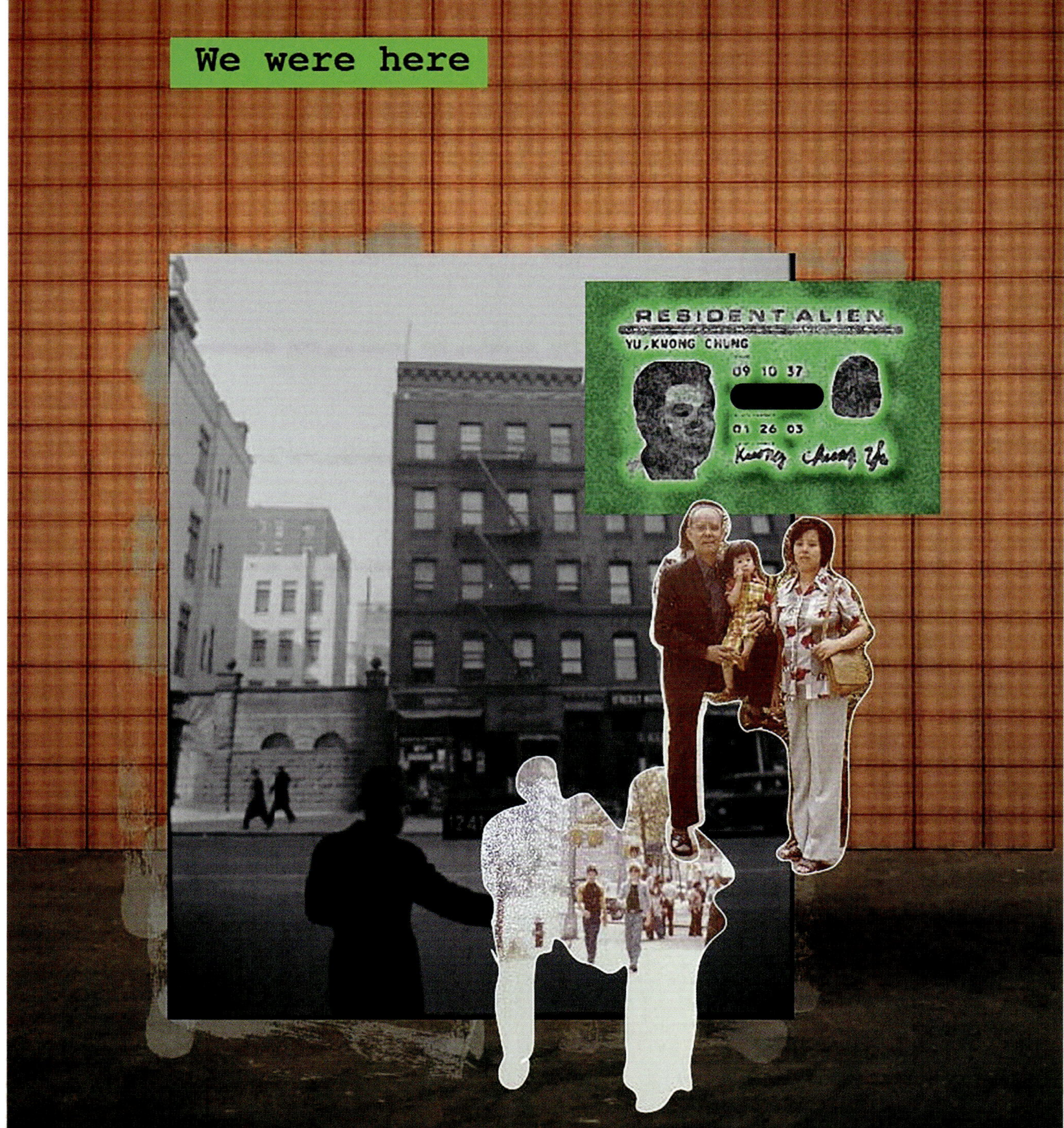

Left: *My dad's US Alien card juxtaposed with me as a baby with my mother and grandpa in NYC*, 2020. Mixed-media collage.

Right: My family and me in the late 1970s and early 1980s in New York City.

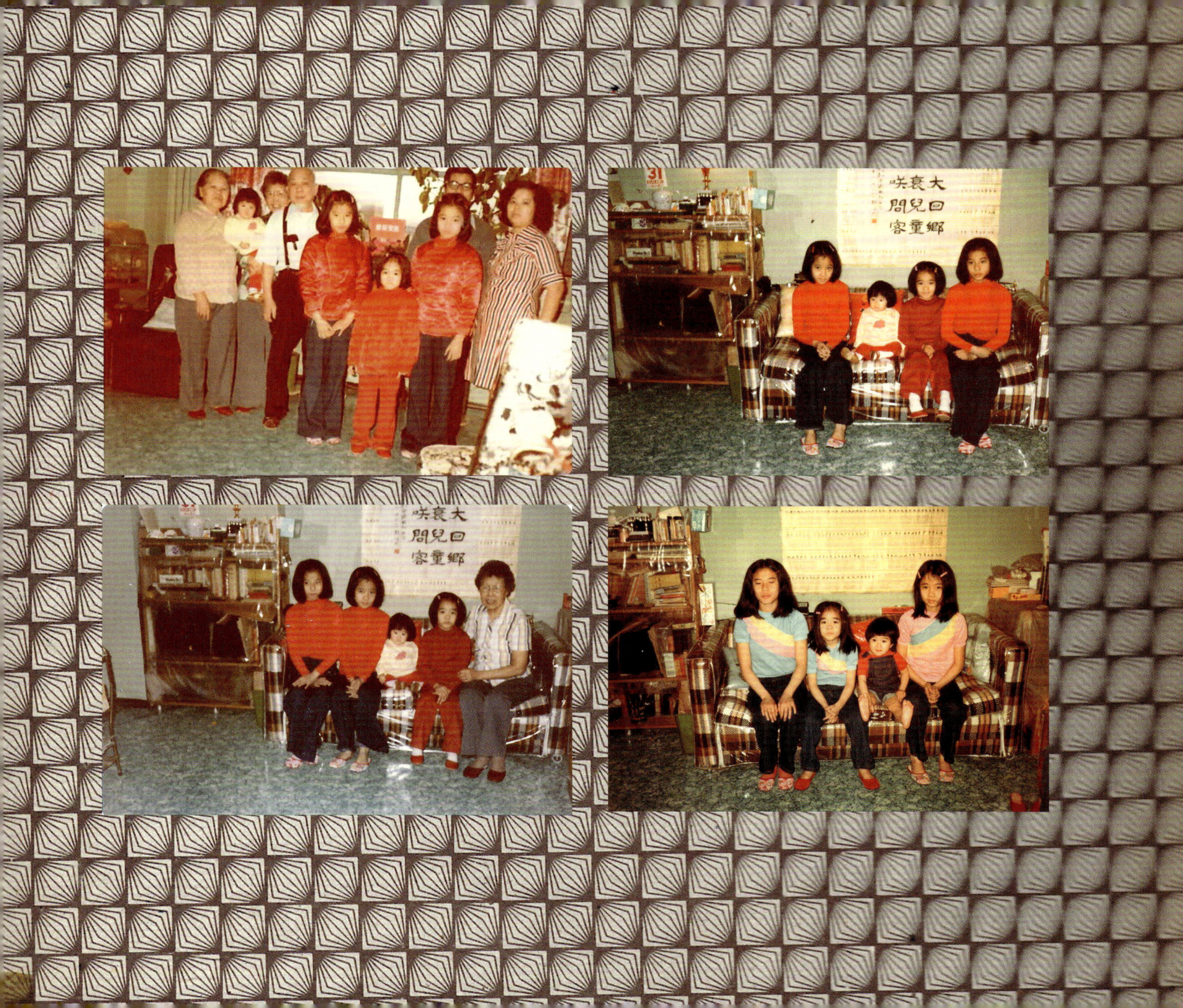
31
大回鄉
衰兒童
咲問客

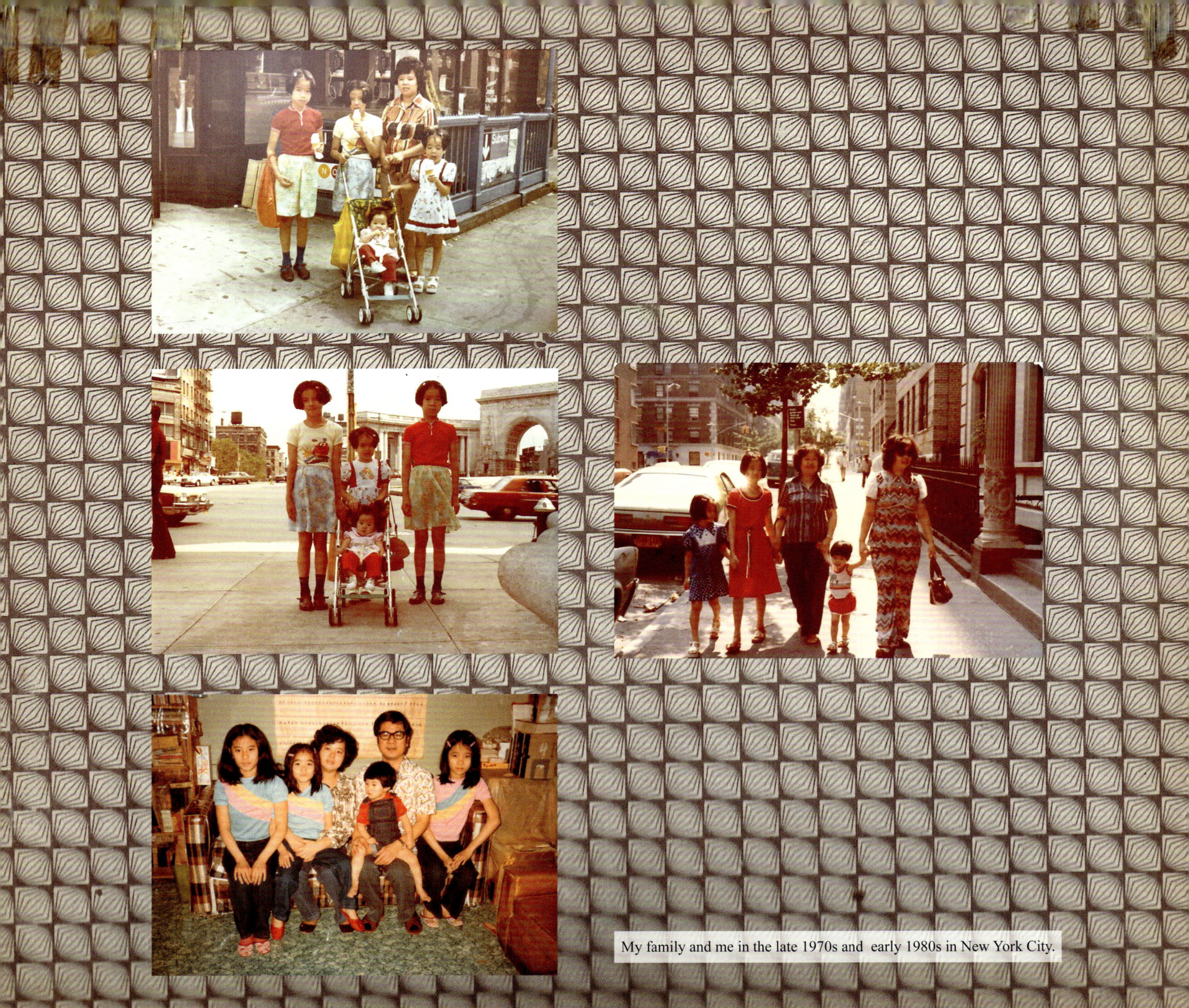

My family and me in the late 1970s and early 1980s in New York City.

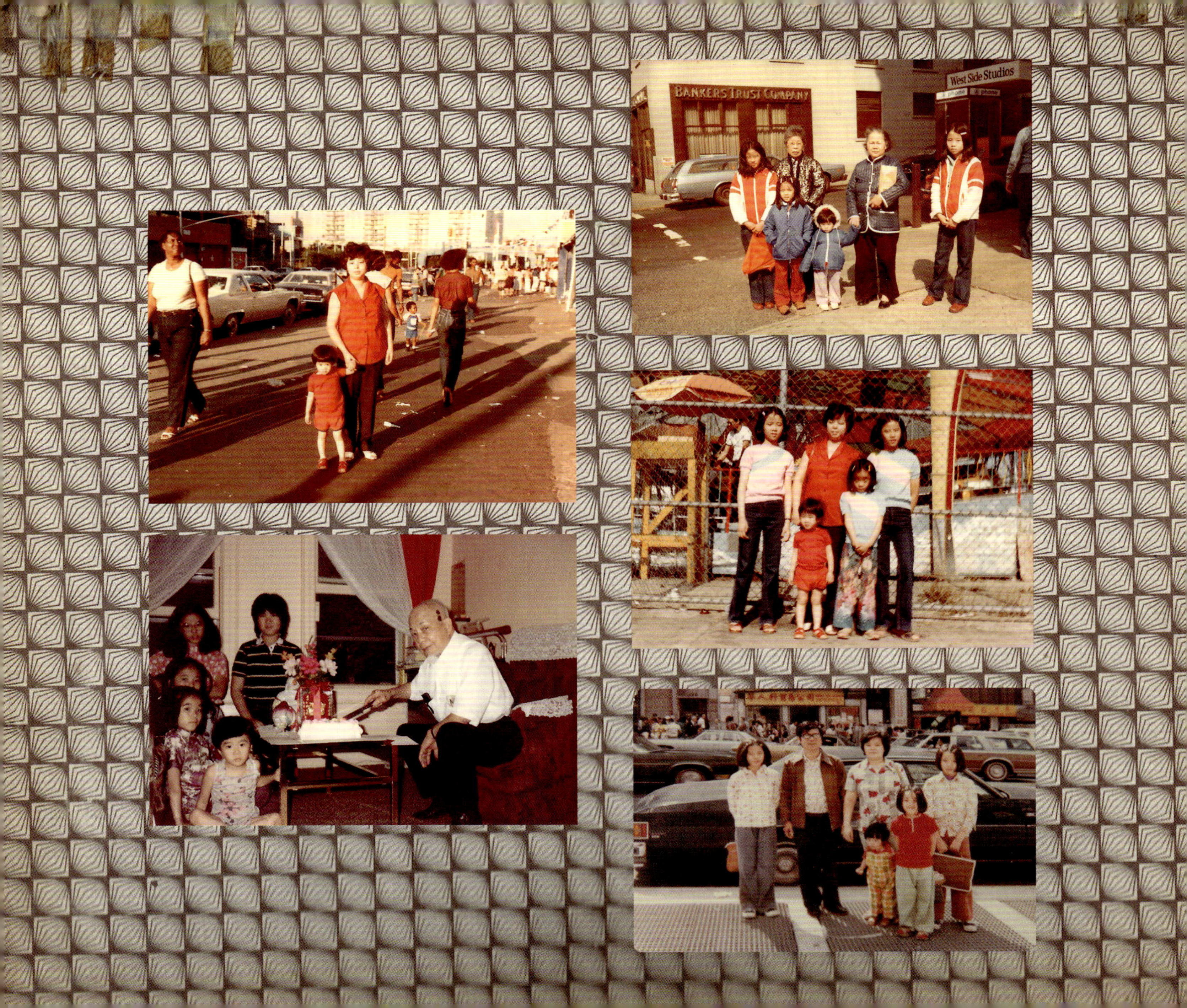
BANKERS TRUST COMPANY
West Side Studios

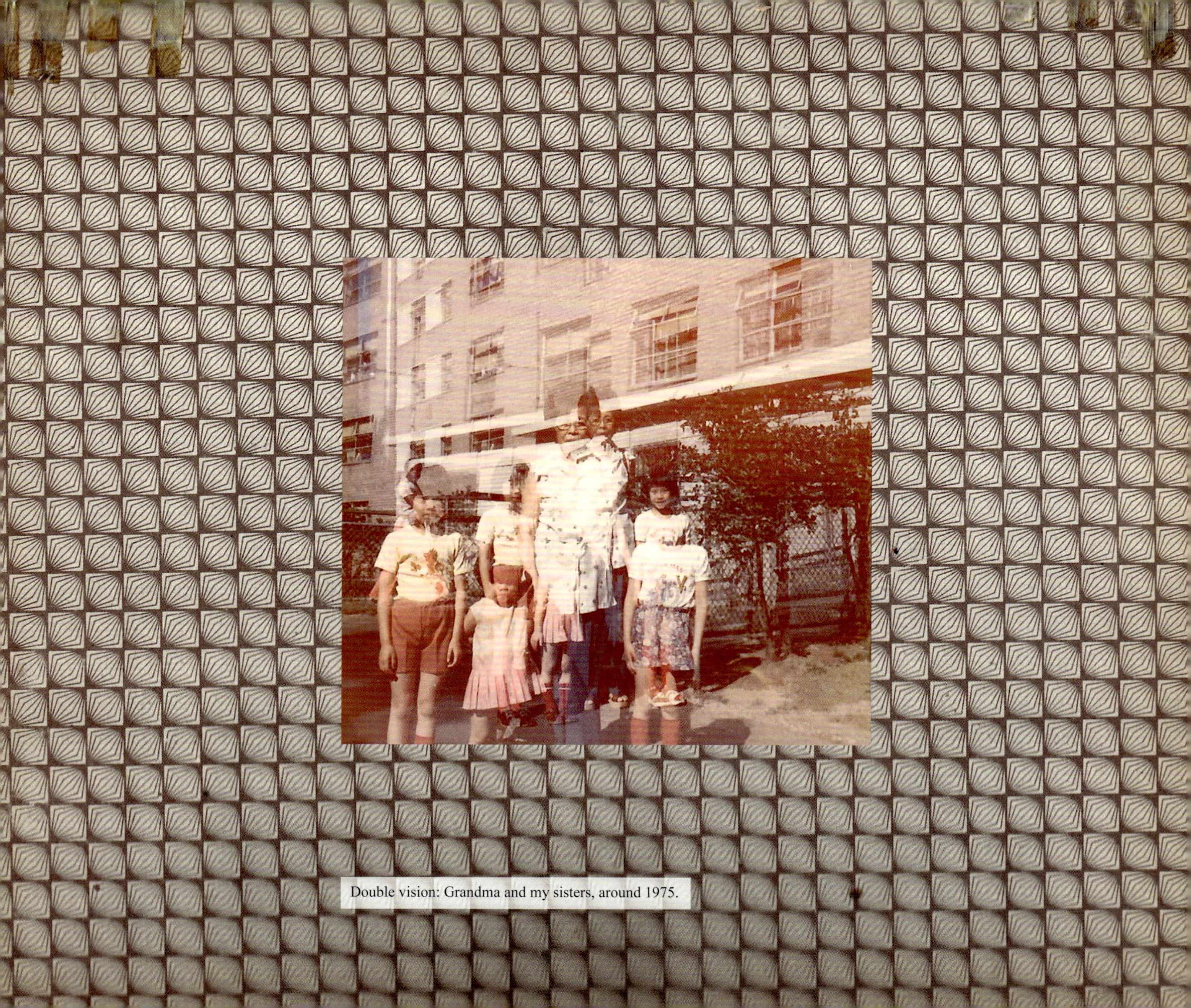

Double vision: Grandma and my sisters, around 1975.

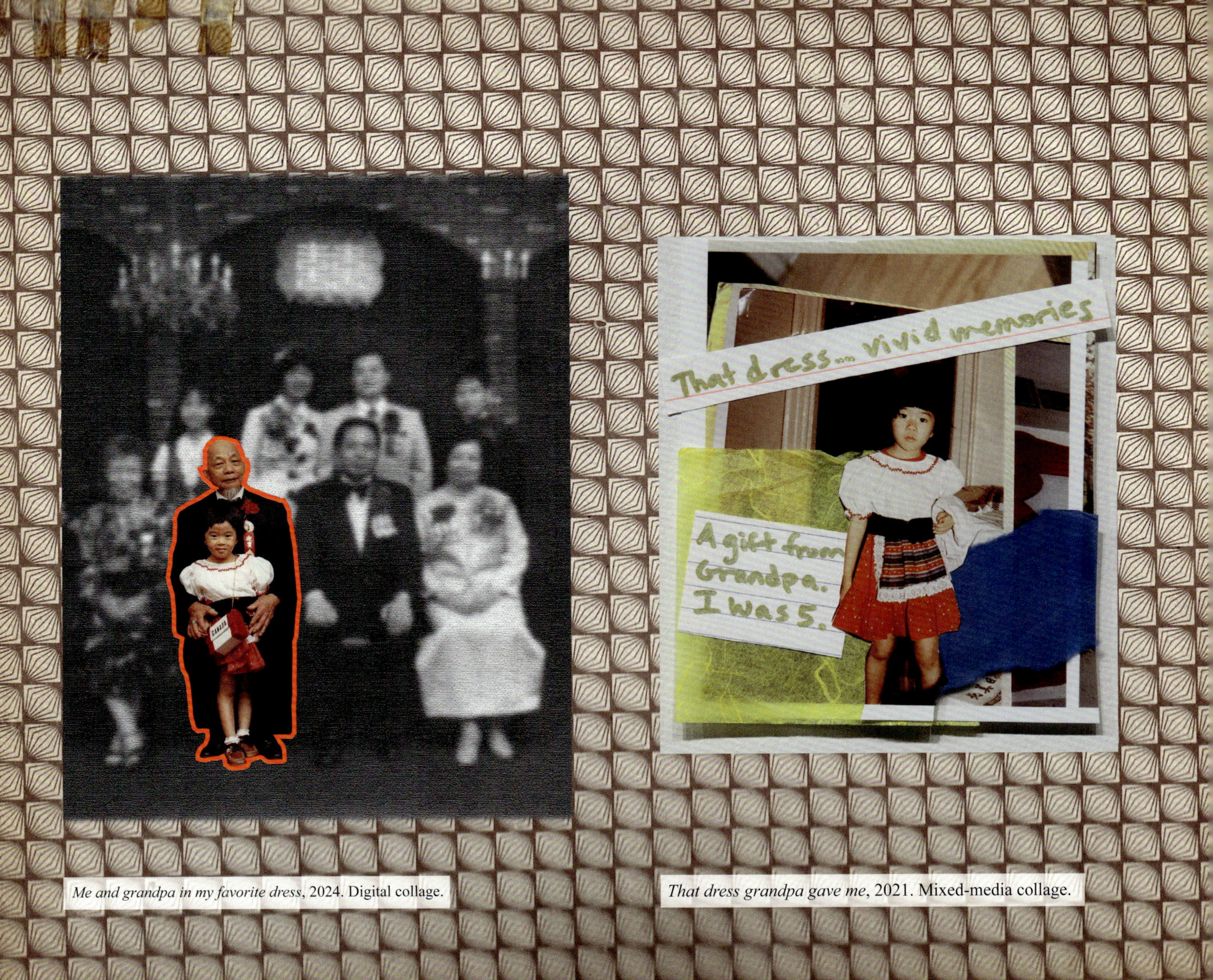

Me and grandpa in my favorite dress, 2024. Digital collage.

That dress grandpa gave me, 2021. Mixed-media collage.

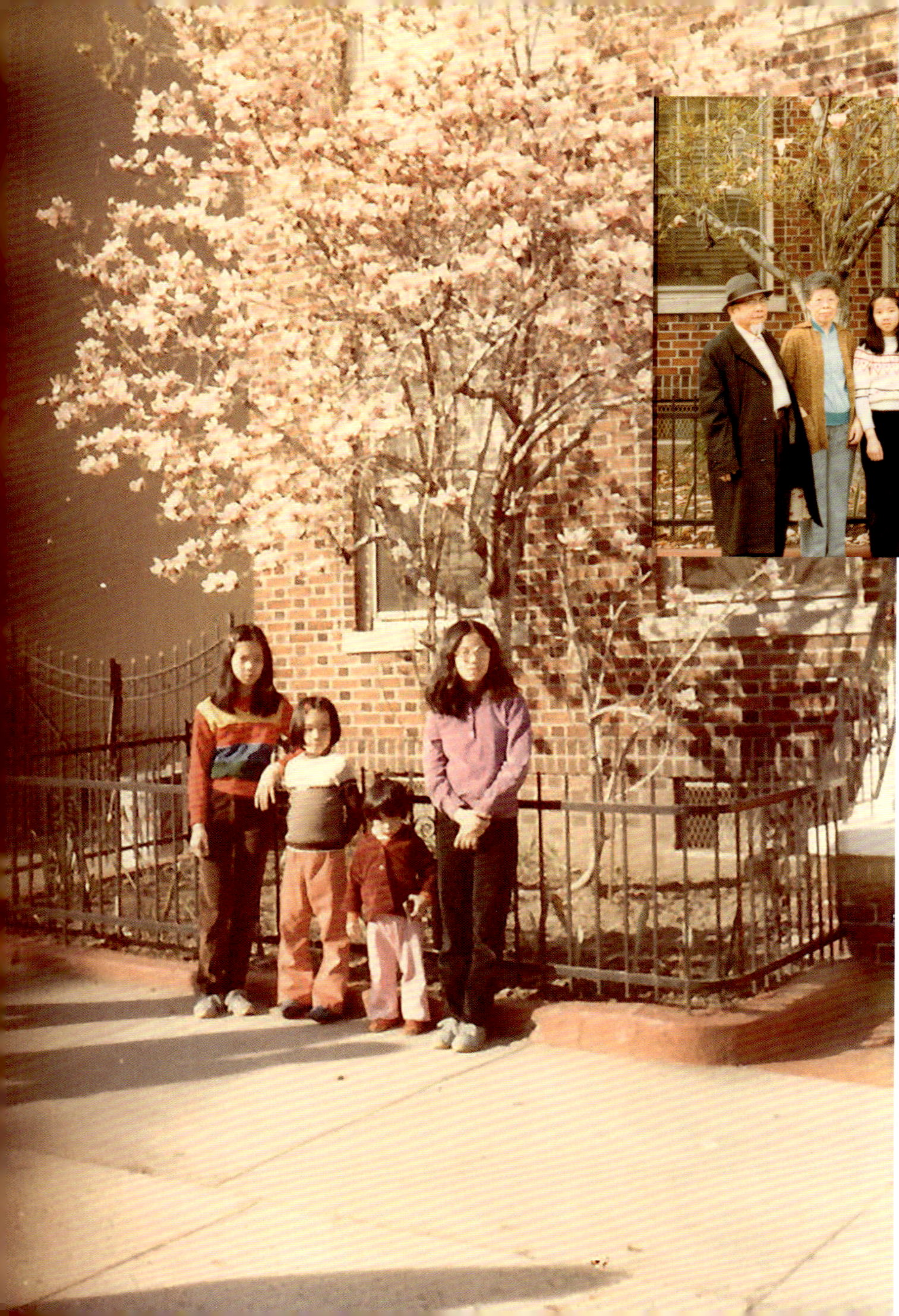

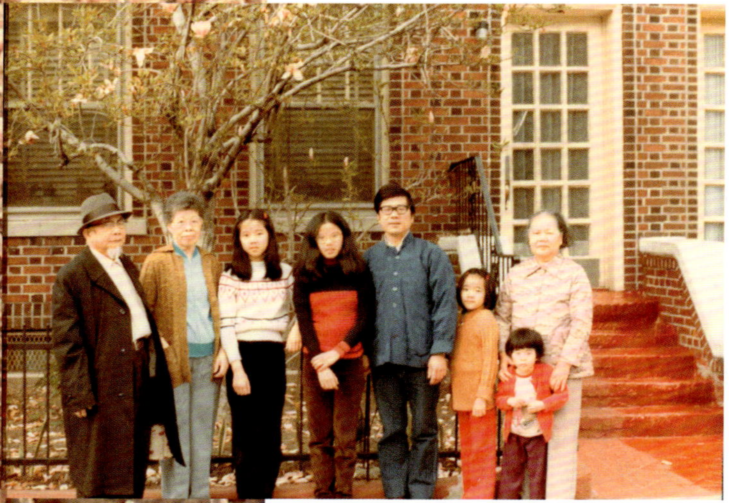

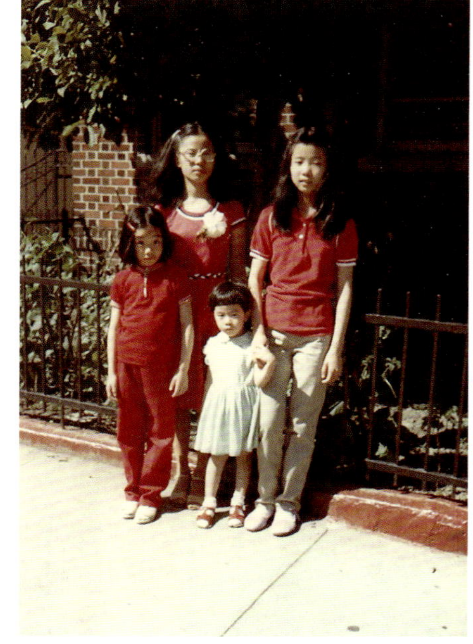

Left: My family and me in the late 1970s and early 1980s in New York City.

Right: *Redlined + Hazardous: my family and me in front of our home in Sunset Park in the early '80s*, 2021. Digital collage.

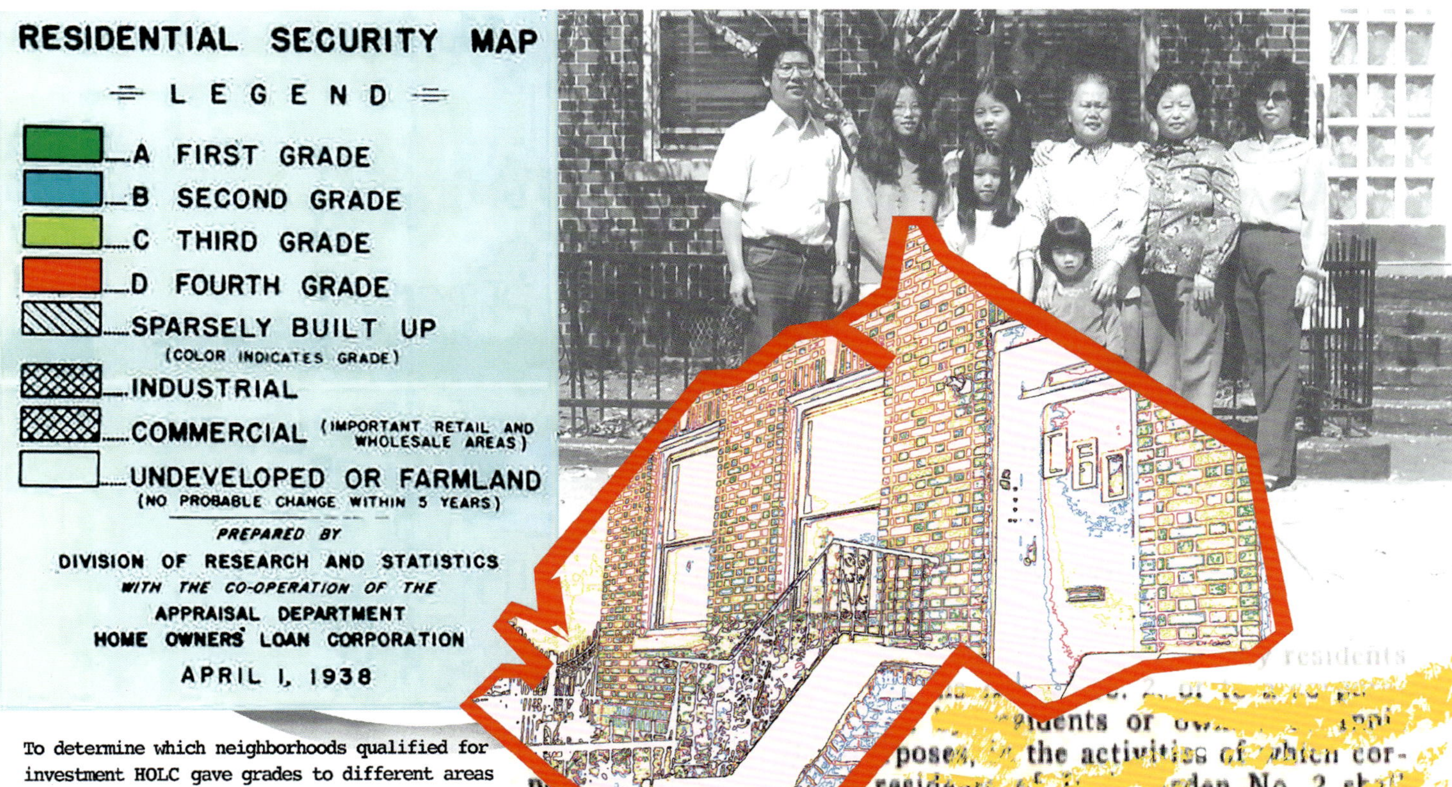

To determine which neighborhoods qualified for investment HOLC gave grades to different areas of the city. On HOLC's maps, an

- "A" neighborhood was green, a best bet for housing investment.
- "B" neighborhoods were blue, meaning "still desirable,"
- "C" neighborhoods were yellow and "definitely declining," and
- "D" neighborhoods were red, or "hazardous."

They evaluated areas based on the "threat of infiltration of foreign-born, negro, or lower grade population." This meant that green areas were green not just because of the quality of the buildings, but because, as Ta-Nehisi Coates reminds us, they lacked "a single foreigner or Negro."

14. *RACIAL RESTRICTIONS*...No property in said addition shall at any time be sold, conveyed, rented or leased in whole or in part to any person or persons not of the White or Caucausian race. No person other than one of the White or Caucausian race shall be permitted to occupy any property in said addition or portion thereof or building thereon except a domestic servant actually employed by a person of the White or Caucausian race where the latter is an occupant of such property.

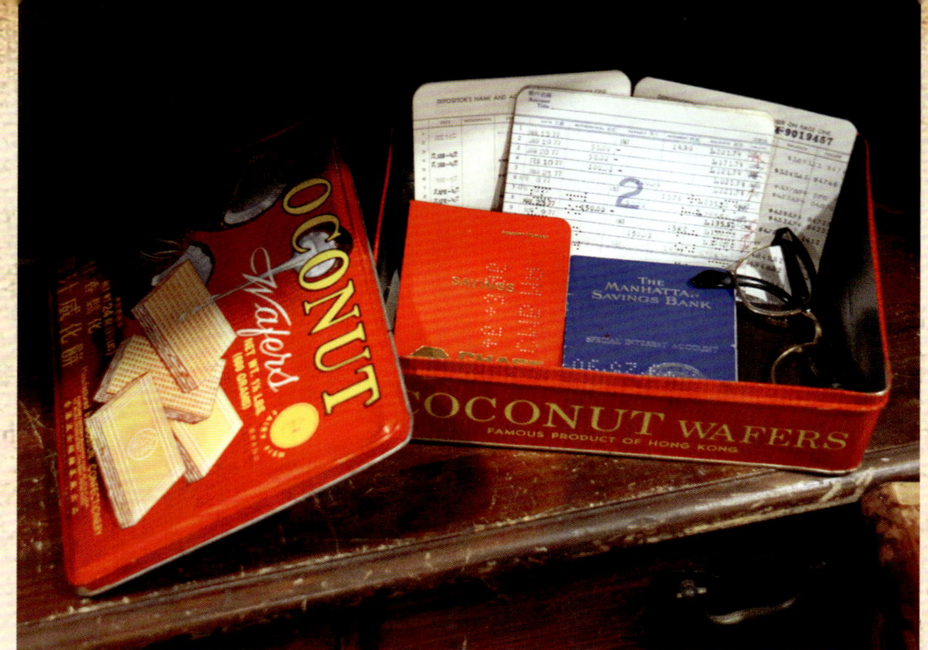

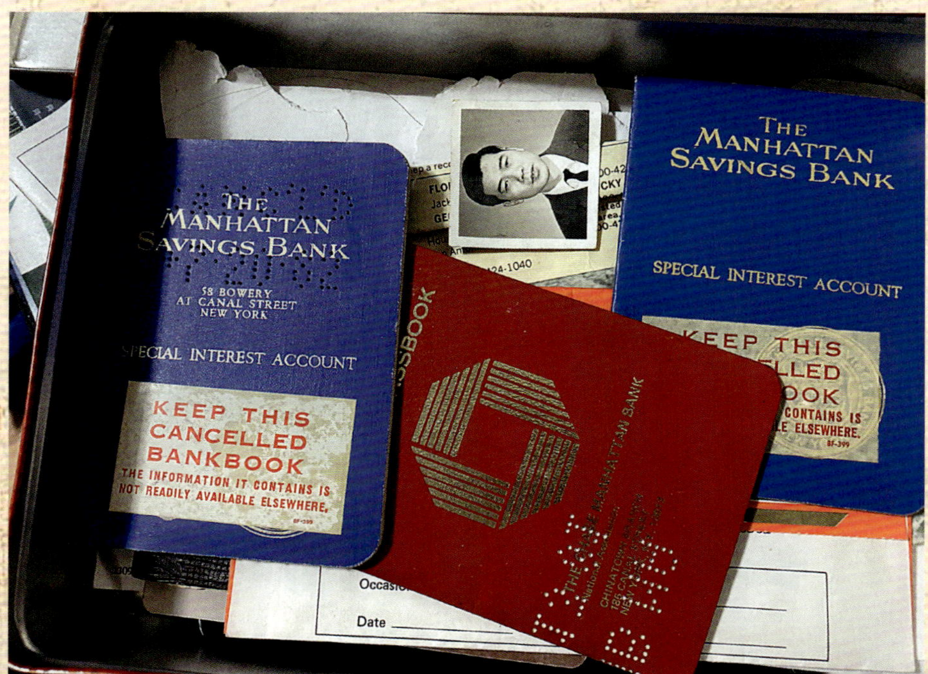

The bin that carries fortunes with my family's banknotes from the 1940s to 1980s, 2024.

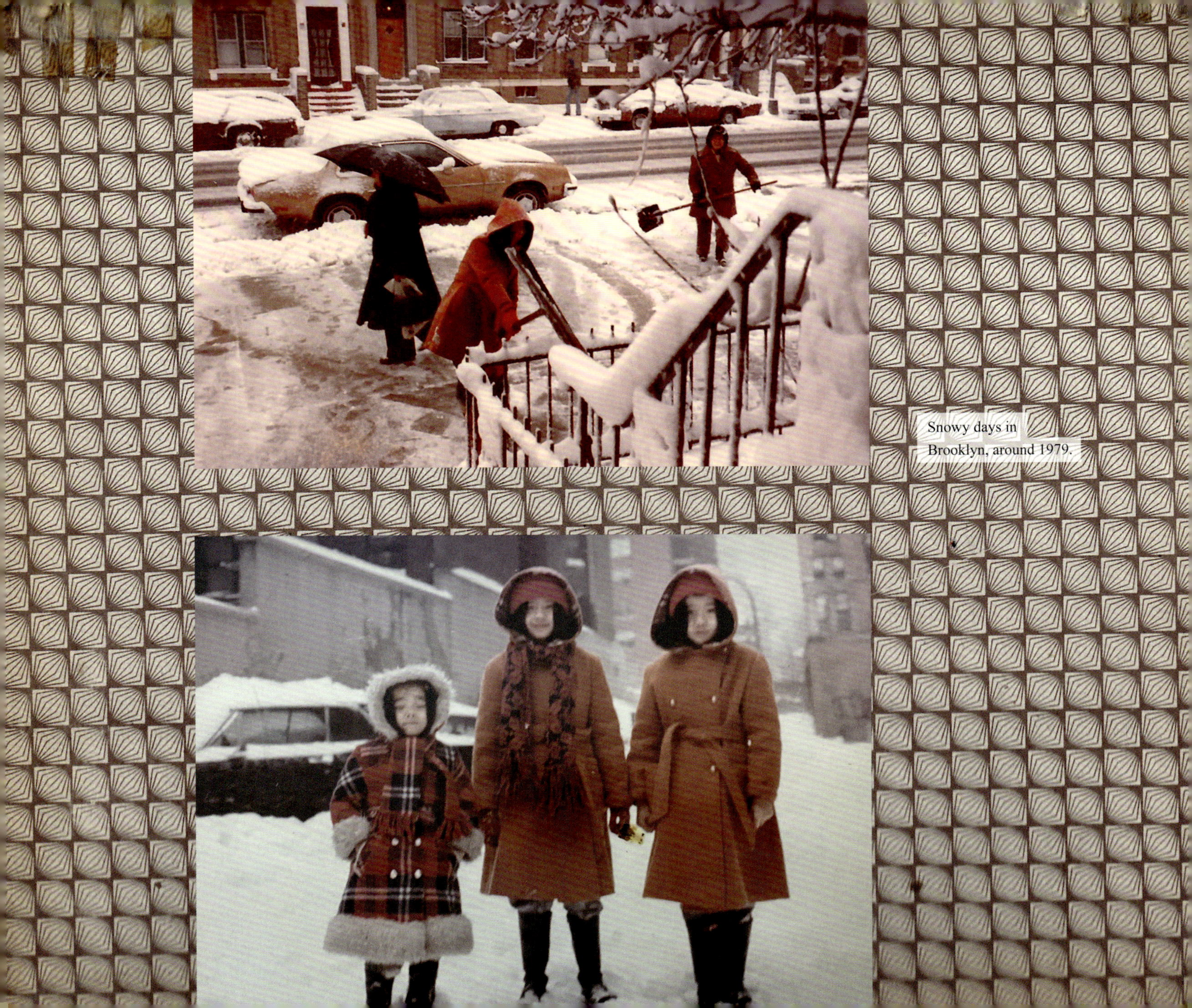

Snowy days in Brooklyn, around 1979.

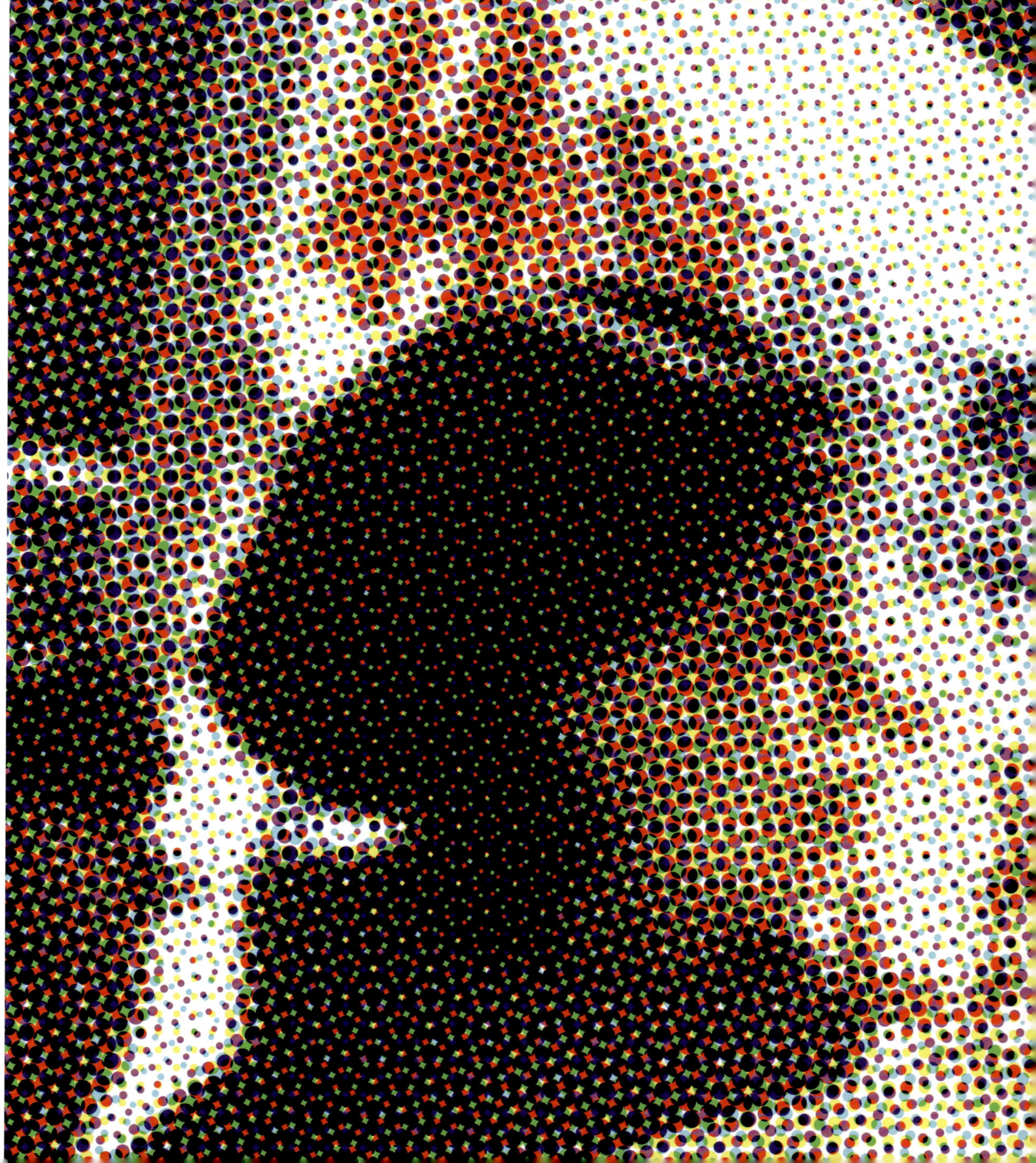

LABOR OF LOVE & OUR ACTS OF RESISTANCE

In the summer of 1995, my college-aged sister, Virginia, decided to go on a hunger strike with other students to expose the inhumane working conditions at Jing Fong restaurant, the largest restaurant on the East Coast, in the middle of NYC's Chinatown. The restaurant owner was paying waiters seventy-five cents an hour, forcing them to work long hours and stealing their tips. Garment and restaurant workers from Chinatown came out to support the students, risking blacklisting and harassment from their own employers. The hunger strike helped expose the existence of sweatshop conditions in the US. It spread into a national movement, emboldening workers from different workplaces to come forward. A year later, nearly sixty Jing Fong workers won back $1.1 million in owed back wages, the largest settlement for restaurant workers at that time.

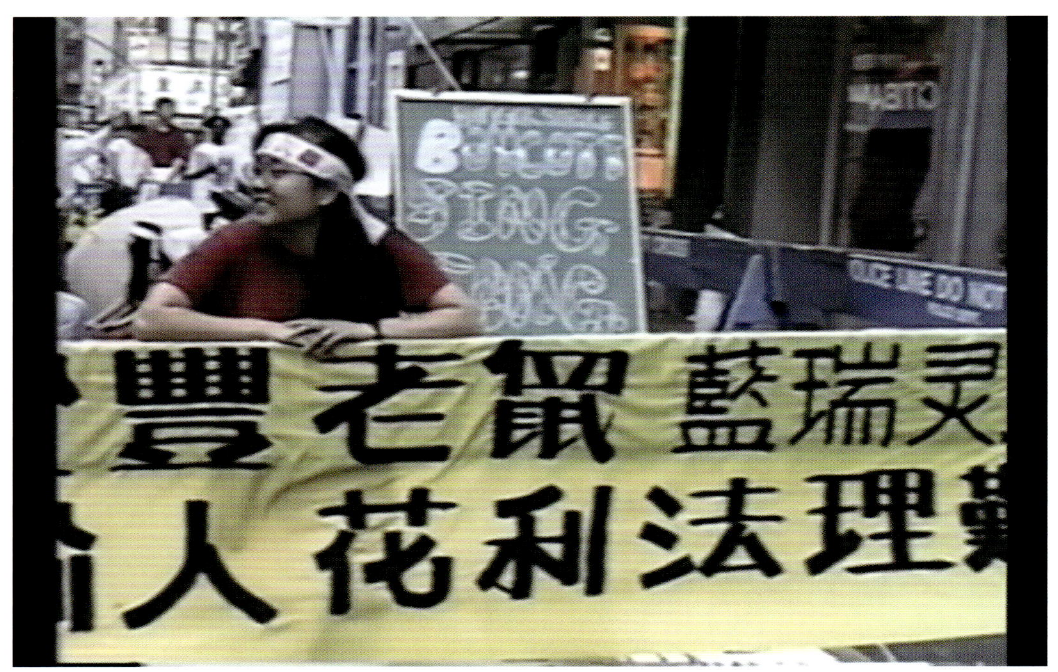

My sister Virginia on a hunger strike in front of Jing Fong restaurant, 1995.

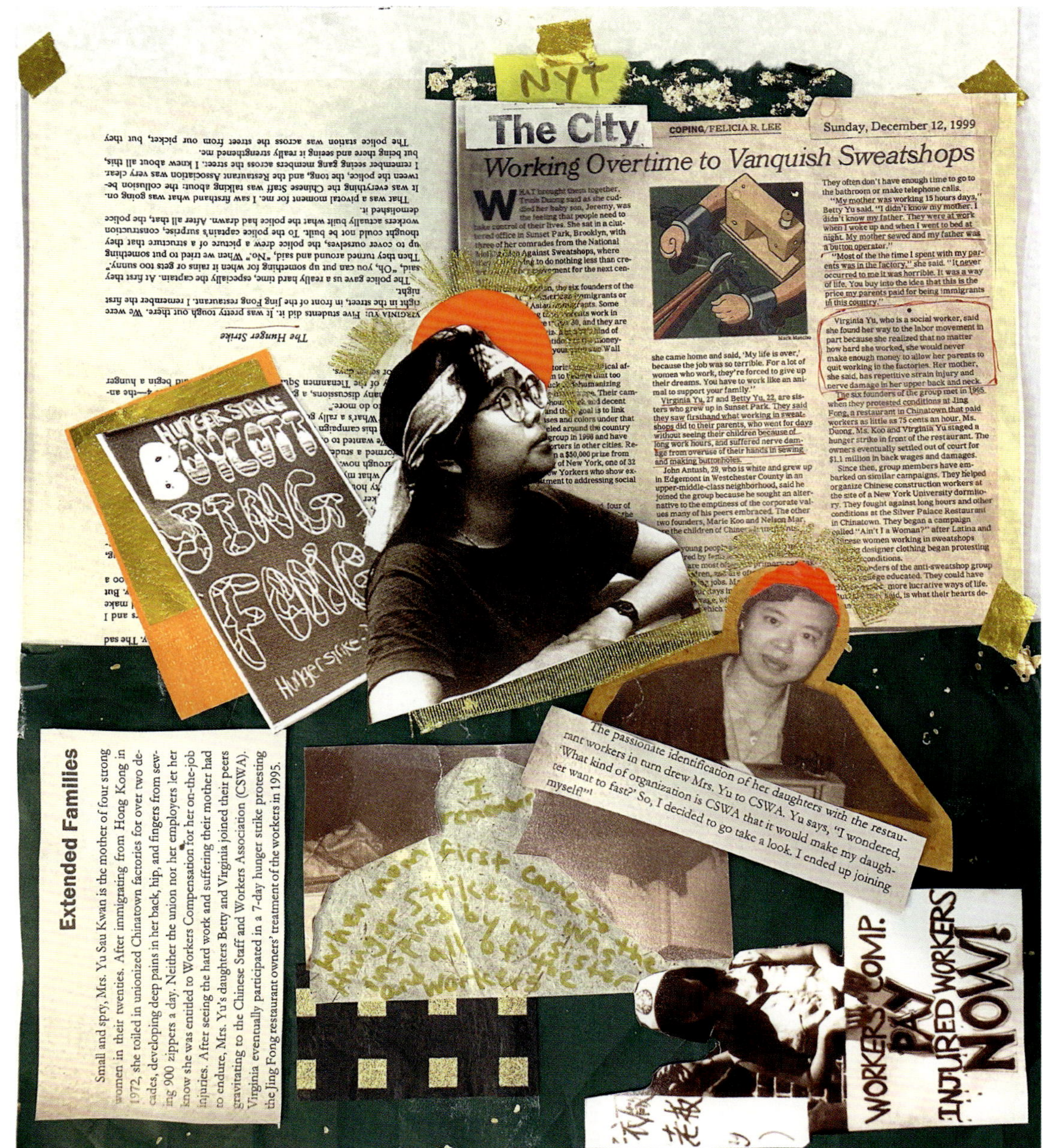

The trio of labor activists - me, my sister and my mom, 2024.
Mixed-media collage.

Love and labor intersect in *Resilience*, a short documentary in which I, the director, document the impact of sweatshop conditions on my family life. The film follows the lives of me, my sister Virginia, and our mother, Sau Kwan, an immigrant from Hong Kong who works in a garment factory. *Resilience* captures Kwan as a passionate leader in the movement against inhumane sweatshop conditions in the United States. 2000.

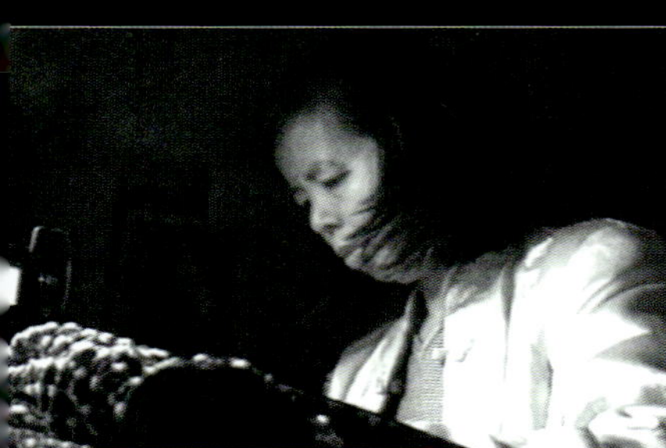

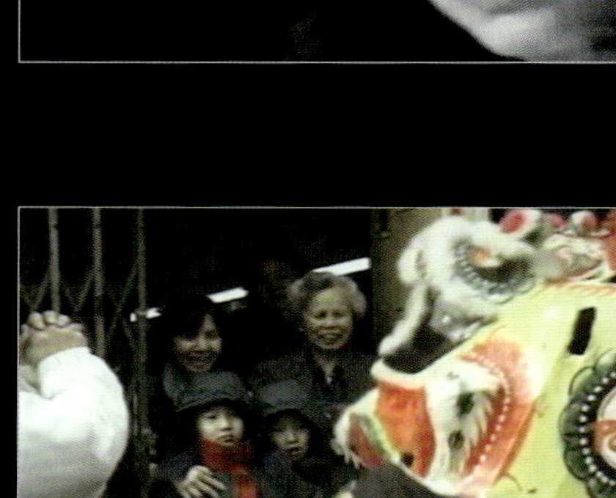

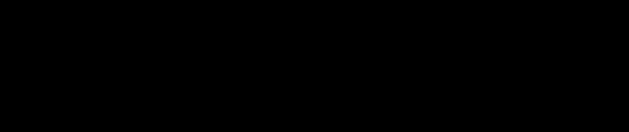

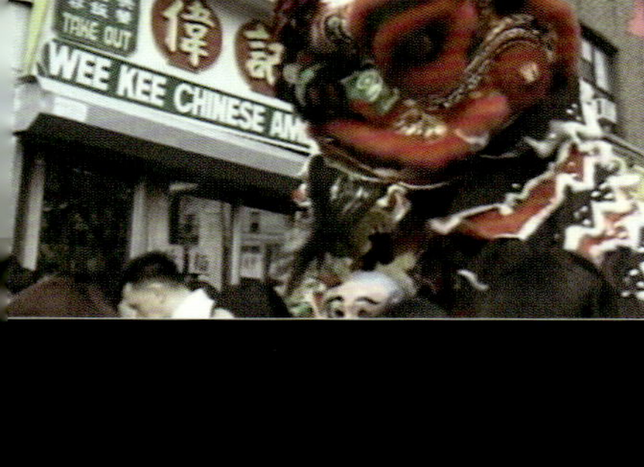

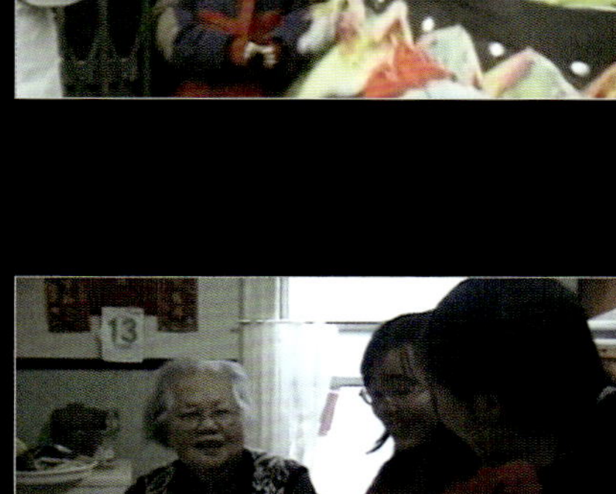

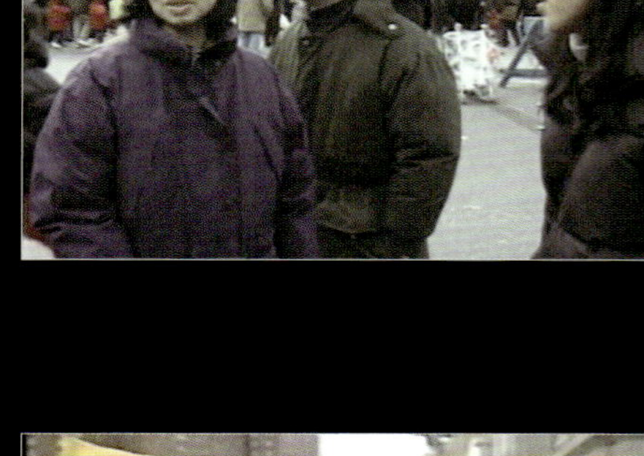

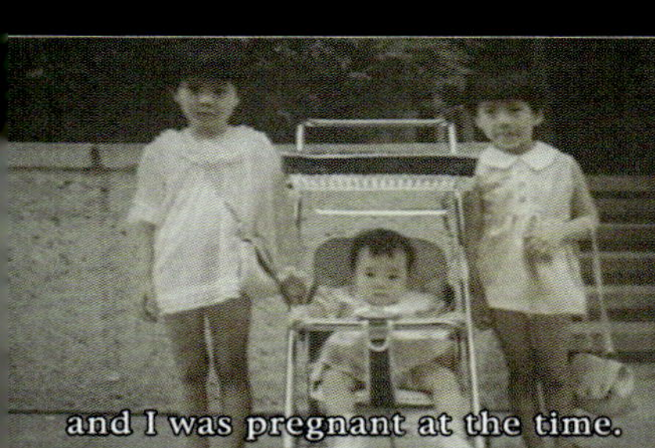

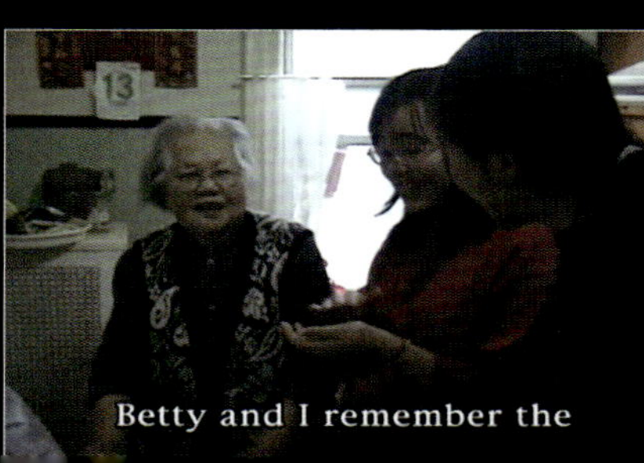

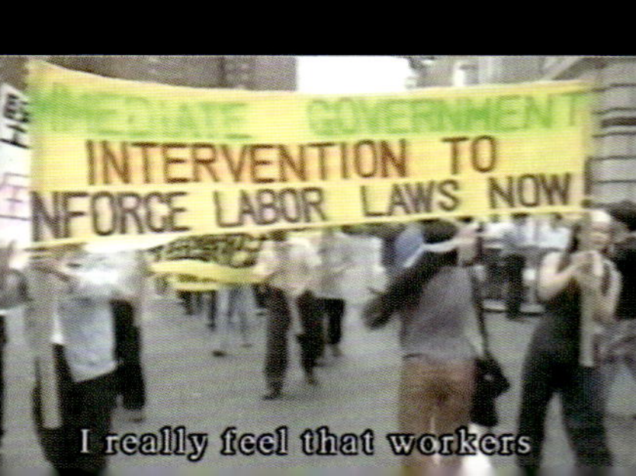

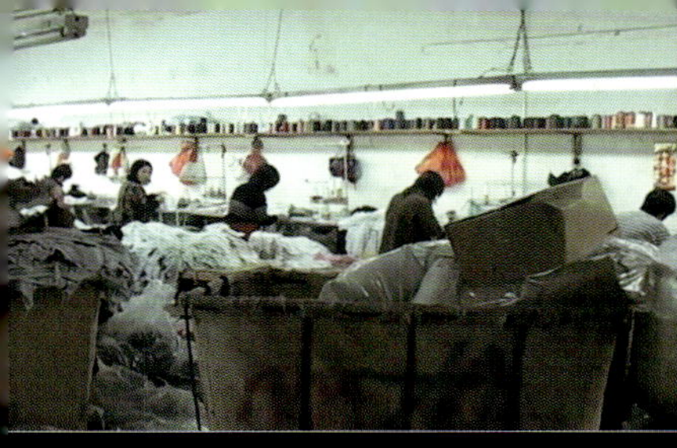
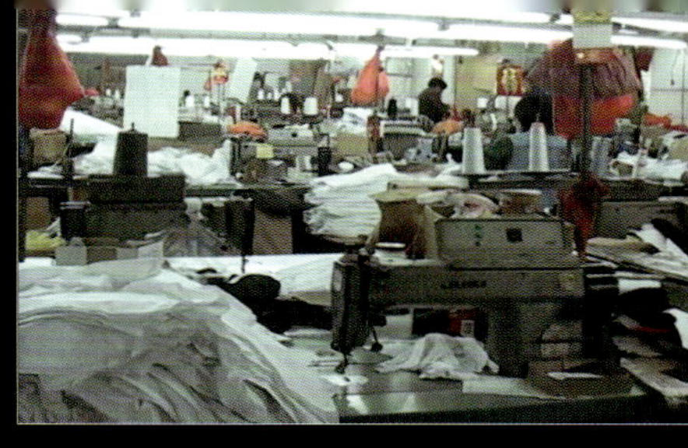
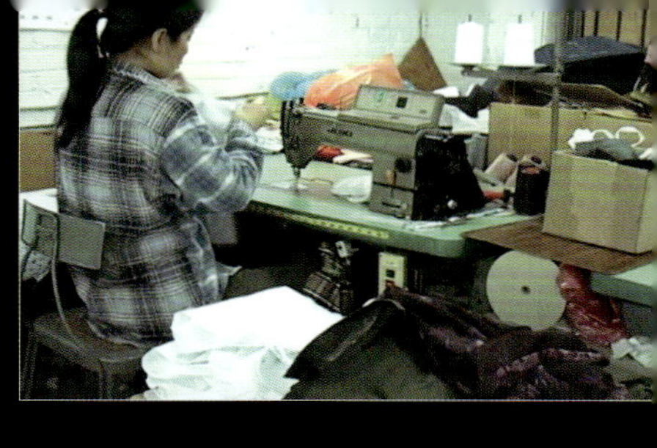
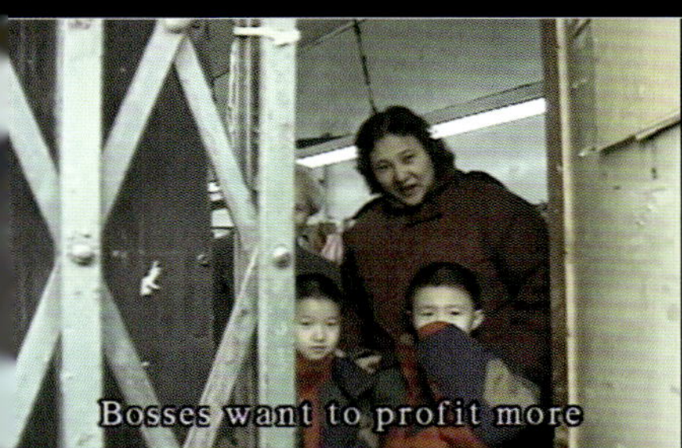
Bosses want to profit more
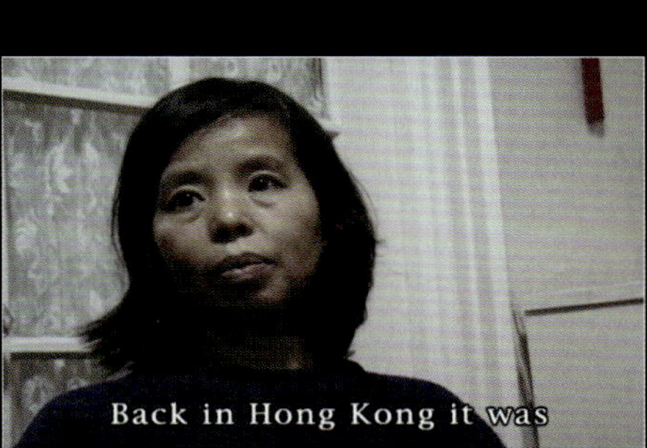
Back in Hong Kong it was
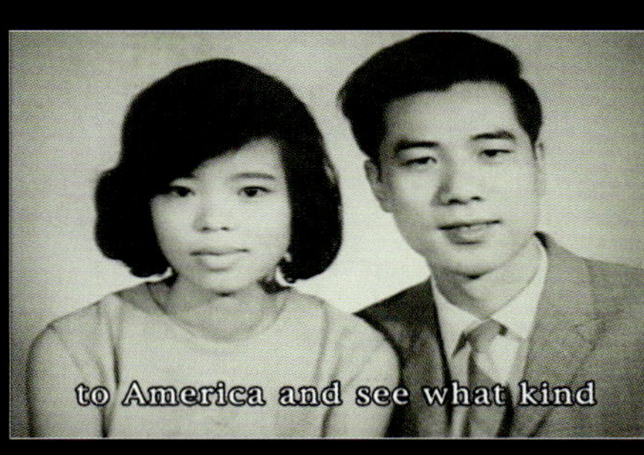
to America and see what kind
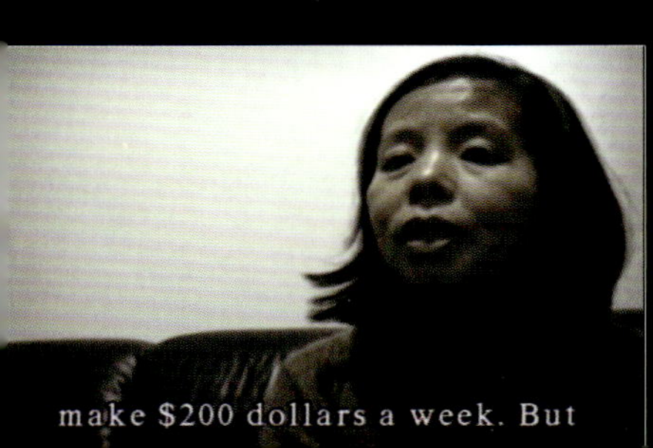
make $200 dollars a week. But
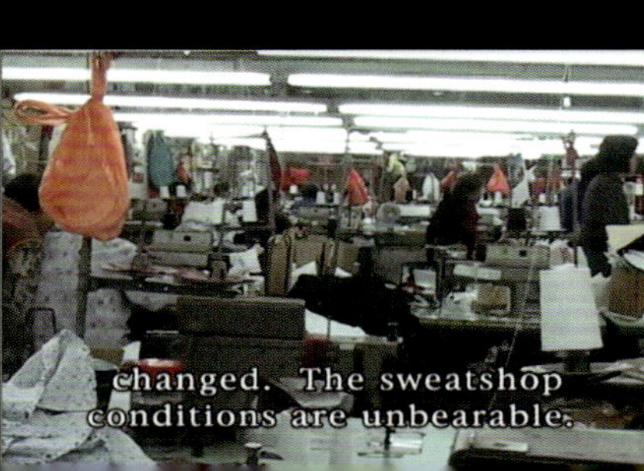
changed. The sweatshop
conditions are unbearable.
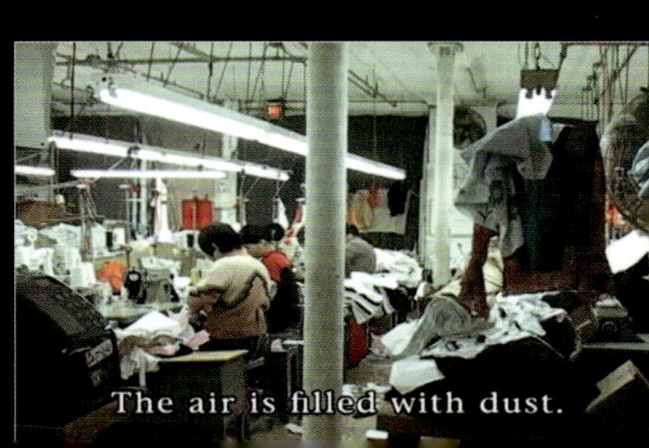
The air is filled with dust.

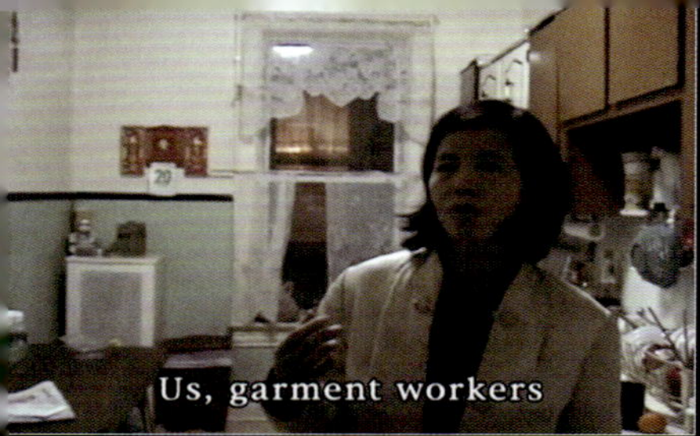
Us, garment workers
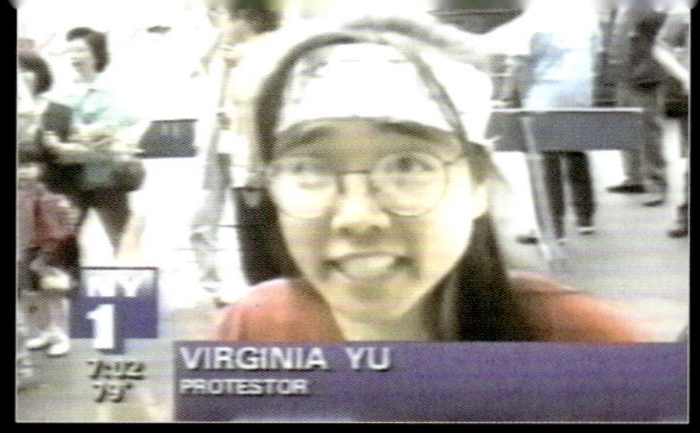
NY 1
VIRGINIA YU
PROTESTOR
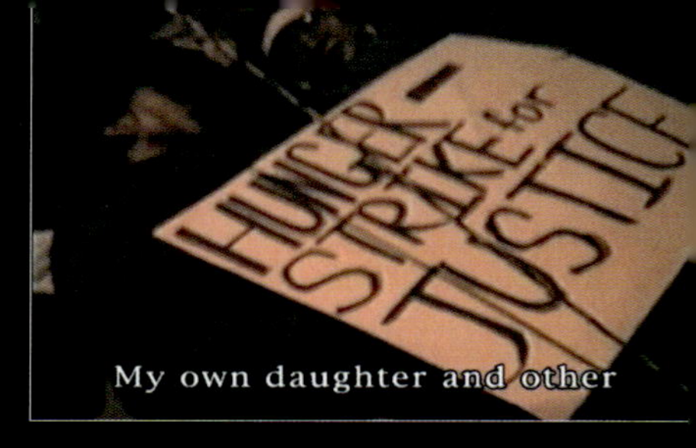
HUNGER STRIKE for JUSTICE
My own daughter and other
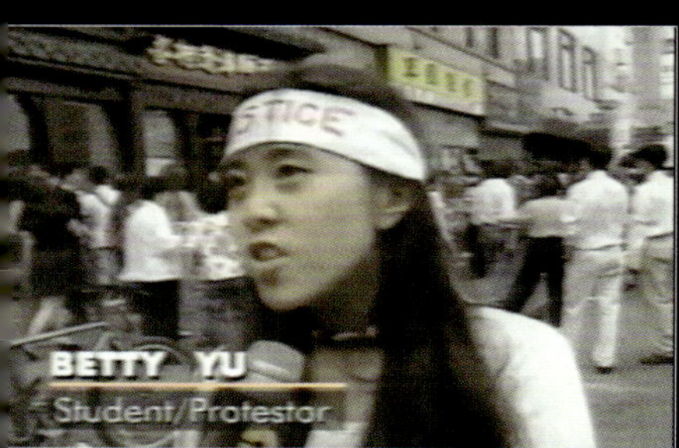
BETTY YU
Student/Protestor
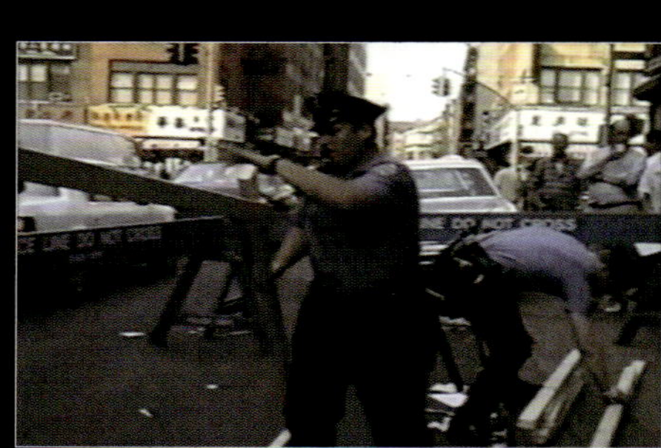
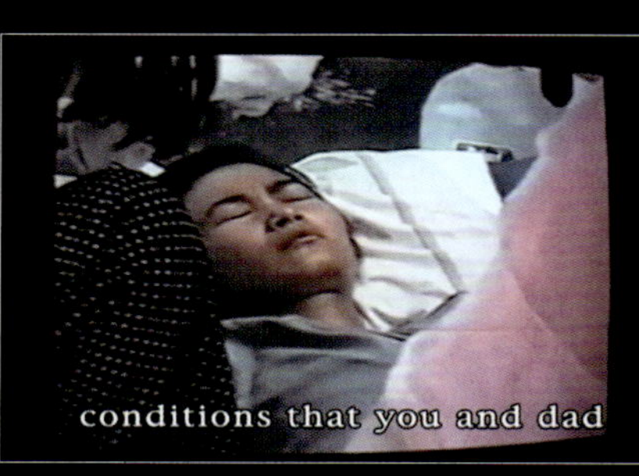
conditions that you and dad
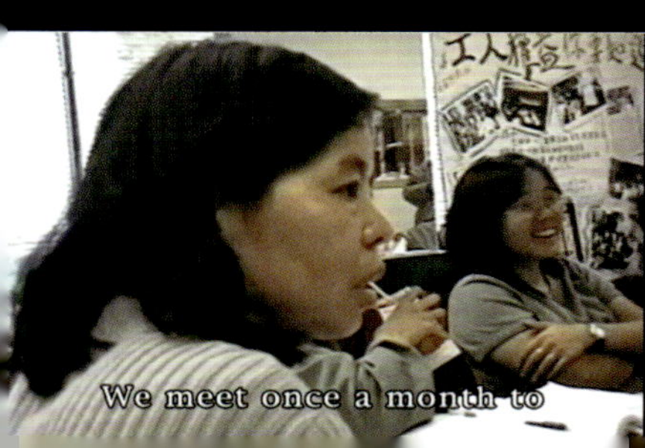
We meet once a month to
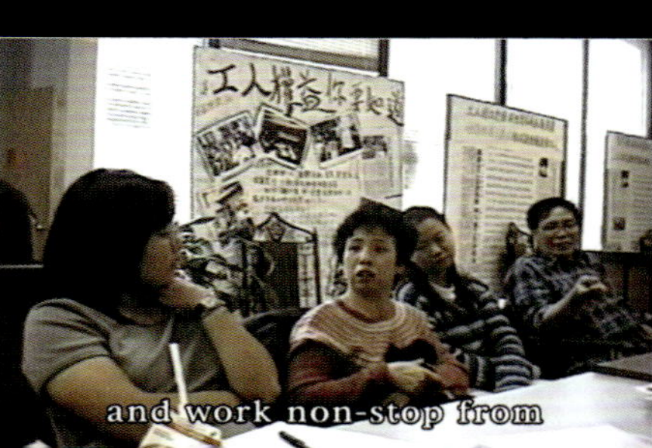
and work non-stop from
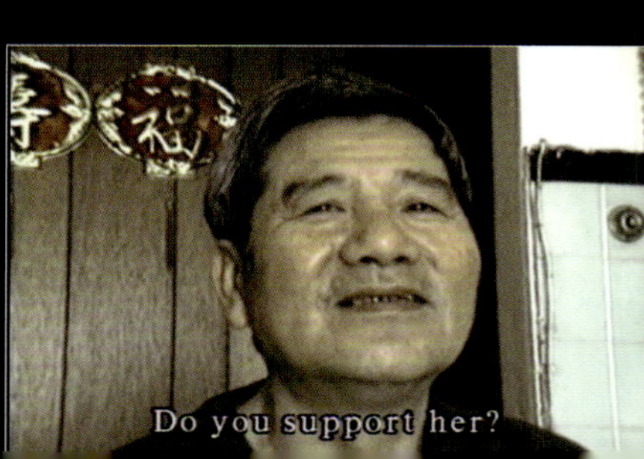
Do you support her?

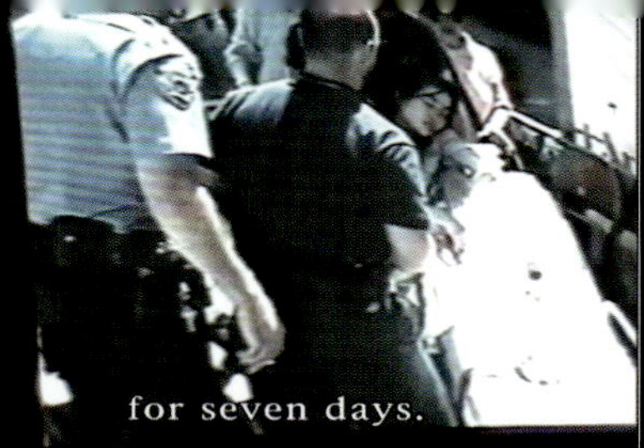

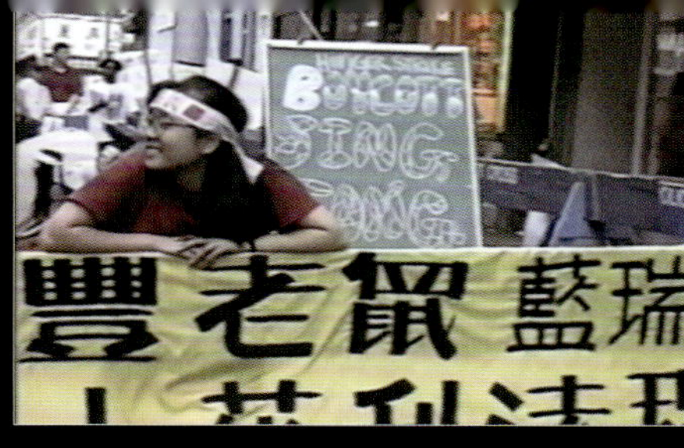

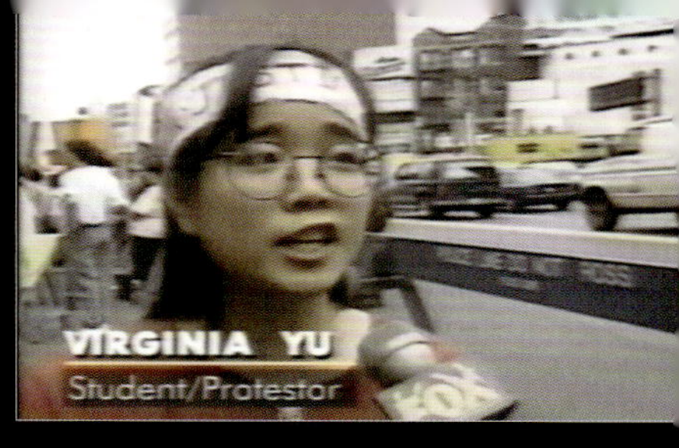

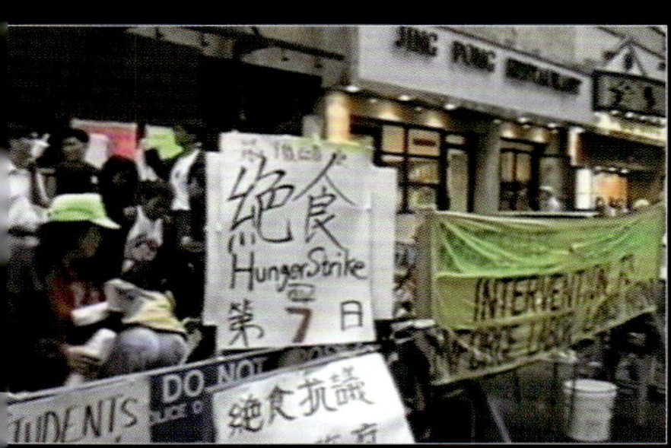

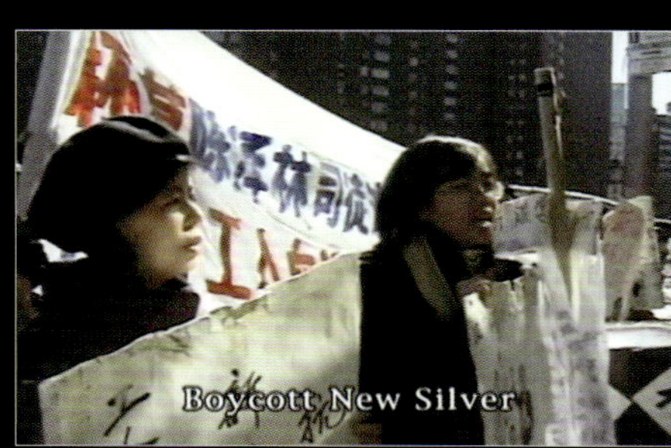

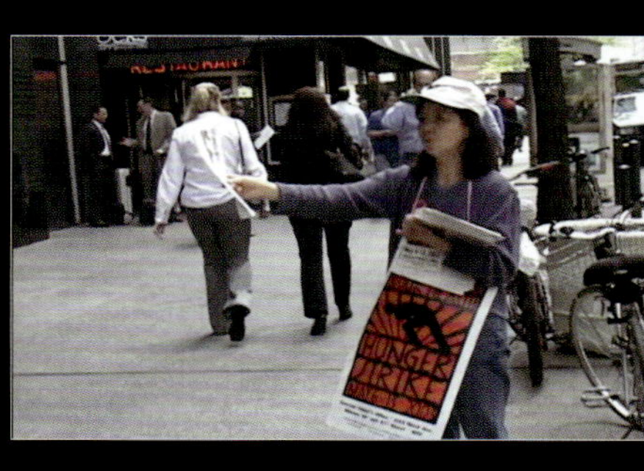

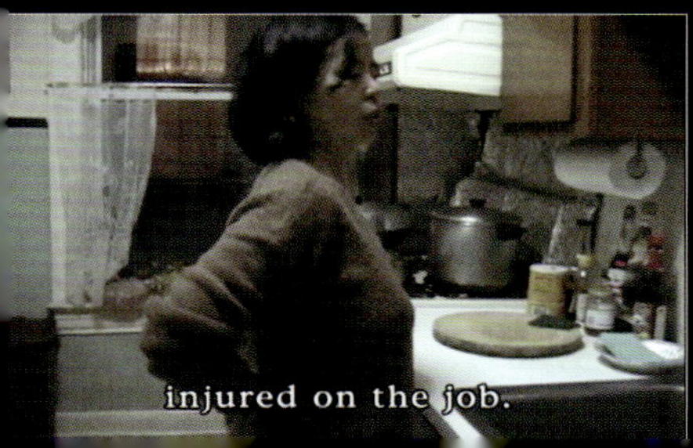

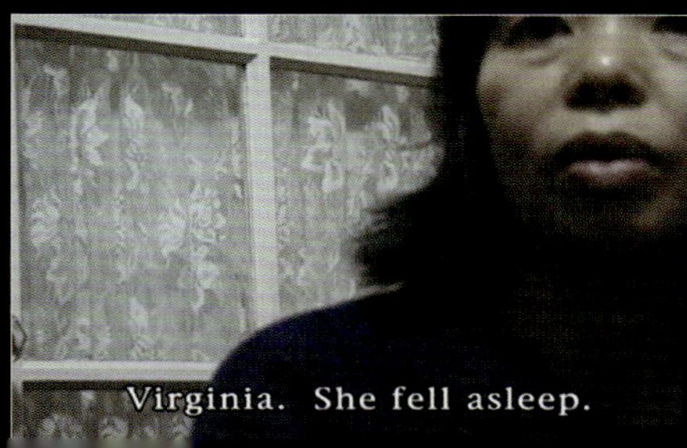

directed, produced, and edited
by
Betty Yu

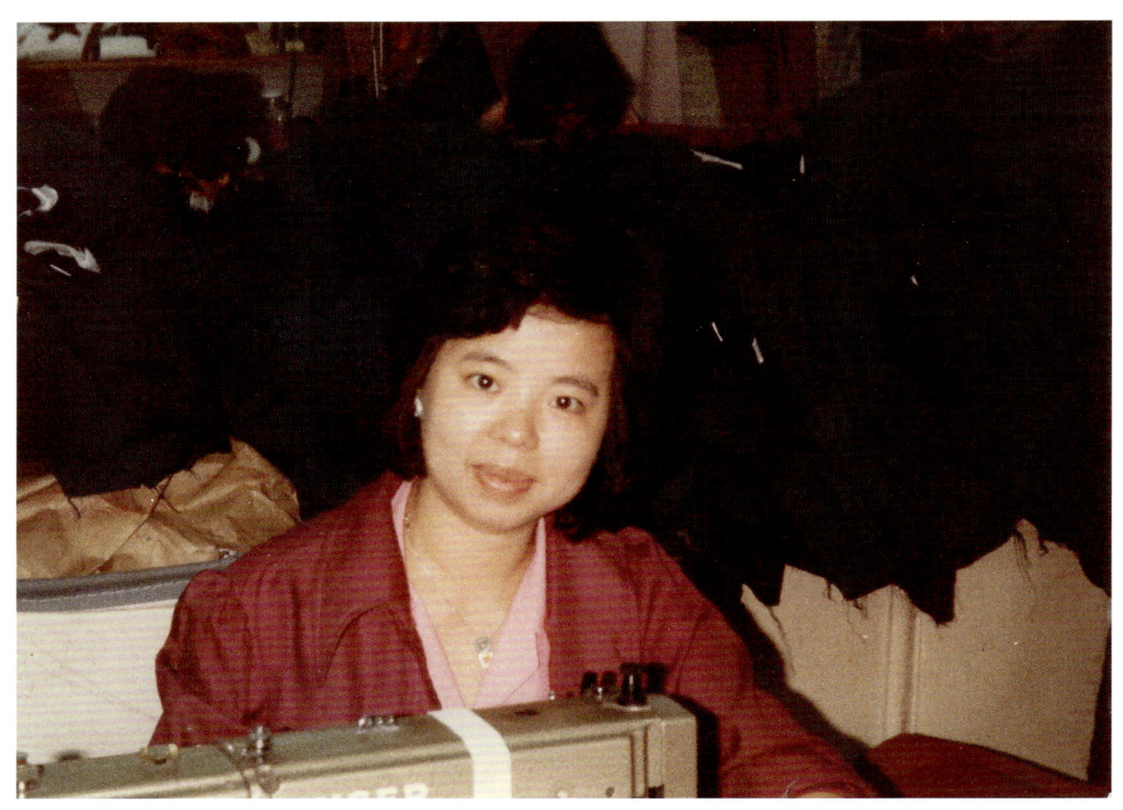

My mom working in a garment factory,
mid-1980s (exact date unknown).

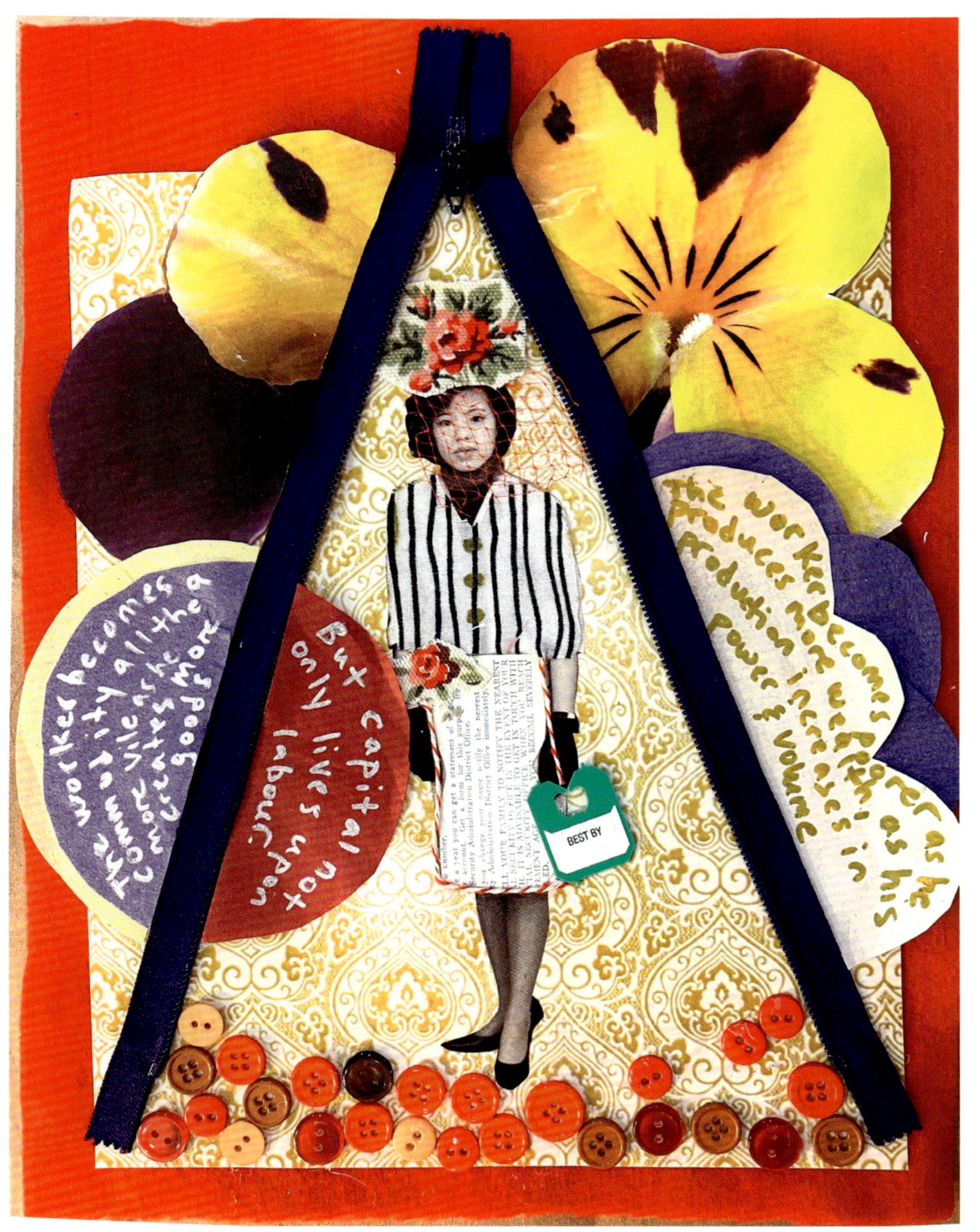

But capital only lives upon labor, 2024. Mixed-media collage.

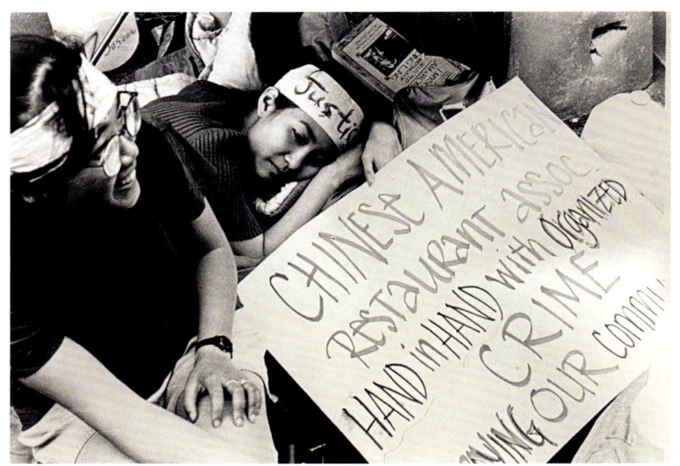

Virginia during the hunger strike in front of Jing Fong restaurant in Chinatown, NYC, 1995.

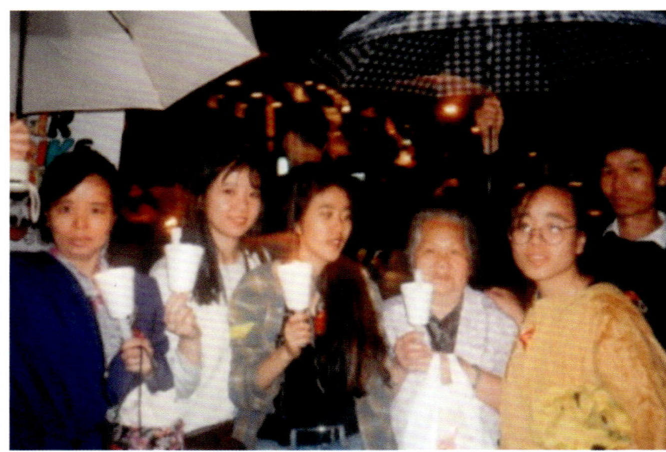

My family comes out to support Virginia during the hunger strike, 1995.

Right: *Piece by piece, one cent at a time*, 2024. Digital collage.

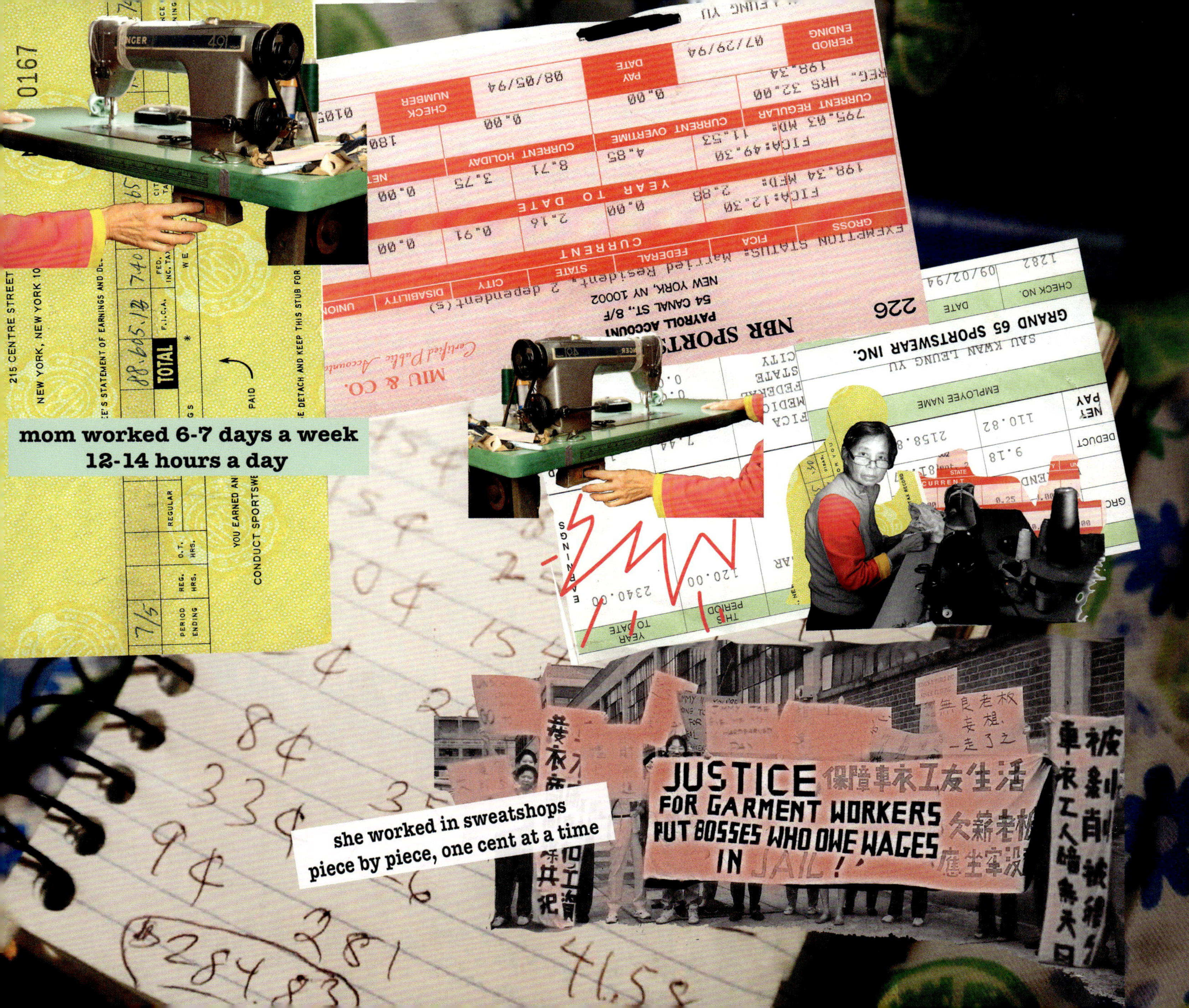
mom worked 6-7 days a week
12-14 hours a day
she worked in sweatshops
piece by piece, one cent at a time
JUSTICE 保障車衣工友生活
FOR GARMENT WORKERS
PUT BOSSES WHO OWE WAGES
IN JAIL!
欠薪老板
應坐牢

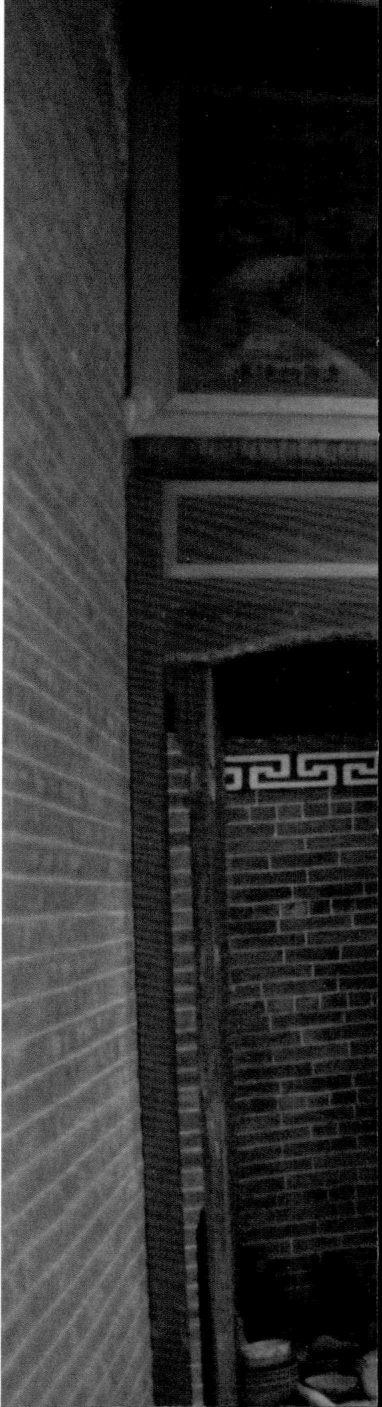

Interior of my dad's house, built in the 1930s in Taishan, China.

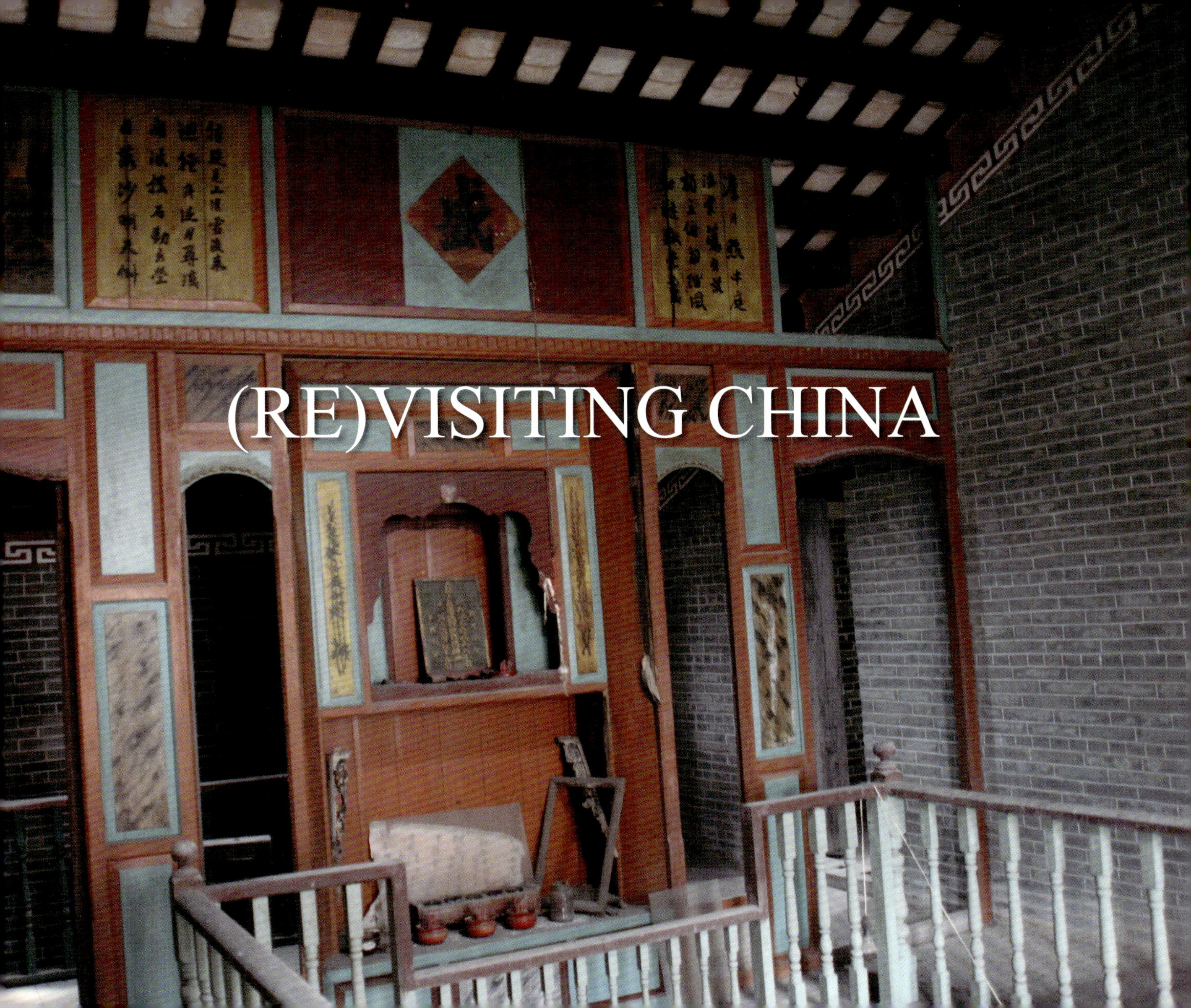

(RE)VISITING CHINA

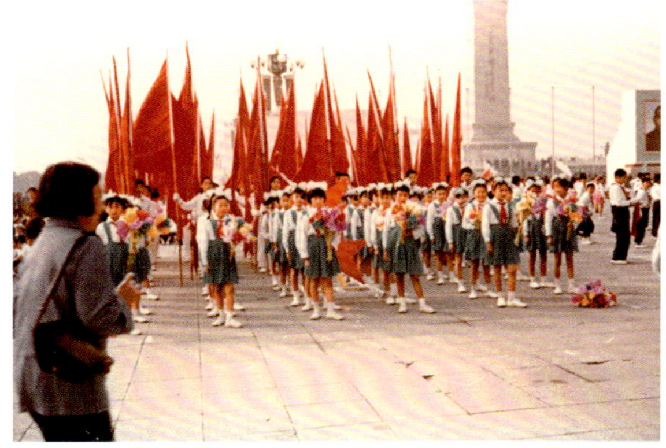

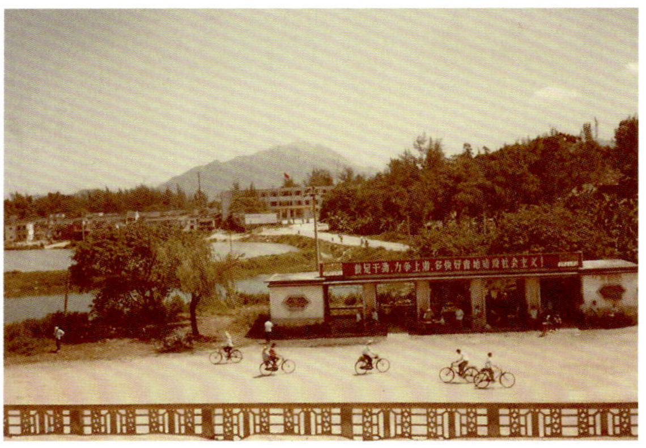

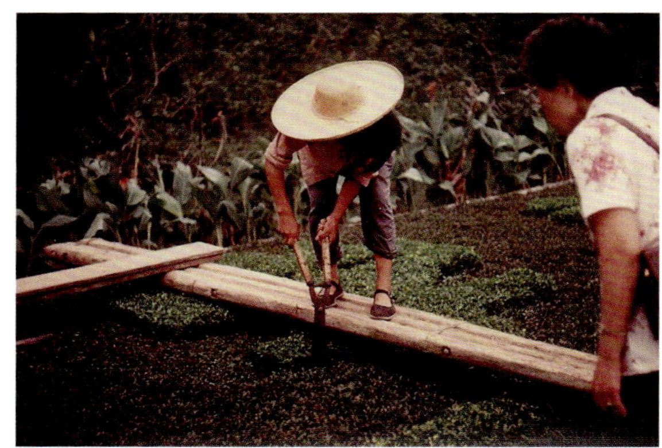

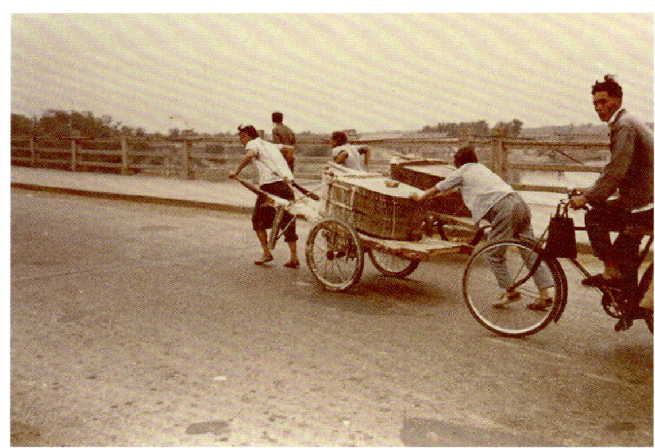

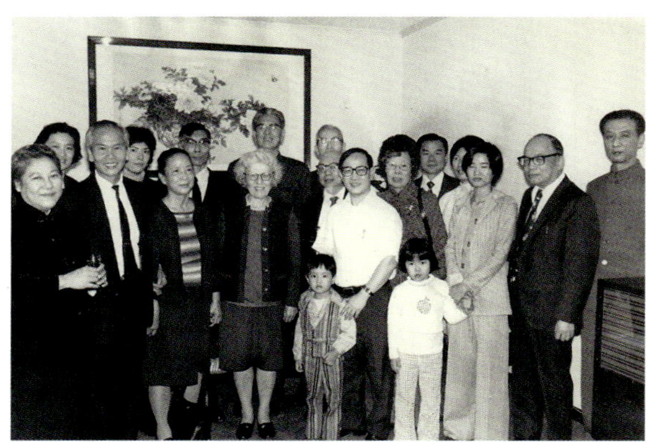

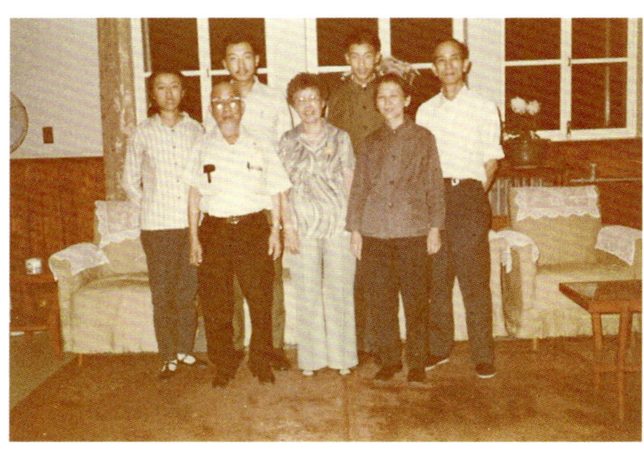

Photos from my grandparents' trip to China in the late 1970s.

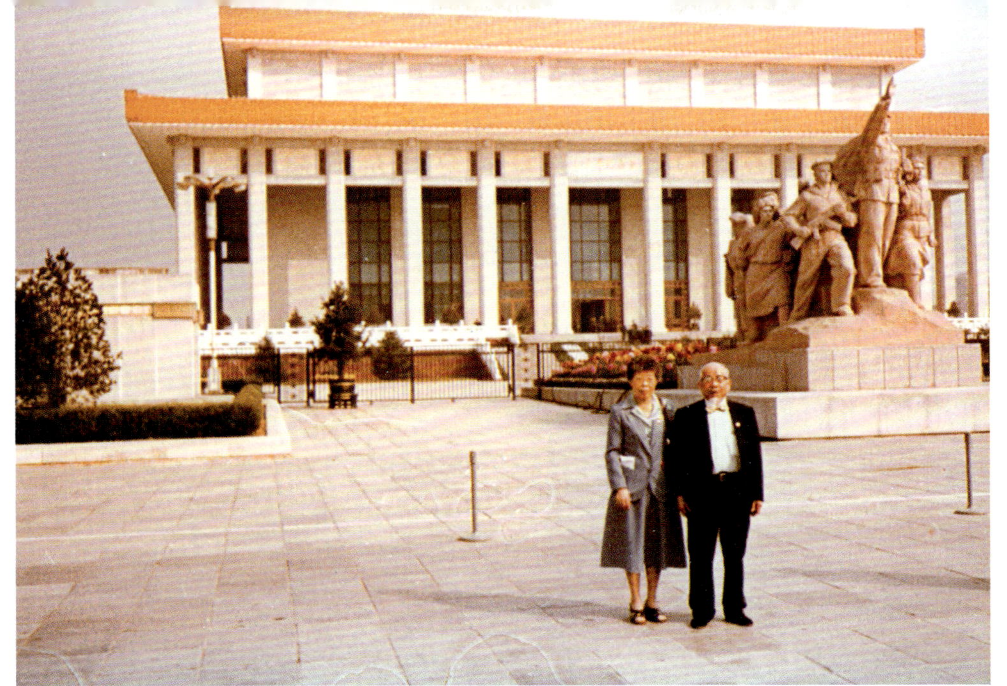

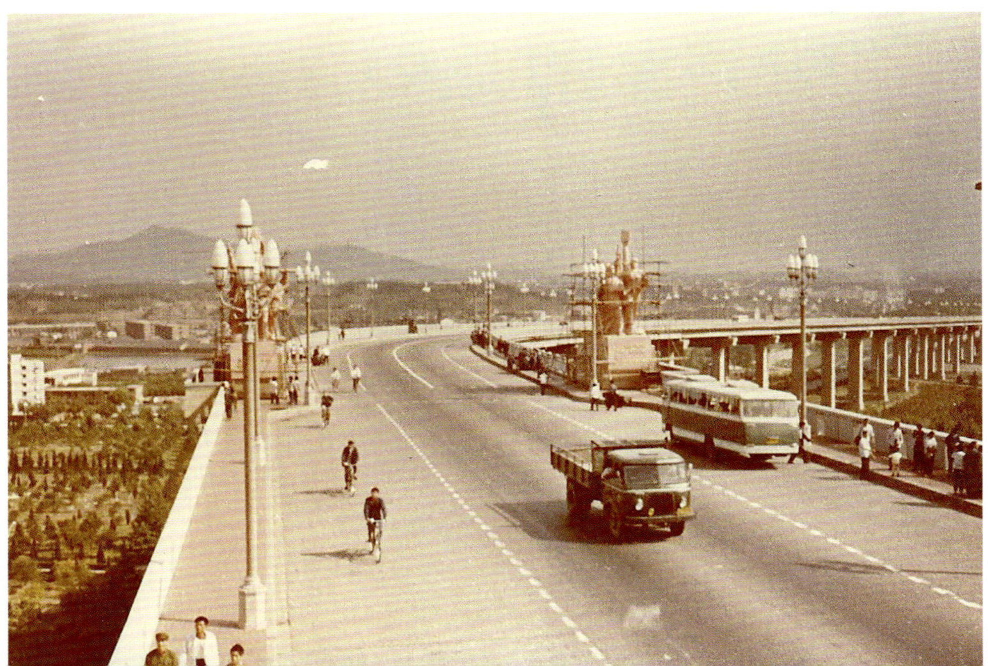

From 1949 to 1976 China was largely closed off from the West. The 1978 reforms in China allowed for people like my grandparents to visit their homeland. Judging from these photographs and accounts from the Chinese Hand Laundry Alliance (CHLA), I believe my grandparents visited China around 1978. The same photographs from my grandpa's archive matched those in the CHLA materials. CHLA members were open supporters of the Chinese Communist Party. The trip was part of an organized delegation of people from the US.

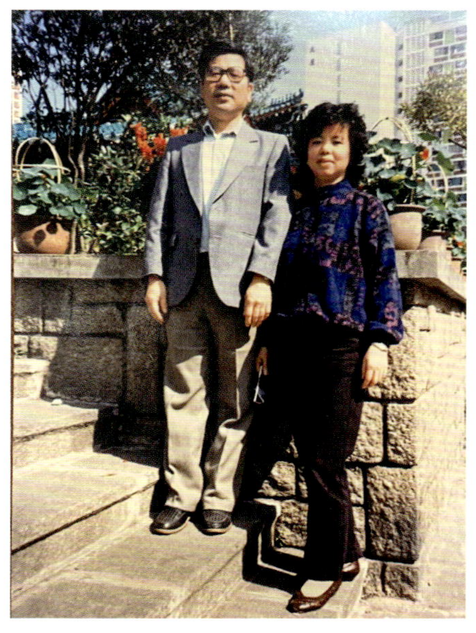
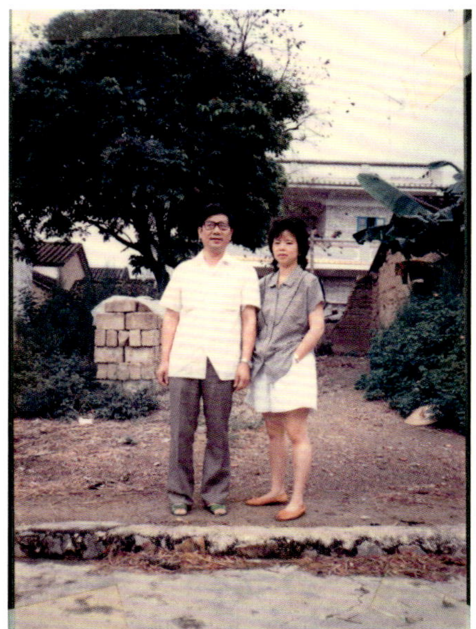
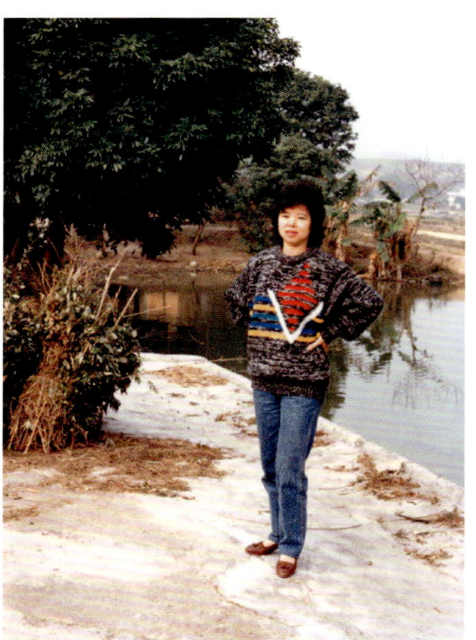

Photos from my parents' trip in the 1980s.

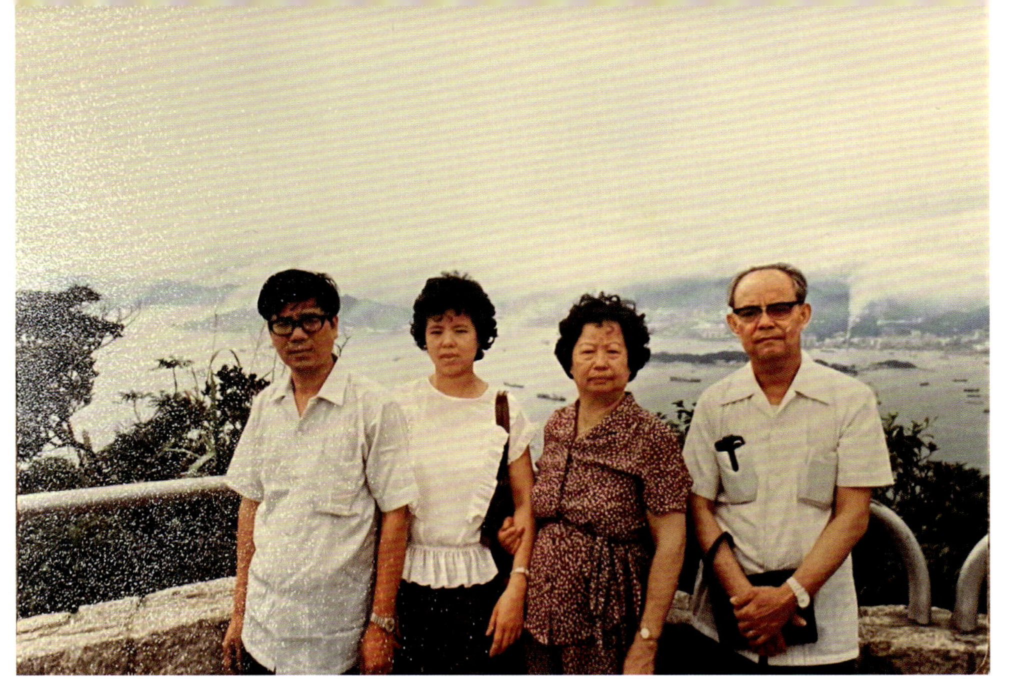

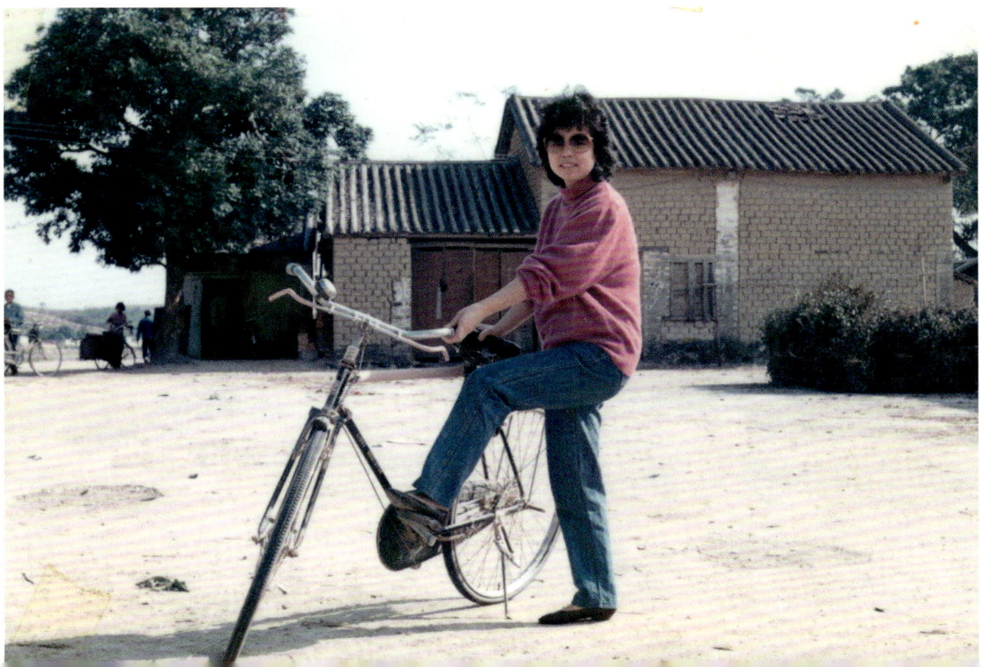

My mother's family fled the Heshan village of Jiangmen in southern China in the 1940s to Hong Kong during China's civil war. My mom shared the deep regret that her father had when he never returned to China to retrieve his eldest daughter (my mom's sister). My parents visited China and Hong Kong back around 1989.

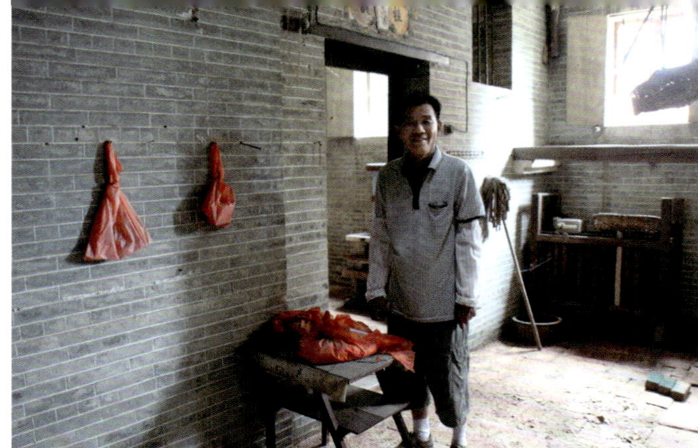

Mr. Hoi, the caretaker of the house.

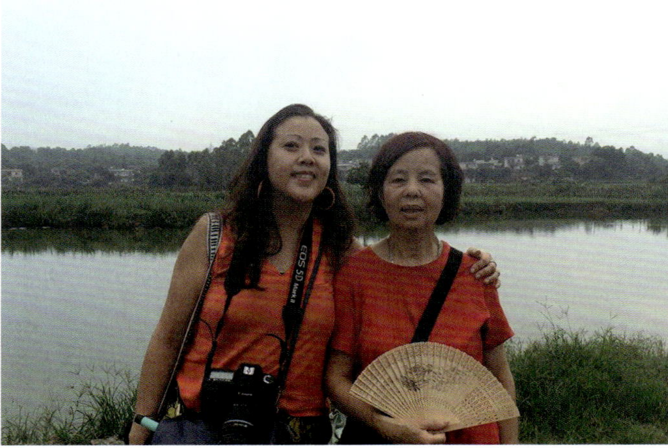

Mom and me in my dad's village in Taishan.

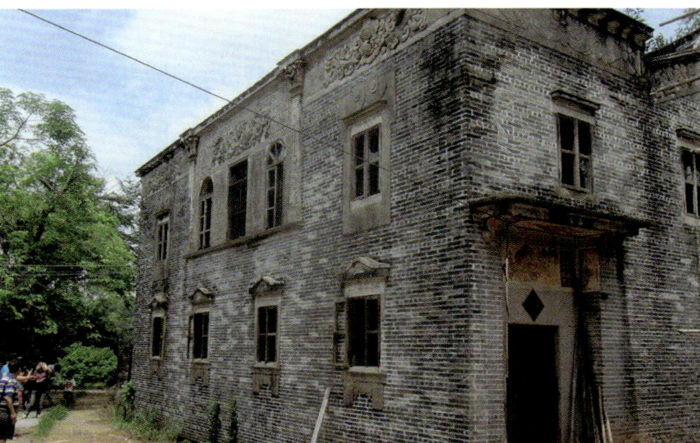

Exterior of my dad's house in Taishan.

In 2016, I traveled with my mother back to her hometown in Kowloon, Hong Kong, and visited her parents in the southern China village of Heshan, where her sister lives. The last time she had seen her sister was 1989, so nearly thirty years had passed. During this trip my mother expressed so much regret that her sister had to stay in China and live under the Communist regime, but her sister harbored no resentment. To our surprise, she talked about how the lives of people in the countryside improved after the agrarian land reforms. She shared how she, her family, and village benefited. We also made a trip to my dad's village where he grew up in Taishan, in southern China. We visited the 100-year-old house my grandfather built with the money that he and his father (my great-grandfather) earned working in the US. This was the same house that they had to escape during World War II. My dad didn't join us for the trip to China. He is very ill these days, but also was adamant that he had no desire to go back to that dark period of his life. I met villagers who were now in their seventies and remembered my dad from when they were little kids. One man said, "I remember your dad; he was about ten years older than me, but I remember he really liked birds and had them as pets." I ended up making a short film about our trip, mainly to have as an archive for our family. I showed my dad footage of his village from our visit and he couldn't stop smiling and laughing. He pointed out all the places that look the same, as it brought up childhood memories that he had forgotten. It was a full-circle moment for me. The following pages capture some images from that short film, *An Unknown Home*.

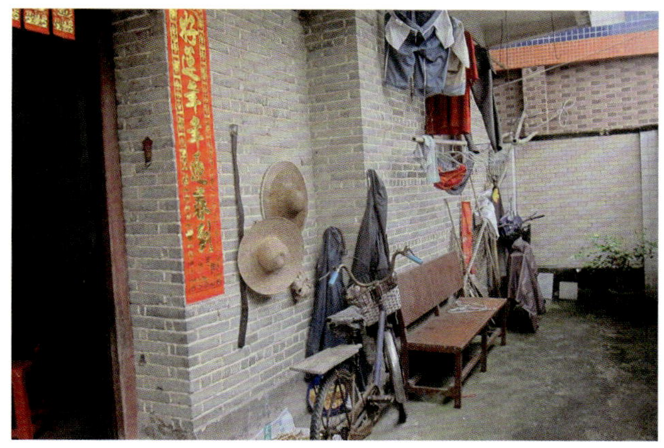

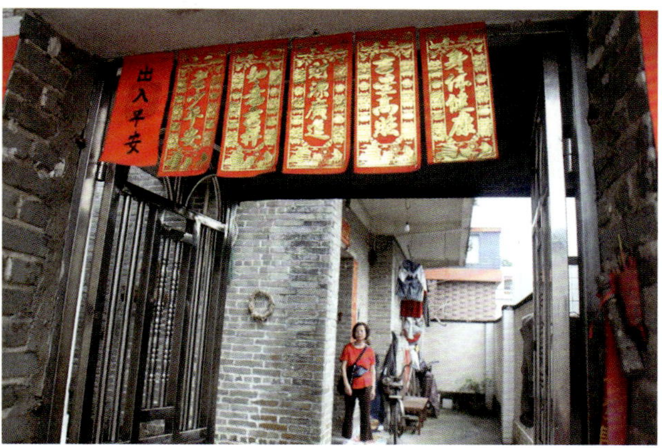

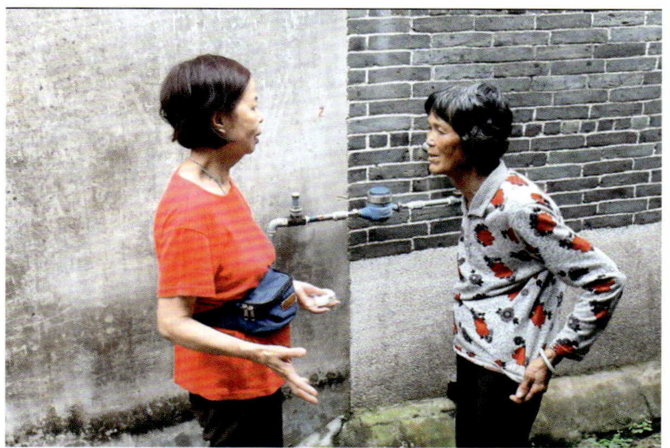

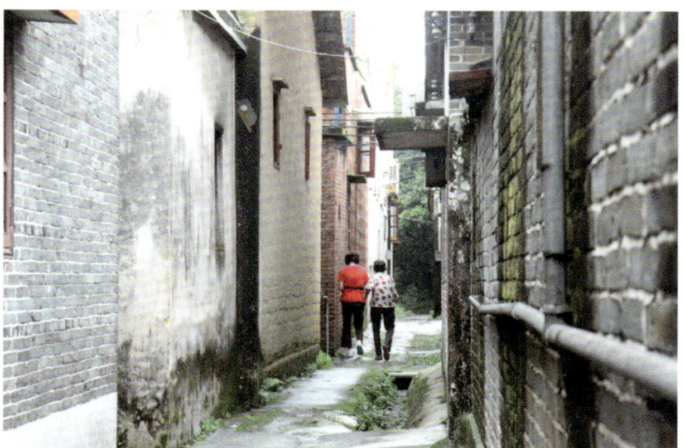

Photos from my aunt's home and my mom's family's hometown in Heshan.

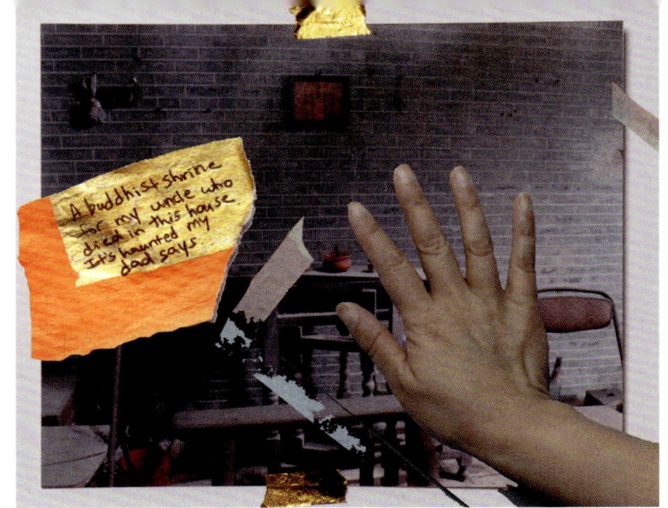

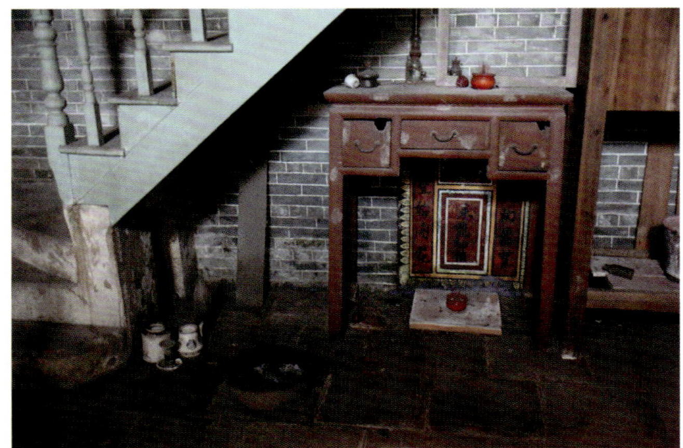

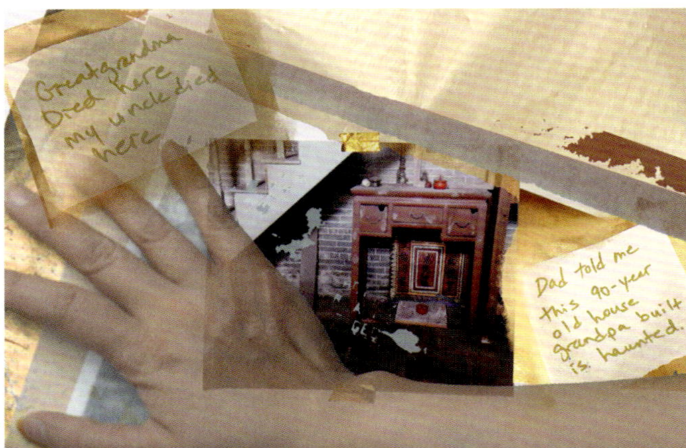

Top: *The haunted house*, 2020. Mixed-media collage.

Middle: An altar in memory of my uncle who died when he was ten. This altar has been in the same spot in the house for over seventy years.

Bottom: *The shrine in my family house back in Taishan, China, that dates back eighty-five years*, 2017–2020. Digital collage.

Right: *Grandpa's eighty-five-year-old deed for his house in Guangdong, China; Dad says the house is "haunted"*, 2020. Mixed-media collage.

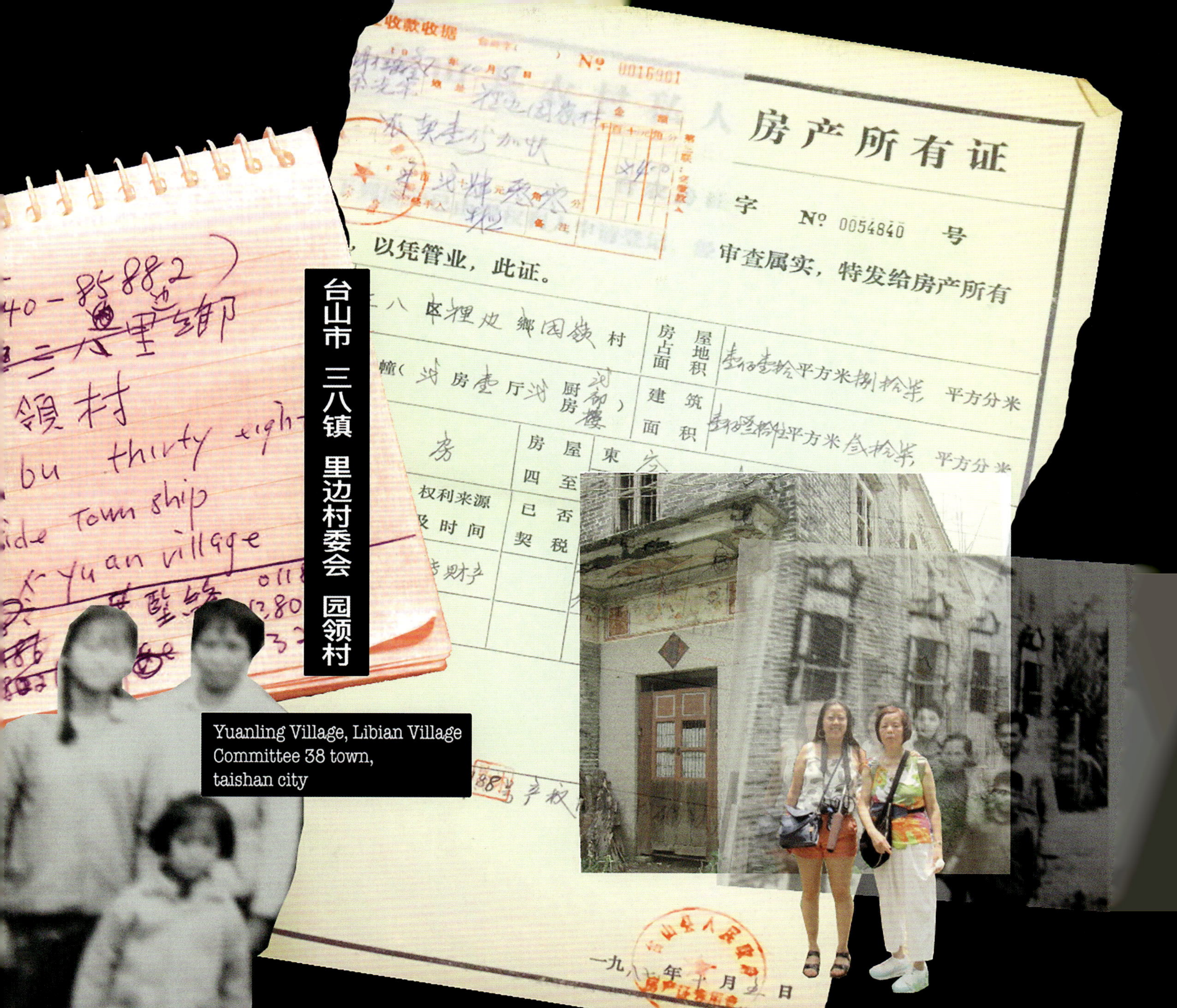
房产所有证
字 № 0054840 号
审查属实，特发给房产所有
以凭管业，此证。
台山市 三八镇 里边村委会 园领村
Yuanling Village, Libian Village Committee 38 town, taishan city

An Unknown Home is a short documentary film about my journey to my father's hometown in Taishan, China. I deepen my understanding of my family's roots and past through his eighty-year-old home. 2017.

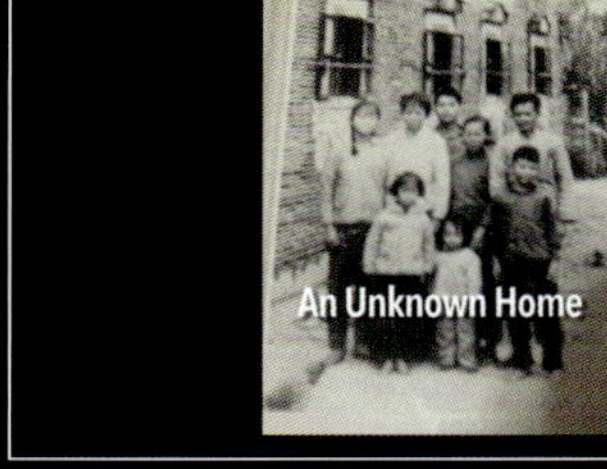

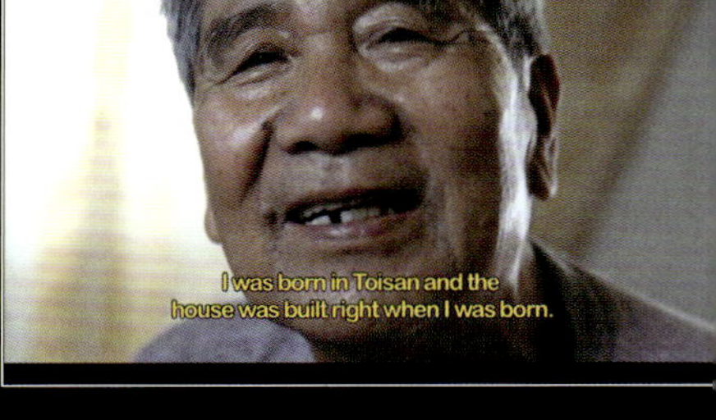

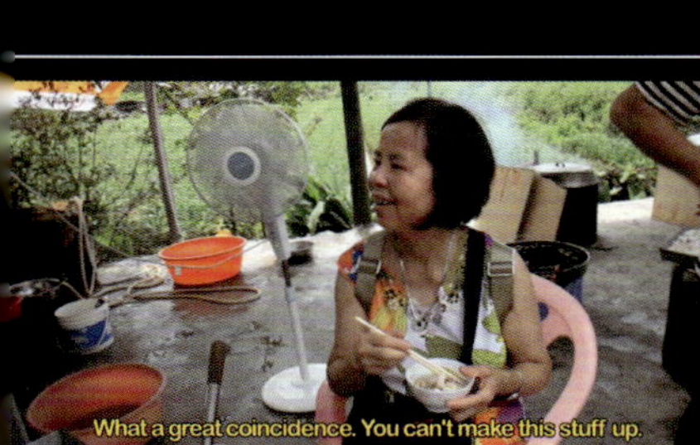

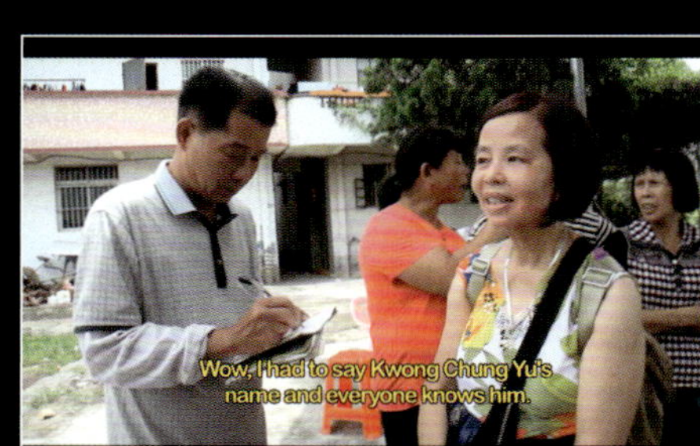

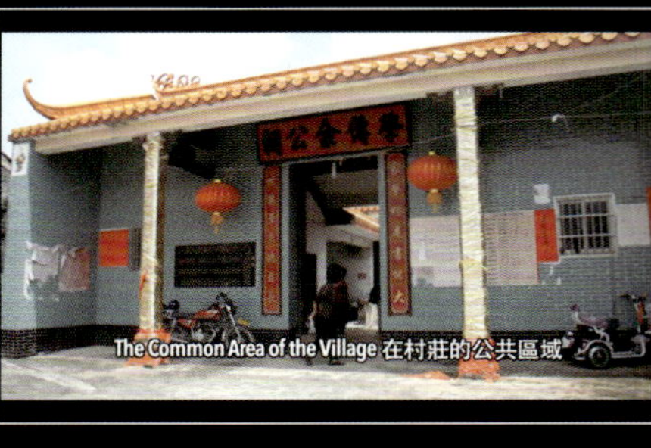

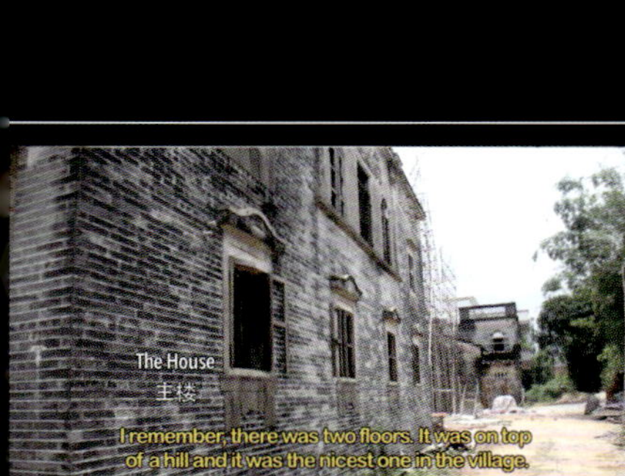

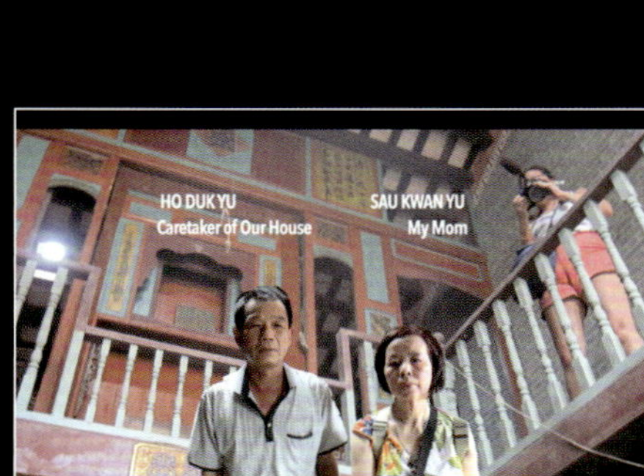

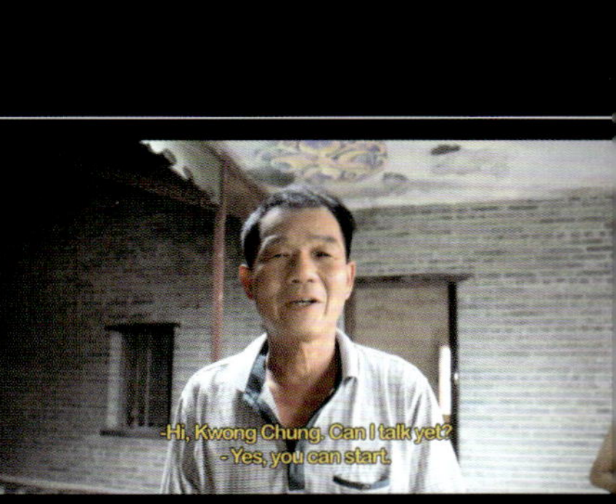

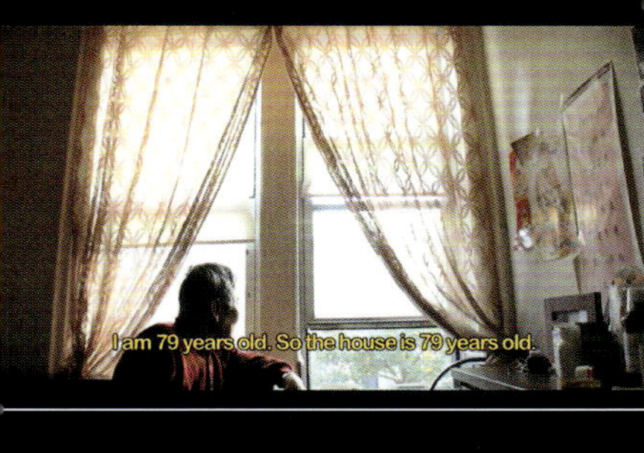
I am 79 years old. So the house is 79 years old.

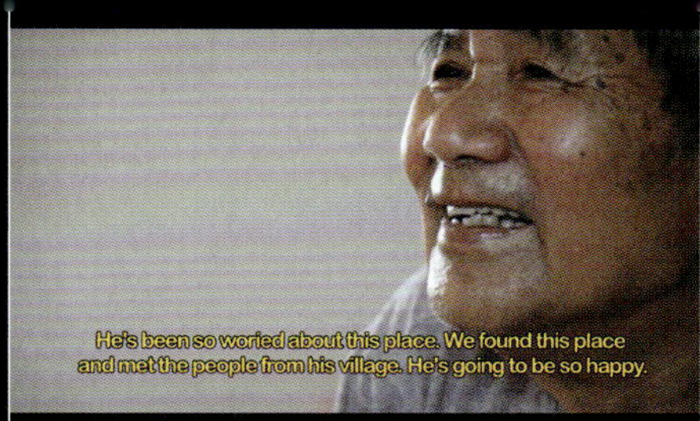
He's been so worried about this place. We found this place
and met the people from his village. He's going to be so happy.

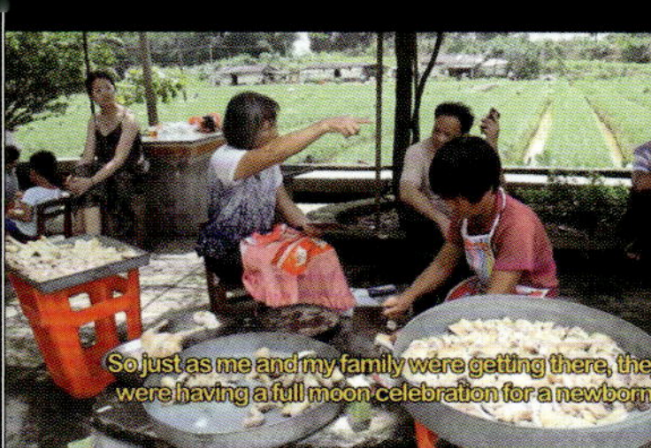
So just as me and my family were getting there, they
were having a full moon celebration for a newborn.

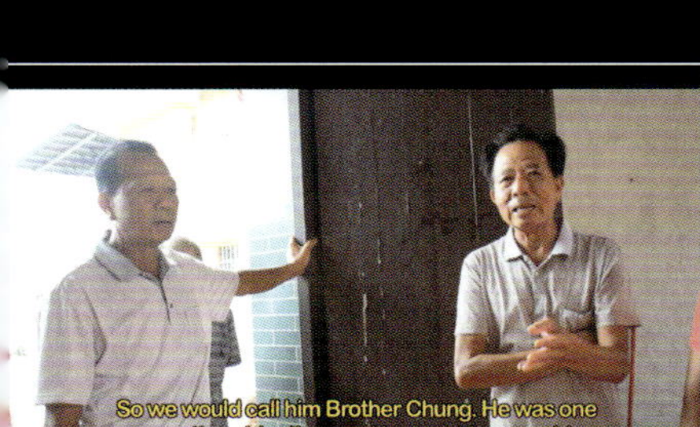
So we would call him Brother Chung. He was one
generation older than us. He was 10 years older.

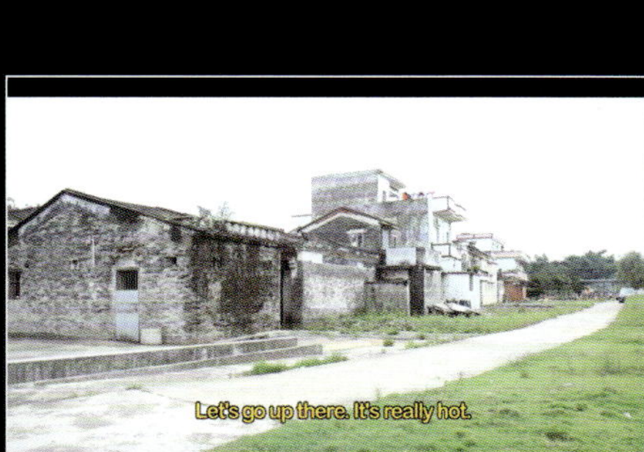
Let's go up there. It's really hot.

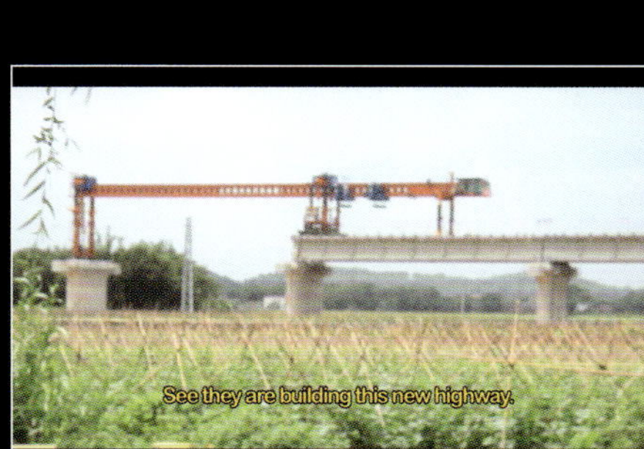
See they are building this new highway.

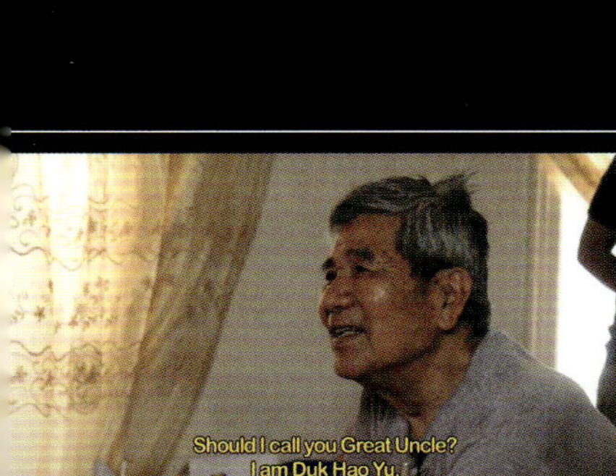
Should I call you Great Uncle?
I am Duk Hao Yu.

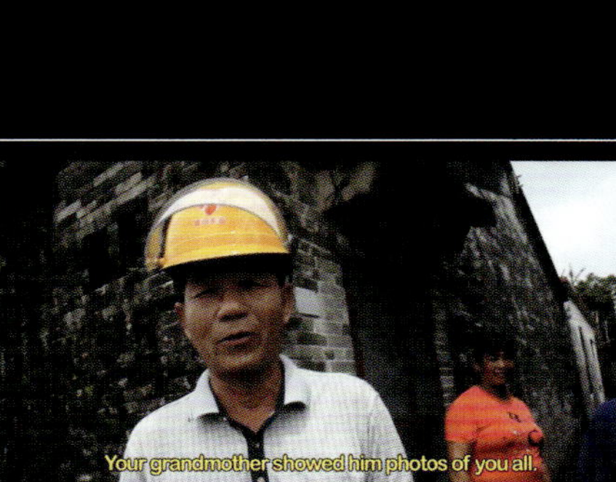
Your grandmother showed him photos of you all.

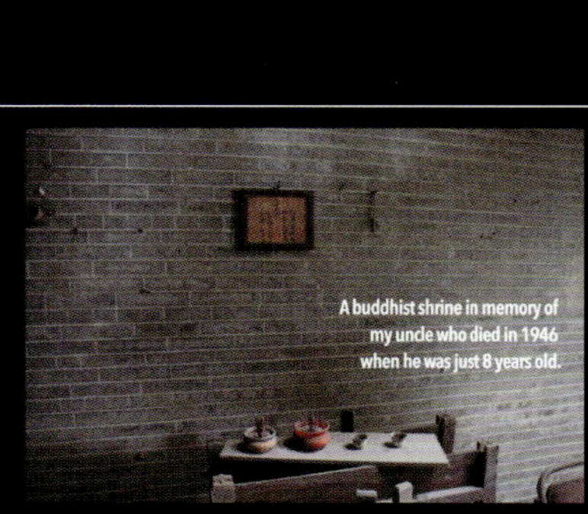
A buddhist shrine in memory of
my uncle who died in 1946
when he was just 8 years old.

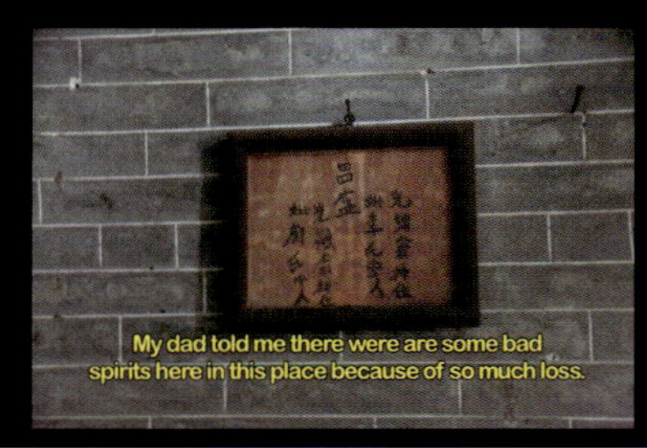
My dad told me there were are some bad
spirits here in this place because of so much loss.

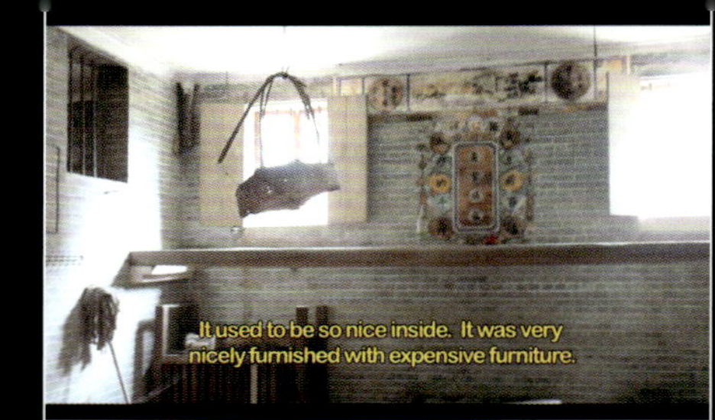
It used to be so nice inside. It was very
nicely furnished with expensive furniture.

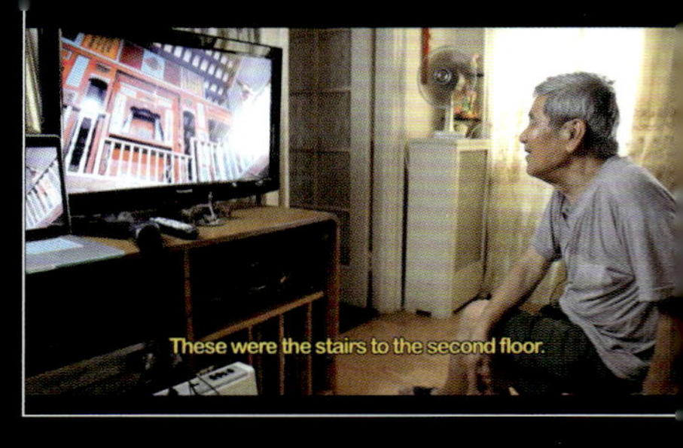
These were the stairs to the second floor.

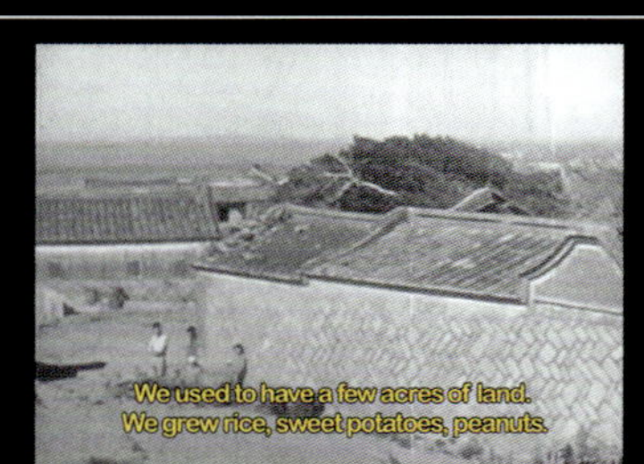
We used to have a few acres of land.
We grew rice, sweet potatoes, peanuts.

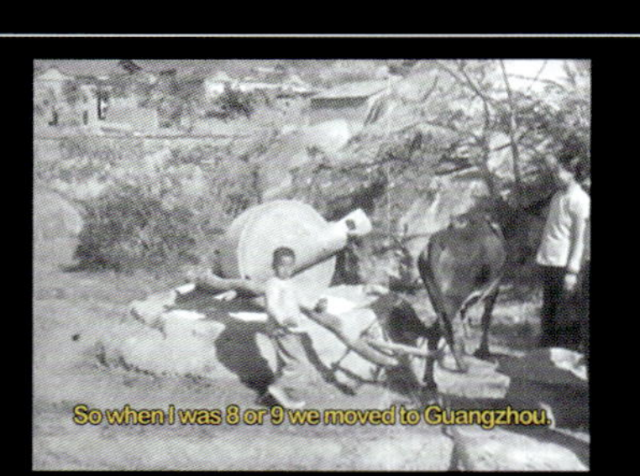
So when I was 8 or 9 we moved to Guangzhou.

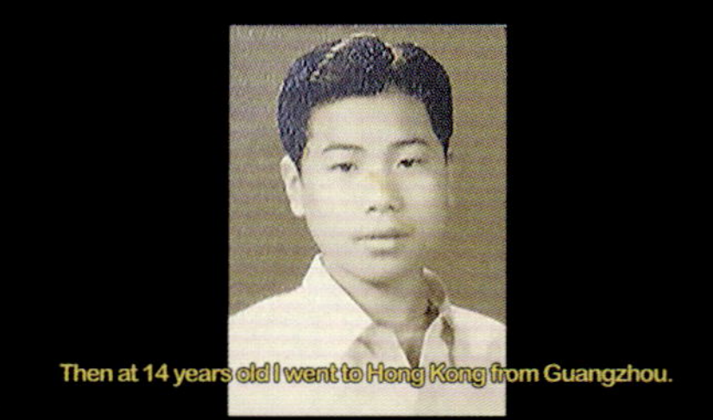
Then at 14 years old I went to Hong Kong from Guangzhou.

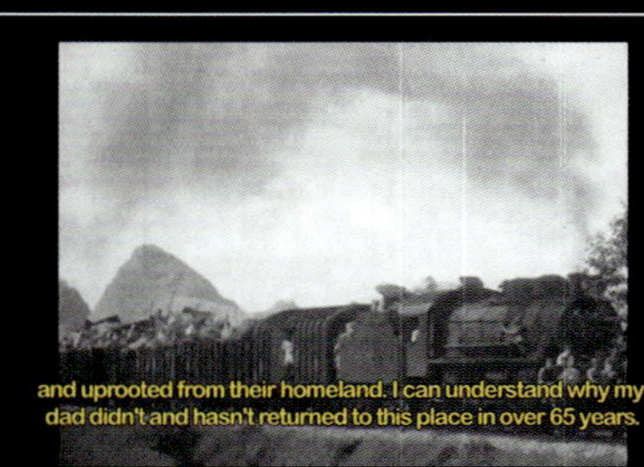
and uprooted from their homeland. I can understand why my
dad didn't and hasn't returned to this place in over 65 years.

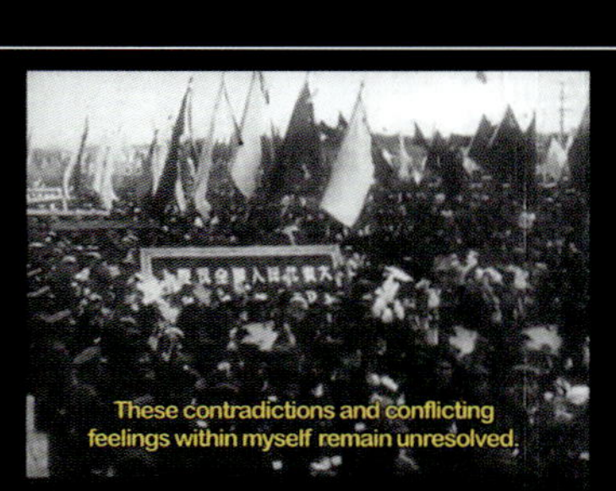
These contradictions and conflicting
feelings within myself remain unresolved.

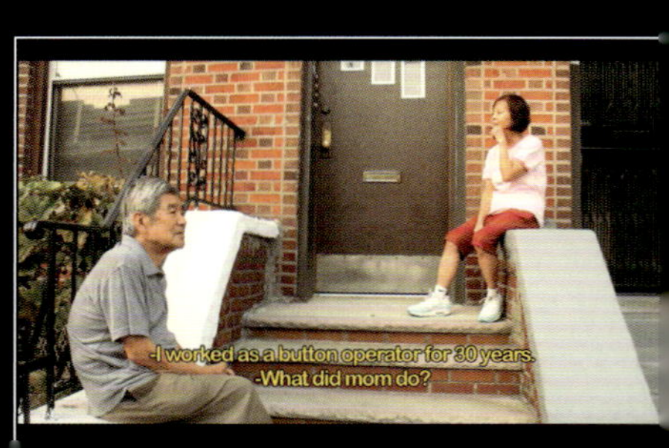
-I worked as a button operator for 30 years.
-What did mom do?

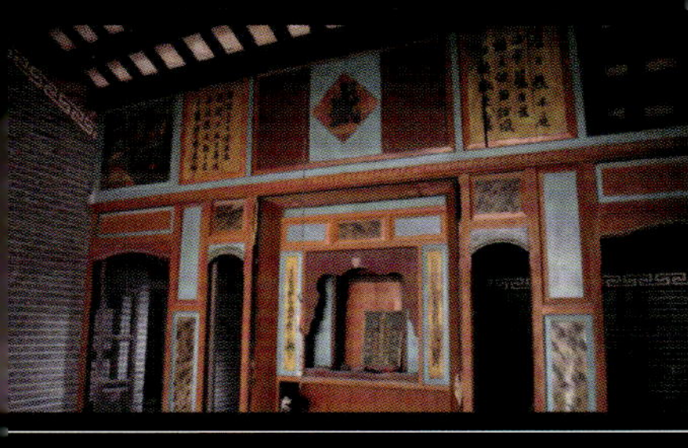

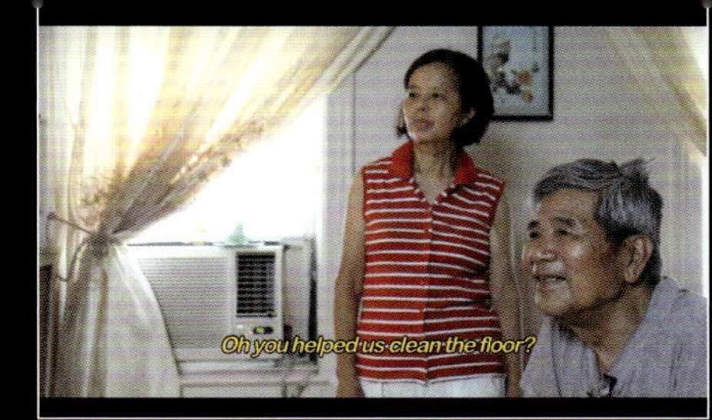
Oh you helped us clean the floor?

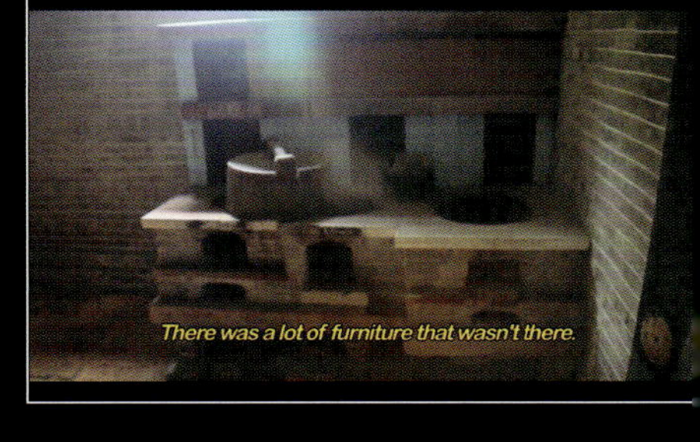
There was a lot of furniture that wasn't there.

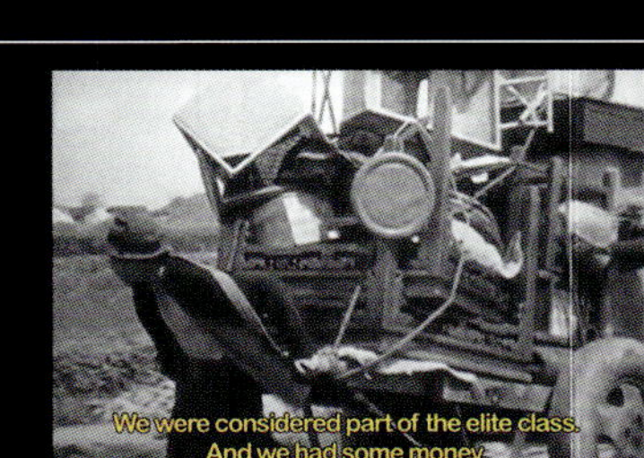
We were considered part of the elite class.
And we had some money.

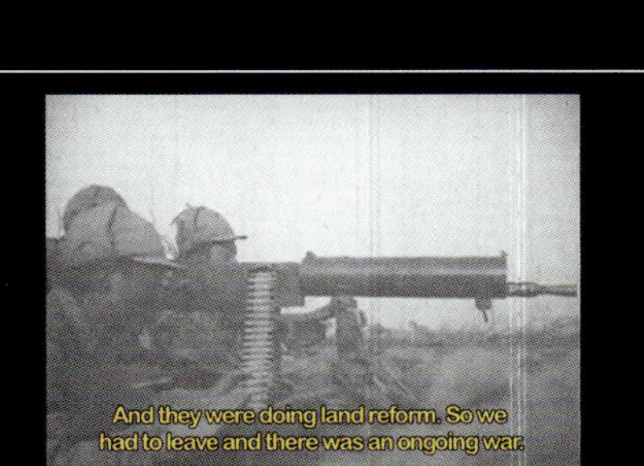
And they were doing land reform. So we
had to leave and there was an ongoing war.

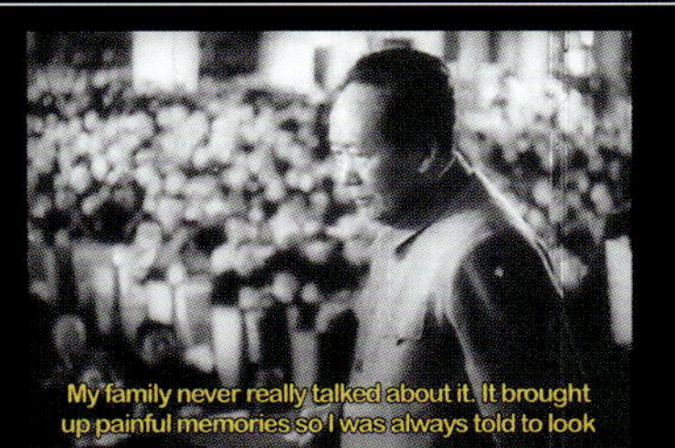
My family never really talked about it. It brought
up painful memories so I was always told to look

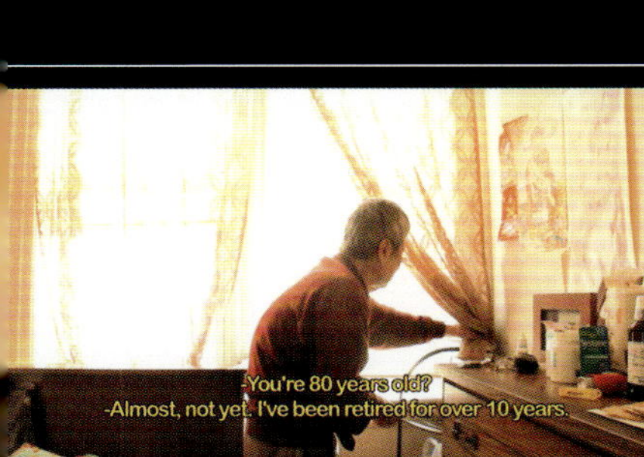
-You're 80 years old?
-Almost, not yet. I've been retired for over 10 years.

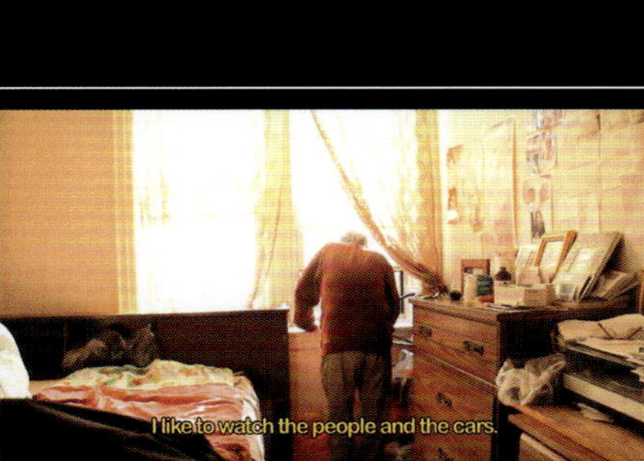
I like to watch the people and the cars.

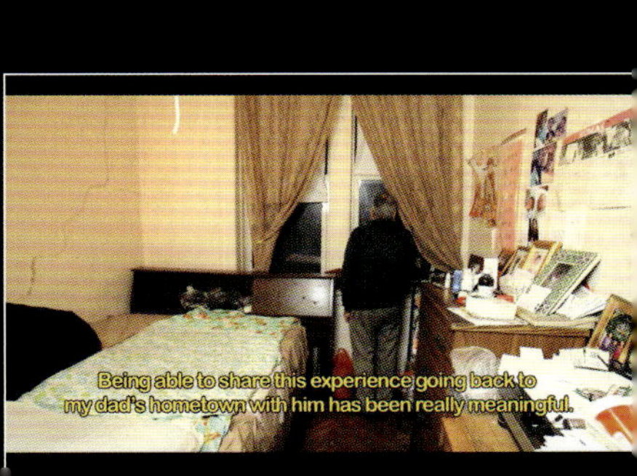
Being able to share this experience going back to
my dad's hometown with him has been really meaningful.

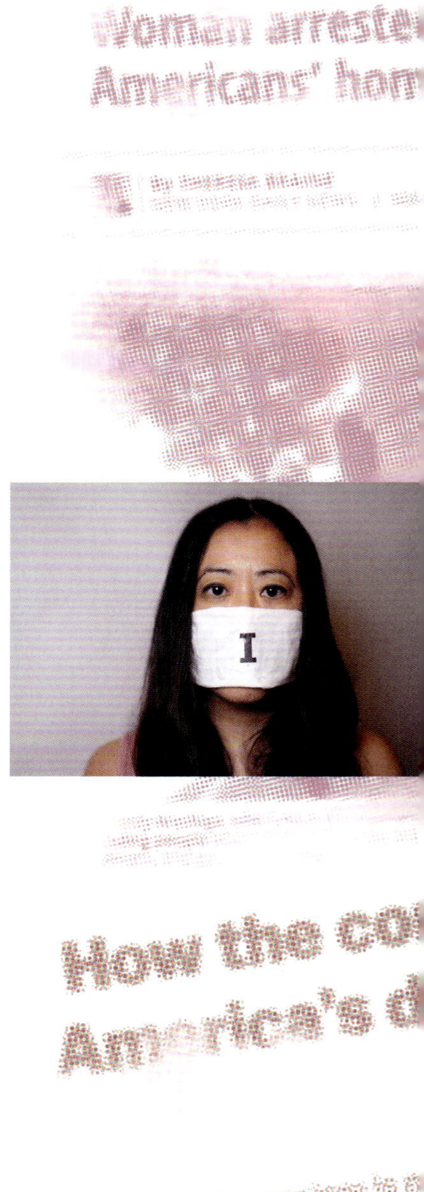

I am not a virus, 2020. Digital collage.

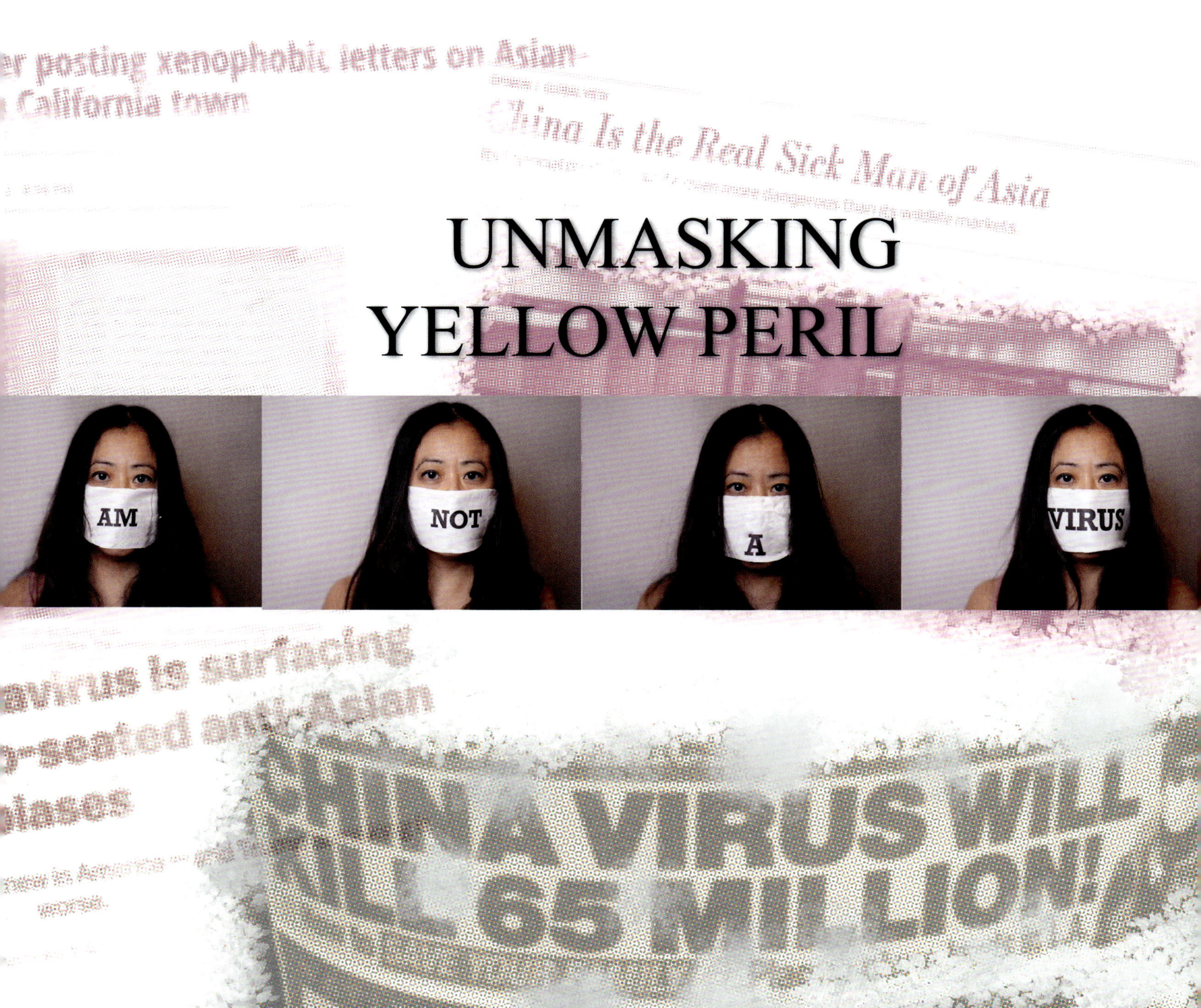
er posting xenophobic letters on Asian-
California town
hina Is the Real Sick Man of Asia
UNMASKING
YELLOW PERIL
AM
NOT
A
VIRUS
virus is surfacing
-seated anti-Asian
biases
HINA VIRUS WILL
LL 65 MILLION!

Right: *The artist wearing a mask with the printed text "Chinese Must Go," a popular slogan used during the rise of anti-Asian violence in the US in the 1870s; 150 years later the author contemplates today's similar climate*, 2020. Mixed-media collage.

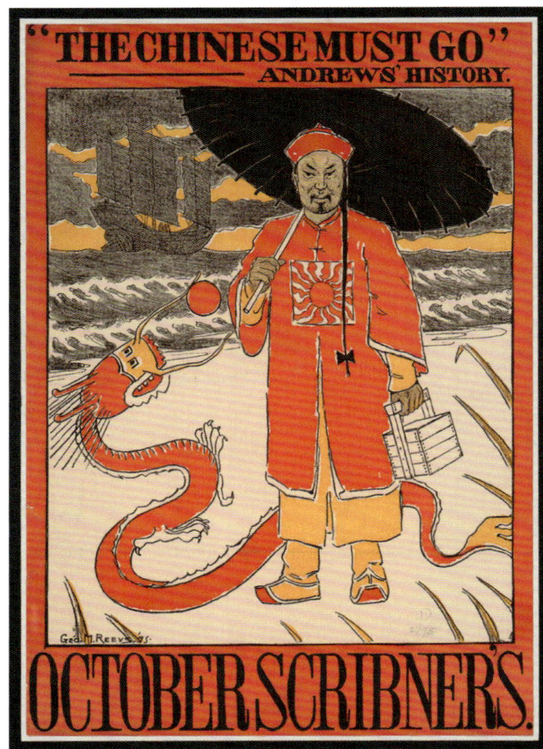

"The Chinese must go," Andrews' history. October Scribner's, 1895. Library of Congress, Washington, DC.

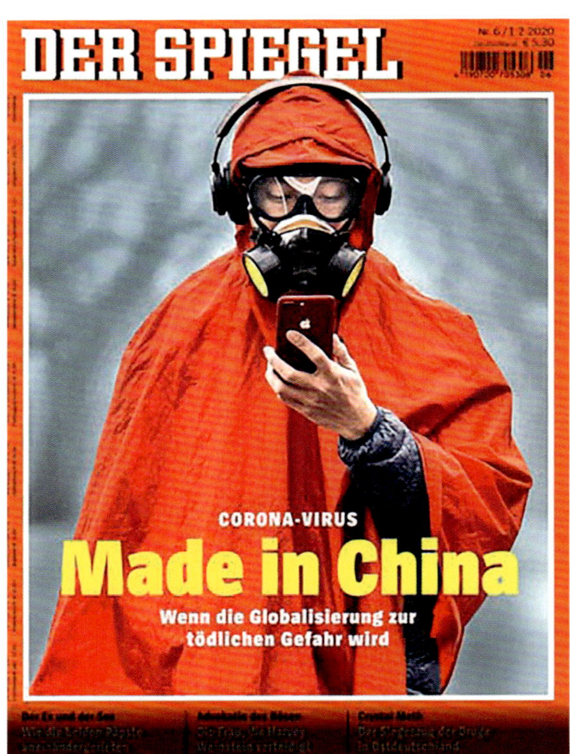

Magazine cover of German magazine *Der Spiegel*, which ran a front-page report in issue 6/2020 (February 1, 2020) featuring a man wearing red protective clothing, goggles, and earphones, with the headline "Made in China." (Photo Credit: Der Spiegel.)

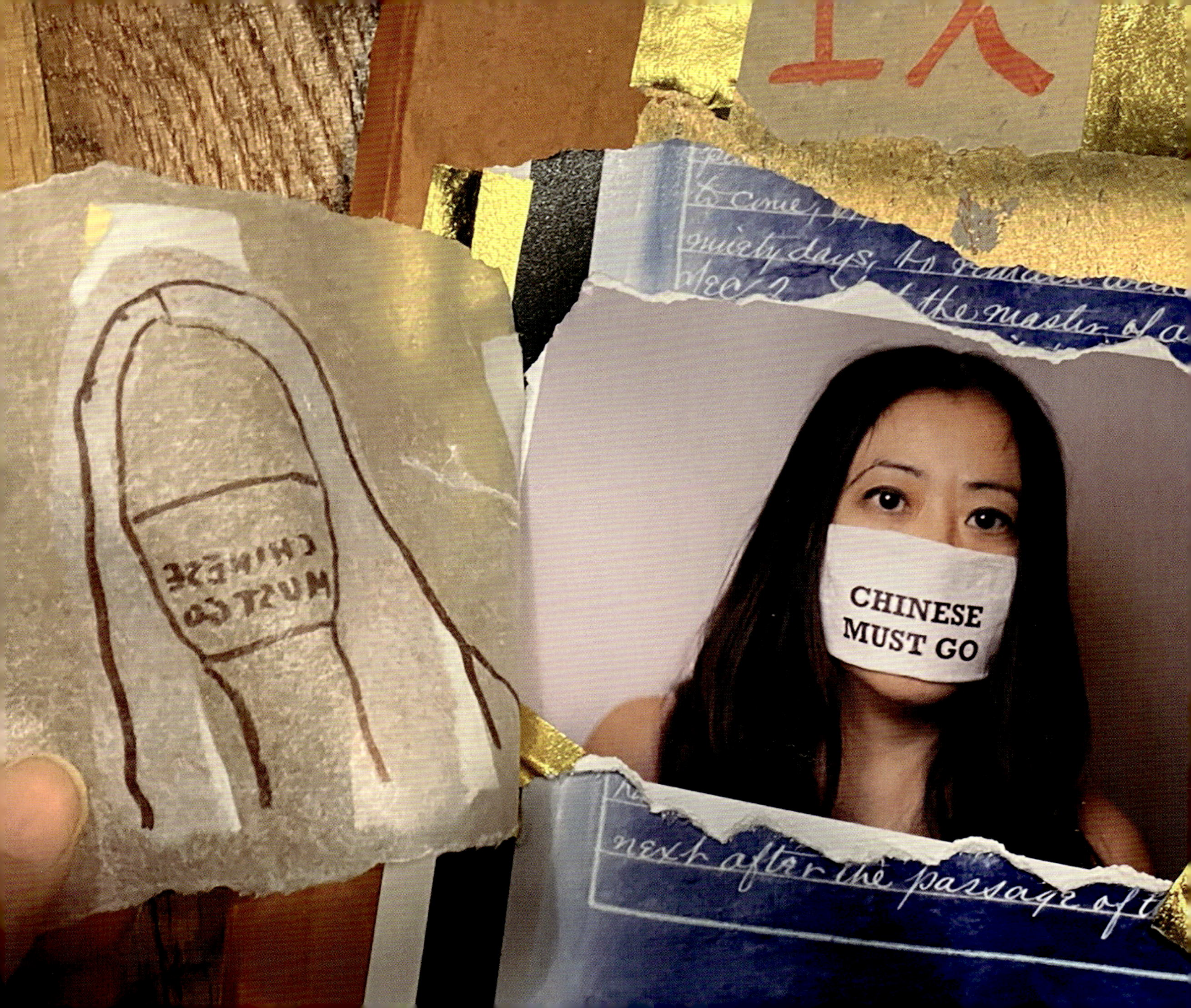
ninety days, to
the master of
CHINESE
MUST GO
next after the passage of

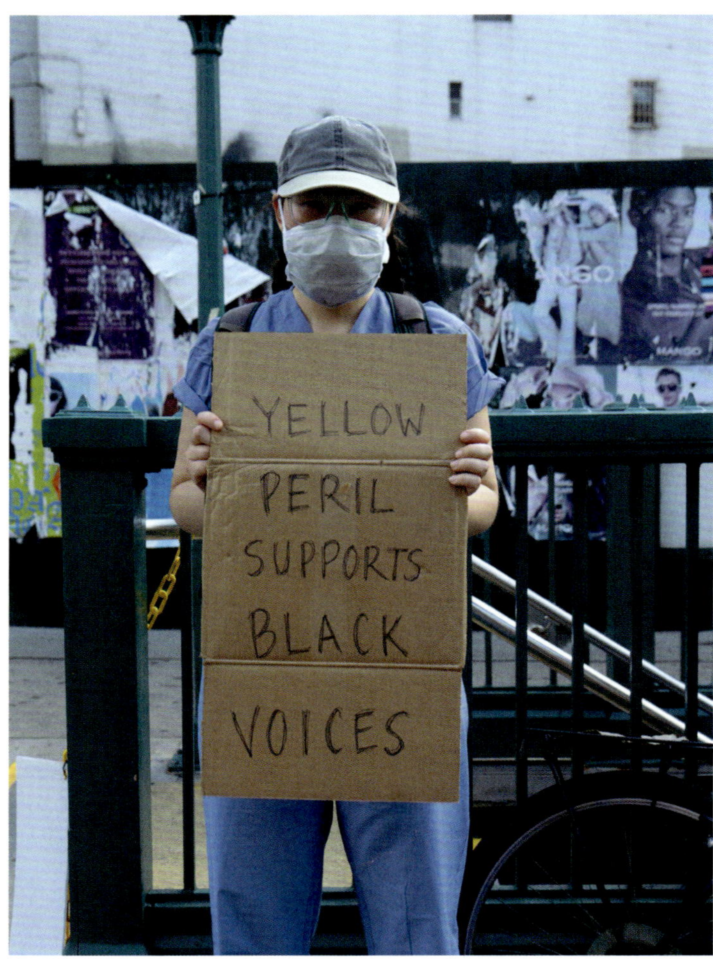

Top: Yellow Peril Supports Black Voices, 2020.

Right: *"You can't have capitalism without racism"—Malcolm X,* 2020. Digital collage.

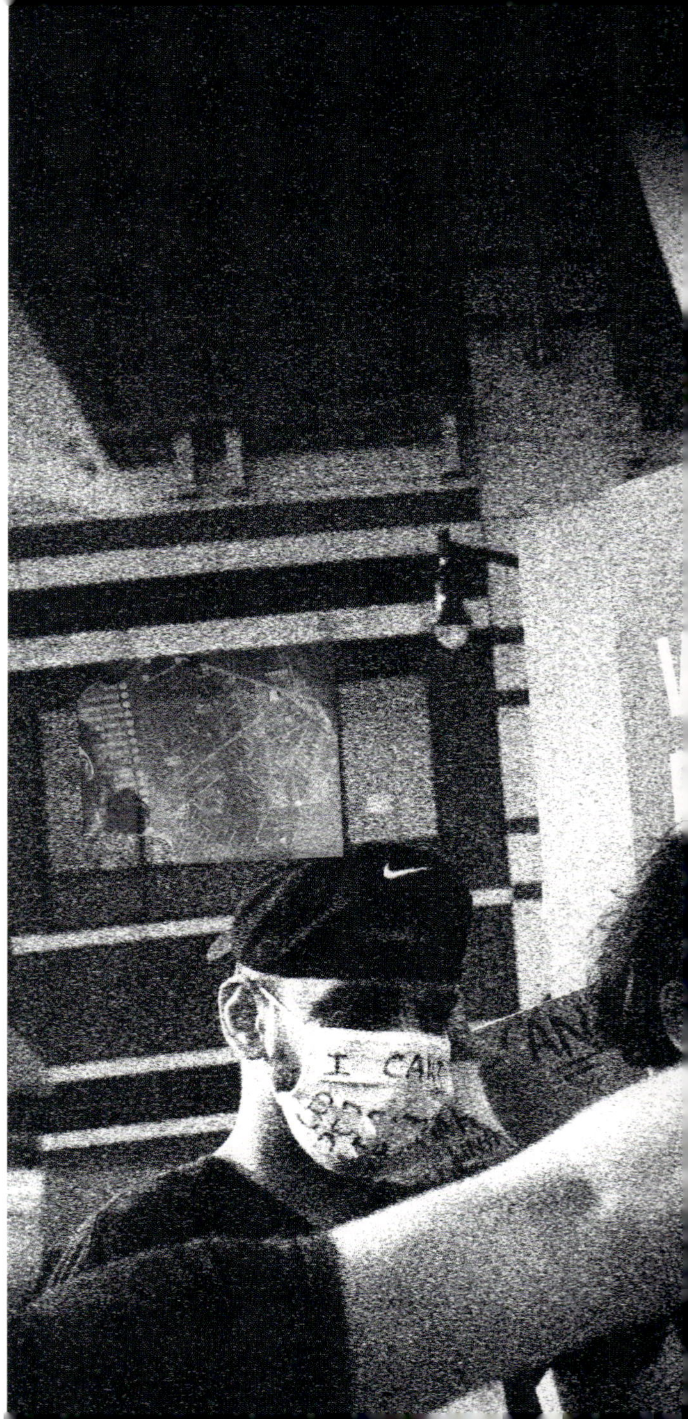

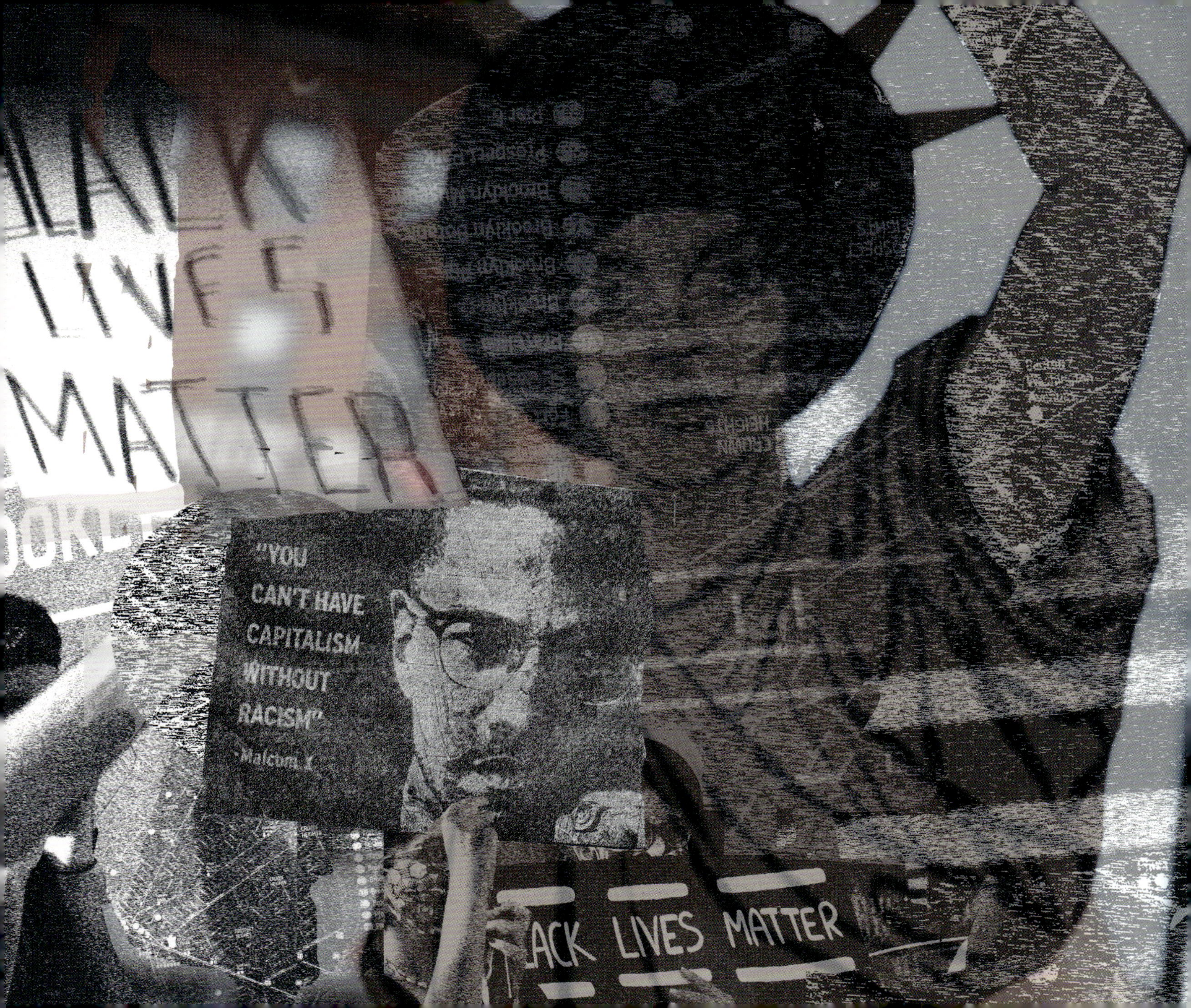

LIVES
MATTER

"YOU
CAN'T HAVE
CAPITALISM
WITHOUT
RACISM"
-Malcolm X

ACK LIVES MATTER

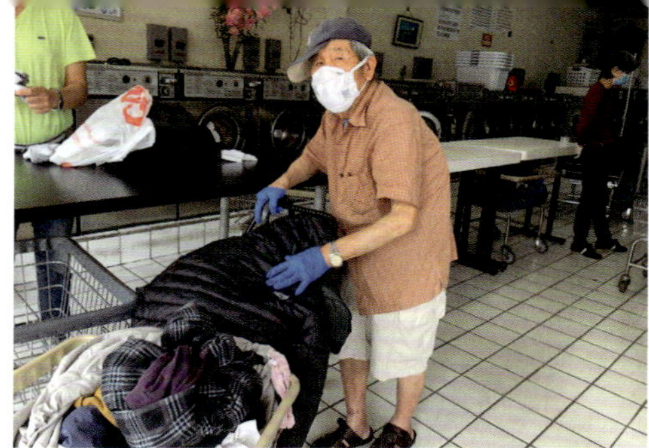

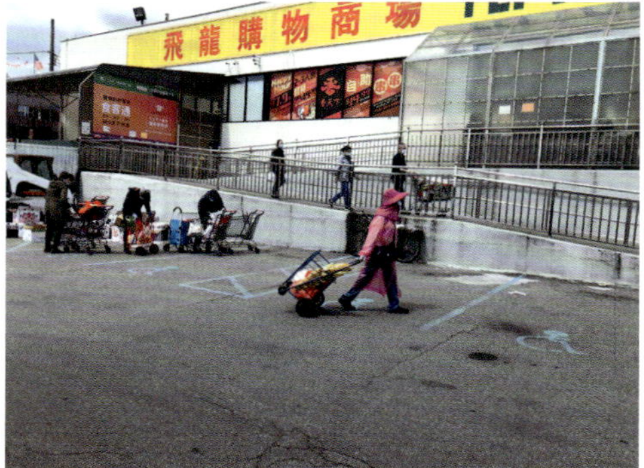

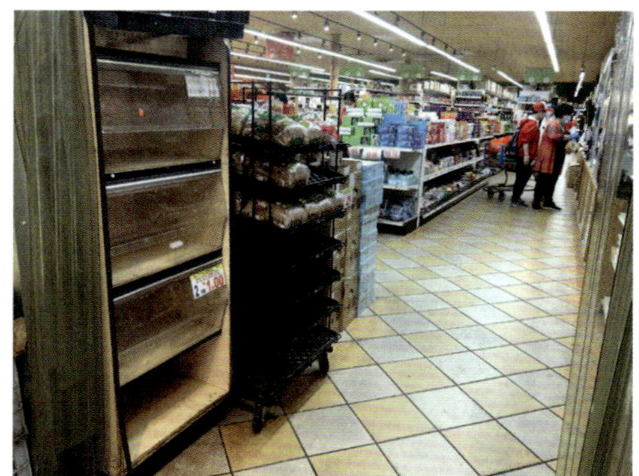

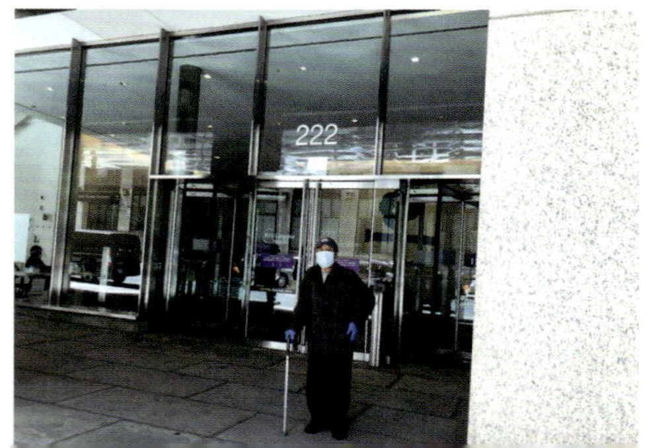

My parents have been together for over fifty-five years. They have had a difficult relationship for as long as I can remember. Back in 2020, during the COVID-19 pandemic lockdown, they had already been socially distancing from one another for many decades, before it was the norm.

Yes, COVID-19 changed their relationship. For months my parents were inseparable whether they liked it or not. They were terrified of contracting the virus, and became increasingly distressed as anti-Asian violence and hate crimes escalated. In order to stay connected, I had to rely on FaceTime calls and my mom's cell-phone images to stay connected to them. I collaborated with my mom on documentation. Every day, she used her cell phone to document their daily lives, essential doctors' appointments, laundromat trips, and the eerily empty streets of Brooklyn's Chinatown during the pandemic.

Right: My parents: 1966 to 2020.

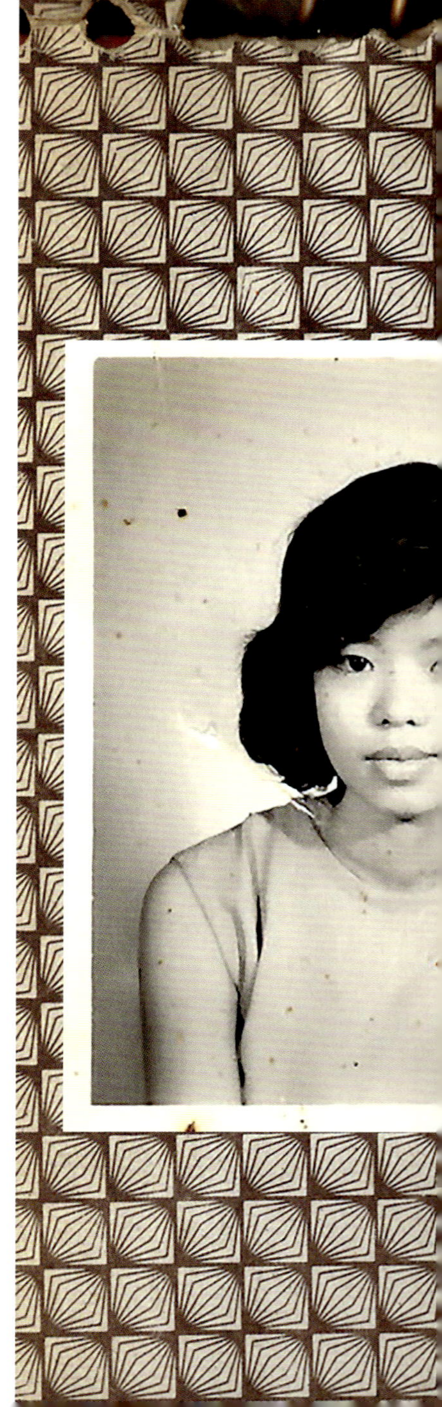

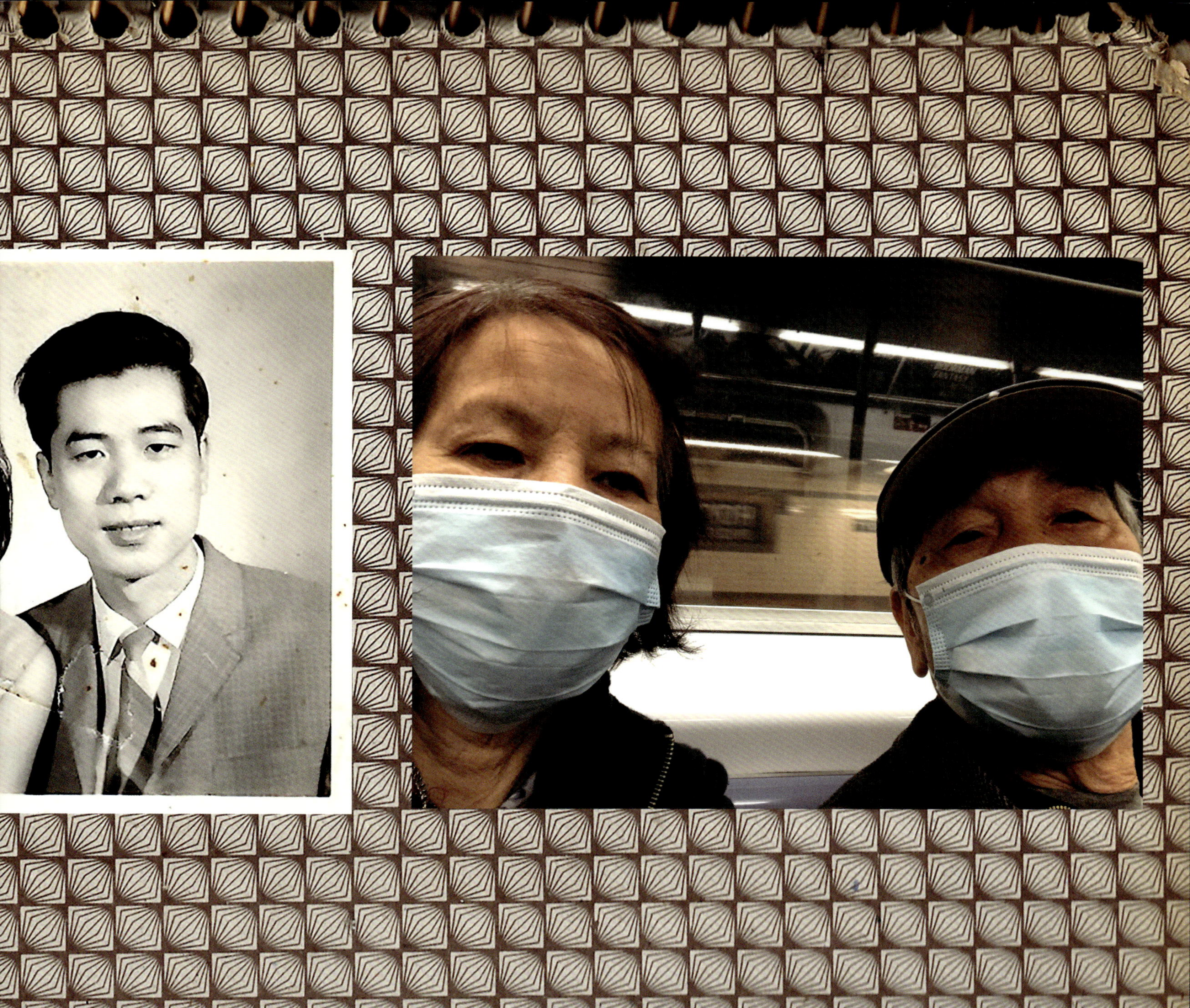